Joss Whedon

Manchester University Press

series editors

JONATHAN BIGNELL
STEVEN PEACOCK

former editor

SARAH CARDWELL

already published

Paul Abbott BETH LOUISE JOHNSON

Alan Bennett KARA MCKECHNIE

Alan Clarke DAVE ROLINSON

Jimmy McGovern STEVE BLANDFORD

Andrew Davies SARAH CARDWELL

Tony Garnett STEPHEN LACEY

Trevor Griffiths JOHN TULLOCH

Troy Kennedy Martin LEZ COOKE

Terry Nation JONATHAN BIGNELL AND ANDREW O'DAY

Jimmy Perry and David Croft SIMON MORGAN-RUSSELL

Lynda La Plante JULIA HALLAM

Jack Rosenthal SUE VICE

MATTHEW PATEMAN

Joss Whedon

Manchester University Press

Published by Manchester University Press
Altrincham Street, Manchester M1 7JA

www.manchesteruniversitypress.co.uk

British Library Cataloguing-in-Publication Data
A catalogue record for this book is available from the British Library

ISBN 978 0 7190 7781 4 paperback

ISBN 978 0 7190 7780 7 hardback

First published 2018

Typeset
by Toppan Best-set Premedia Limited
Printed in Great Britain
by CPI Group (UK) Ltd, Croydon, CR0 4YY

In loving memory of Monty:
faithful, loving, joy-bringer. Sorely missed.

Contents

Figures and tables

Figures

Tables

General editors' preface

Television is part of our everyday experience, and is one of the most significant aspects of our cultural lives today. Yet its practitioners and its artistic and cultural achievements remain relatively unacknowledged. The books in this series aim to remedy this by addressing the work of major television writers and creators. Each volume provides an authoritative and accessible guide to a particular practitioner's body of work, and assesses his or her contribution to television over the years. Many of the volumes draw on original sources, such as specially conducted interviews and archive material, and all of them list relevant bibliographic sources and further reading and viewing. The author of each book makes a case for the importance of the work considered therein, and the series includes books on neglected or overlooked practitioners alongside well-known ones.

In comparison with some related disciplines, Television Studies scholarship is still relatively young, and the series aims to contribute to establishing the subject as a vigorous and evolving field. This series provides resources for critical thinking about television. While maintaining a clear focus on the writers, on the creators and on the programmes themselves, the books in this series also take account of key critical concepts and theories in Television Studies. Each book is written from a particular critical or theoretical perspective, with reference to pertinent issues, and the approaches included in the series are varied and sometimes dissenting. Each author explicitly outlines the reasons for his or her particular focus, methodology or perspective. Readers are invited to think critically about the subject matter and approach covered in each book.

Although the series is addressed primarily to students and scholars of television, the books will also appeal to the many people who are interested in how television programmes have been commissioned, made and enjoyed. Since television has been so much a part of personal and public life in the twentieth and twenty-first centuries, we hope that the series will engage with, and sometimes challenge, a broad and diverse readership.

Jonathan Bignell
Steven Peacock

Acknowledgements

This book has taken a long time to complete so I would like to thank Matthew Frost of Manchester University Press for his patience and continuing enthusiasm for the project over all these years. I also owe great debts of gratitude to colleagues at the Universities of Hull, Kingston and Sheffield Hallam. In particular, I would like to thank Martin Arnold, Charles Mundye, Martin McQuillan, Lorna Severn, Ian Brown, Katharine Cox, Simon Nolan and Natalie Jeffcock. The community of Whedon and TV scholars is a large and varied one, and I have received great intellectual and personal nourishment from a great many of the people in it. In particular, I would like to thank Stacey Abbott, Simon Brown, Lorna Jowett, Mike Starr, James Zbrowski, Casey McCormick, Julie Hawk, Steve Halfyard, Marcus Recht, Beth Johnson, Alison Peirse and Bronwen Calvert. The world of Whedon scholarship owes a huge amount to Rhonda Wilcox and the late David Lavery. Thank you, both. Without the joint support and trust of Jen Hale and Nikki Stafford, I would have abandoned this book long ago. I cannot overstate my thanks.

For the drafts; the scripts; the emails of such insight, candour and knowledge; and the sheer thrill of correspondence, thank you, Jane Espenson.

For friendship and support when it seemed this book would never be finished, my thanks go to Kevin Johnson, John McLeod, Amanda Wilcox, and Matt and Vicky Jackson. My parents have supported me through five house moves and three job moves during the writing of this book. Much love and thanks to you, Mum and Dad! On my wall, above the computer where I am typing is a poster of my daughter, stake in hand, posing like Buffy and photoshopped into a *Buffy*-style set. Thank you to her mother, Kelly, and her partner Andy for this constant source of joy. And to Ellie for being the funniest, lovingest, brightest

Captain Seaweed – and for loving the *Buffy* musical and *Commentary!* so much.

And for inviting me to a conference on Jean-Francois Lyotard and going on to become my rigid designator, thank you, Heidi: we'll run like we're awesome, totally genius.

Introduction

'Art and feminism; my little show that changed things.'
(Whedon in Lavery and Burkhead, 2011: 40)

When asked in an interview what he was most proud of, Joss Whedon replied with the above comment. The (anything but) little show was *Buffy the Vampire Slayer* (The WB/UPN 1997–2003) and it did, indeed, change things. It changed Whedon's career; it changed the lives of tens of thousands of those who watched it; it established an expectation from fans and viewers of high quality writing on television long-form serial dramas; and much else besides. And it did this by treating television serial drama as 'art' and imbuing that art with a politics, in this case, 'feminism'. He ensured that his television show (and all his later projects, too) told stories that were both artistically rewarding and politically engaged.

Whedon is a liberal in the American sense, which makes him more likely to support the Democrats than the Republicans, but also places him to the left edge of mainstream political action. Far from a radical in the British tradition of an Alan Clarke (Rolinson, 2005), he is nevertheless a radical voice in American mass entertainment, and part of that radicality derives from the fact that his works are mass art in the sense of striving to engage the viewer, reader, listener and draw out a genuinely important aesthetic-affective response. His work presents through its formal choices a polyglot sensibility that is axiomatically democratic. While he explicitly seeks to change the world ('The idea of changing culture is important to me, and it can only be done in a popular medium' [Lavery and Burkhead, 2011: 65]), his work is not didactic, though this is as much a pragmatic decision as a political or aesthetic one: 'If I made "Buffy the lesbian Separatist", a series of lectures on PBS[1] on why there should be feminism, no one would be

[1] PBS is Public Broadcast Service, a non-profit public broadcaster and television show distributor and is commonly perceived as offering high quality educationally oriented content.

coming to the party, and it would be boring' (Lavery and Burkhead, 2011: 65). While he does not make the connection explicit, his 'little show' as both an aesthetic object (art) and a democratic politics (feminism) contributes (and by implication is successful only if the art and politics work equally strongly) to 'changing culture'.[2]

This book is concerned with exploring how the questions of storytelling, art and politics intersect and interact in Whedon's works. Working across a range of media including television, film, comic books, the web and music, Whedon's writing has helped to shape the popular aesthetic landscape since the late twentieth century. In television, his shows (*Buffy*, *Angel* [The WB 1999–2004], *Firefly* [Fox 2002], *Dollhouse* [Fox 2009–10], *Agents of S.H.I.E.L.D.* [ABC 2013–present]) have received massive critical and popular acclaim by virtue of their willingness to devise formats that knowingly merge, re-shape, subvert, celebrate and invigorate genre drama with excellent writing and production standards that had been less usual in the medium in the thirty years or so leading up to *Buffy*. In addition, his well-publicised disputes with the American television networks have led to unprecedented industrial innovation – the moving of *Buffy* from The WB to UPN being the prime example. His web work (*Dr. Horrible's Sing-Along Blog* [2008]) heralded an as-yet undeveloped model of creative control and distribution that could still prove to be one of his most lasting innovations. Similarly in film, the quality of his writing in movies as diverse as *Toy Story* (directed by John Lasseter), *Speed* (Jan de Bont), *Alien Resurrection* (Jean-Pierre Jeunet), *The Avengers* and *The Cabin in the Woods* (Drew Goddard) has made him a hugely high-grossing and much sought after creative force: boxofficemojo.com estimate the total amount the films he has written has grossed at the truly quite staggering amount of over US$3 billion (boxofficemojo.com, 2017). Turning the less than celebrated *Buffy the Vampire Slayer*

[2] Whedon's feminism is not a theoretically consistent one, but rather a broadly articulated challenge to the inequalities between the genders that he perceives. Strongly influenced in his political views by his mother ('a radical feminist, a history teacher and just one hell of a woman' [in Pascale, 2014: 30]), it was his surprise at attitudes at his private liberal arts university, Wesleyan, that prompted him to use writing as a vehicle through which to address these issues in order to help 'empower and protect them so they could in return empower and protect me' (in Pascale, 2014: 31). The writing however needed not just to offer strong women, but also to unsparingly address places that are 'dark' and have to do with passion and lust and things you don't want to talk about like 'the murderous gaze and ... objectification' (Pascale, 2014: 31). So Whedon's feminism, while clearly intellectually and politically understood and motivated has, in its artistic manifestations, an emotional core that is created through the mobilisation of the full array of televisual storytelling mechanisms.

(Fran Rubel Kazui) movie (1992) into the iconic television series, and then re-fashioning the critically acclaimed but short-lived *Firefly* in to the award winning film *Serenity* (2005) demonstrates that it is not just in the art itself, but in the processes surrounding the art that Whedon is so innovative. Setting himself up as a 'micro-studio' in order to produce his version of *Much Ado About Nothing* (2012) illustrates this point further. And moving away from film and television, Whedon has also sought media that are often even less highly prized as art forms through which to tell his stories. Continuing the narratives of all of his television shows in comic book form, Whedon not only allowed for the continuation of these narratives that had, in some cases, become so central to parts of popular culture, but did so in a way that promoted the comic book as a medium to those previously disinclined to treat it as a serious aesthetic form.

Despite his extraordinary range and depth across a host of media, this book will primarily focus on his television shows. The very concept of what a television show is has been challenged with the advent of web series, such as Whedon's own *Dr. Horrible,* and platforms, such as Netflix and Amazon Prime. For the purposes of this book, I am classifying a Whedon television show as something designed for television or small screen viewing (tablet, phone) and which is in episode form. This means that films, comic books, short web-based interventions, such as his attack on Mitt Romney during the 2012 presidential campaign (Whedon, 2012) and his 2017 video for Planned Parenthood, while being part of the broader discussion, will not form the main argument of the book.

This book, then, is going to try to provide an account of Whedon's career to date. It is not, though, a biography. My concern is not primarily with his life but with his works and the ways in which those works have had such an important influence in the ways outlined above.[3] Whedon is a writer, first and foremost, and his writing traverses song, film, television, comic books; it ranges across comedy tragedy, drama, horror, romance, science fiction, westerns, farce, melodrama, history; it blends genres, styles and modes; insists on emotional realism within fantastical fictional worlds, employs narrative complexity, character memory and development; it demands attention of its viewers and, in turn, respects

[3] One way in which his life has become pertinent to discussion of his work is through the accusations made by his ex-wife Kai Cole about his sexual behaviour with female co-workers. This came to light after the current book was in publication so I cannot develop an argument here, However, I wrote a blog and posted a vlog that deal with the issue. These can be found at http://patemanponders.blogspot.co.uk/2017/09/brand-whedon-feminism-and-damage-done.html and https://www.youtube.com/watch?v=KNd1_fozoZo&t=510s.

them with careful, textured, subtle stories; and it is also a writing that moves beyond the page and into the studio where his linguistic skills are allied to his directorial, musical and acting skills, as well as to his capacity to produce. The combination of these skills, in the creation and development of his television series, will be the focus of this book. While I will be asserting the importance of Whedon's work, it is also true to say that in the twenty years since *Buffy* first aired, the kinds of clever, sophisticated storytelling employed by Whedon has become (thankfully) much more common-place. So much so that Jason Mittell (2015) can claim a new level of narrative complexity in the television of the 2010s and beyond. This complexity goes beyond Whedon's self-contained story of the week and its relationship to an overarching seasonal arc, to a show that '*redefines episodic forms under the influence of serial narration* – not necessarily a complete merger of episodic and serial forms but a shifting balance' (Mittell, 2015: 19, emphasis in original).

Following a more-or-less chronological sequence, the three chapters in Part I present analyses of the shows in terms of their relationship with the networks, their story arcs, characterisation and themes (an industrial-thematic approach). Part II presents a series of case studies that pay attention to particularly important aspects of Whedon's aesthetic strategies, especially as they relate to genre and narrative, and these highlight the ways in which Whedon creates a televisual language that allows for his vision to be realised. This second part of the book focuses less on explicit discussions of politics, such as his feminism, and more on the aesthetic-production aspects that serve to realise the core themes of Whedon's works. To this extent, the chapters and case studies contribute to the established critical versions of Whedon, and will both draw from and supplement the already impressive body of Whedon studies. Furthermore, the chapters also seek to address other parts of Whedon's contribution to and importance in a discussion of the development of television more broadly from the late twentieth century.

I will do this by addressing a range of issues. First, the chapters will locate the different series in the broader context of the television industry, in particular paying attention to the importance of the networks and production companies, most notably Whedon's own, but also others. In this way, both the industrial contexts, which allow and impede Whedon's vision to be expressed, and the other people responsible for this process (co-producers, writers, directors, actors and so on), will be included in the discussion. This is not to diminish Whedon's achievements, but it is to insist upon them in more broadly conceived ways. Rhonda Wilcox develops a very useful way of thinking of Whedon's role in producing his shows, by likening him to 'a master builder of a cathedral' having the overarching vision but needing a very large team of talented individuals and artisans to enable that vision to be manifested (Wilcox, 2005: 6). Describing his wife Kai Cole's plans for the house she designed for them, Whedon recasts Wilcox's metaphor saying, 'an architect is just like a filmmaker' (Whedon, 2013: 10).

However, a significant aspect of this book is that I do not want to reduce the shows to the man, or vice versa. A danger with the 'great man' view of any authorship, even if authorship is conceived of in the fashion identified by Wilcox, is that the celebration can become uncritical in the narrowest sense; the analyses can tend to view the product as a *symptom* of the producer. Or, worse, the product is used as a way to discover the 'truth' of the producer (reading a character as 'really' an avatar of the writer – Xander in *Buffy*, Wash in *Firefly*, Topher in *Dollhouse* as 'really' being versions of Whedon); and the opposite error, seeing the writer as offering us the 'truth' about the show (understanding Whedon's relationship with his mother is the key to understanding the characters of Joyce, Buffy's mother, and Maggie Walsh in *Buffy*, for example). The difficulty in such approaches is that they seek to simplify, contain and reduce narratives, characters and shows whose formats, stories and arcs assert complexity, multiplicity and heterogeneity. Whedon's artistic drive, his flair, his motivations are, of course, essential in the shows' construction and development, but it is an error to see an analysis of the shows as being an analysis of the man. Whedon clearly sees some autobiographical aspects to his own writing. He (2013: 9) says, reflecting on his own lack of perspicacity about himself, 'When I find out [things about myself] I usually find I've been writing about them for years.' However, recognising this as a truth about his own work, does not for me, endorse a psycho-biographical approach. To that extent, this book is slightly mis-named. It would be better called, *The Television Shows of Joss Whedon*. He, Joss Whedon, is not the story – his works and their contexts are.

Among these contexts are those people with whom he has created these shows – the actors, editors, set designers, producers, industry champions and, of course, the other writers. Discussions of some of these roles occur throughout the book, and I am indebted to the generosity and insight of Whedon collaborator, television producer and web show creator Jane Espenson for engaging in an email correspondence with me during the Writers' Guild of America strike (2007/08) and then allowing me not only to use the information from the correspondence to inform the main argument of the book, but also to include it as Appendix 1, so that all the information and insight she offered is available to everyone. She also gave me draft scripts of all the episodes she wrote on *Buffy*,

Angel and *Firefly*, and they too have proven to be invaluable in some of the discussion in the current book.

I offer analyses of Whedon's shows that highlight their aesthetic achievements but which also draw attention to some of the most pressing questions in relation to aesthetic judgements of mass art forms, and art that is collaborative and industrial in scale. In order to do this, I will also provide accounts of industrial and production histories that directly influence either what Whedon was able to create or which, through his creations, have been forced to change or engage in debate about their status. Alongside this, the chapters and case studies presented will draw attention to Whedon's remorseless promotion and celebration of cultural literacy – few creators of art are able to span as many media, to engage in as many forms with each medium and to do so with reference to so many other forms, media and styles. The generic commingling that is so central to each of his works is matched by at least as much a sense of the necessary intertwining of the artistic, literary, musical, philosophical and political histories that have led to his creative moment. But while he is very aware of – and clearly inspired by – the 'Great Tradition' version of this history he is equally as inspired by the individuals and, almost more importantly, forms and media that have typically been excluded from that tradition.

The multi-genre conception of each of his artworks, and their investment in a wide range of cultural histories and events, indicate a politics that is also important to an understanding of Whedon's work. This aspect will be a recurring theme in the book, with the claim that his aesthetic strategies are always implicated in a certain politics being fundamental to its argument: aesthetics as praxis.

I (Pateman, 2012: viii) have argued elsewhere that television can be read as always already political, that we need to 'understand television as politics, representation as politics' but that we equally have to recognise 'politics as representation – which is to say that the act of creating a televisual aesthetic ... is understood as a political gesture. This gesture is implicated in histories of television, of art ... of exploitation and liberation.' The general political economy of television (often implicit or subjugated) in Whedon is explicit and central.

However much Whedon has influenced the world of television production and popular aesthetics more generally, his work has also, of course, been created and influenced by the possible conditions in which the work was created. This too will form part of the argument of this book. One of the most significant contexts in which Whedon has been working is the period developed by Creeber and Hills (2007) as 'TVIII'. A critical term open to inevitable contestation, TVIII continues the processes begun in the USA with the de-regulation of the television industry in the 1980s. The movement towards a fragmented market that also carries with it the technological shifts, such as, first, DVD, then Blu-ray, multi-platform access, streaming technologies and the web, opening up much greater levels of fan–producer interaction. An interaction that can be considered both positively, as a democratisation of the production process and a democratisation of voices, or more negatively, as the exploitation of fans' free labour in the service of production companies and networks. In a discussion around the concept of TVIII, Derek Johnson (2007: 68) describes one way of considering the ways that new technologies provide corporations with the capacity to exploit fan enthusiasm as free labour:

> Digital media and their resultant economies afforded the culture industries a source of free labor. Digital and online spaces are largely corporate owned, but grow from the contributions of their users; the skilled and knowledgeable consumption of culture is transformed into productive activities both enjoyed by the consumer and exploited by the industry. Free labor, therefore, is the 'creation of monetary value out of knowledge/culture/affect' (Terranova 2000. 38). The intersection of television and new media via multiplatforming, I therefore argue, enabled the television industry to begin participating in this new economy of free labor.

Johnson (2007: 68) continues his analysis by locating, in particular, the role of advertising and promotion as one way that corporations utilise and exploit this resource:

> As knowledgeable consumers of television culture, fans serve a productive, industrial function. As Murray (2004) argues, this utility is often channeled into the promotional sector to foster 'grassroots' buzz about television properties. This was the case with Universal's motion picture *Serenity*, adapted from the short-lived television series *Firefly*, although it could be argued that some compensation was afforded fan promoters. According to *Entertainment Weekly*, Universal offered fans prizes for exposing new viewers to the content stream (Jensen 2005, p. 20).

So, part of this book will engage, explicitly or implicitly, with the changing industrial and technological contexts within which Whedon has been working, as well as the effects these changing contexts have had on the production and the reception of his output.

In the year of Whedon's first television output, a script (see below), Ronald Reagan came to the end of his second term as president. His economic policies (often referred to as Reagonomics) had contributed to some de-regulation of the television industry, a process that continued over the next decade. It was one of Reagan's appointees, Mark Fowler, who, as chairman of the Federal Communications Commission approved Rupert Murdoch's News Corp.'s purchase of Metromedia, which gave him access to national VHF television stations, and control of 20th Century Fox – one of the major film production companies in the USA. The newly rebranded Fox Inc. soon had a television aspect, Fox Television Network, and the first new major network in over thirty years was soon to be born (Kimmel, 2004). Not only a new network, but a massive increase in cable networks meant that there was more and more air time to be filled, and a greater sense of consumer choice and market segmentation.

Fox Television's success, as the fourth network, bolstered the belief that a fifth and even a sixth network would be viable and it was within this climate that The WB and UPN networks came into existence. While smaller than their more established rivals (Fox, ABC, NBC and CBS) it is worth noting that The WB was part of Time Warner. The WB was launched just eight months before the repeal of the Financial Interest and Syndication (Fin Syn) rules on 21 September 1995 (Holt, 2003: 16). These rules, which had limited the amount of content a network could produce for its own prime-time audiences, had been a source of consternation for the industry since their inception. With their repeal, the major media corporations began a flurry of mergers and take overs as each bid to develop fully vertically integrated conglomerations capable of producing distributing and broadcasting shows. The WB, although new, was no small concern. Ten years previously, Ted Turner of Turner Broadcasting had bought MGM/UA for US$1.5 billion. He had to re-sell a huge amount of the assets due to financial difficulty, but he kept the film library, which included, among others, *Gone with the Wind* (1939, Victor Fleming), *Citizen Kane* (1941, Orson Welles), *The Wizard of Oz* (1939, Victor Fleming) and *Casablanca* (1942, Michael Curtiz) (Holt, 2003: 17). These films, along with the Hanna-Barbera library of cartoons, which he acquired in 1991, became central to syndicated viewing as well as to his own range of channels including WBTS, TNT, Carton Network and Turner Classic Movies, which launched the year before the Fin Syn repeal. Just two days after the Fin Syn repeal, and seven months after the launch of The WB, Time Warner merged with Turner Communications creating a US$7.6 billion:

> Colossus that encompassed a vast array of entertainment properties from Warner Bros. film and television production, HBO, CNN, TBS, TNT ... to Warner Bros. Records, Time Life, Turner's world-class film library, the Atlanta Braves, and Atlanta Hawks and Time Warner Cable ... it brought a much larger magnitude [than Disney/ABC] and range of assets under the same corporate insignia greater potential for vertical arrangements. (Holt, 2003: 18)

Viewed in this context, the emergent network that would launch Whedon's executive producer career seems less vulnerable.

The role of the networks and other giant media conglomerates in Whedon's career means that any assessment of Whedon has to include discussion of their development, and his relationship with them. Not only that, but the complex financial relations between Whedon as executive producer and Mutant Enemy, his production company, alongside other vested interests will be, at least, in the background of much of the discussion. As Catherine Johnson (2007: 7) discusses, in relation to *Buffy*:

> However, in the era of TVIII, branding is not simply a feature of television networks. The dominant practice of co-producing means that one programme could potentially be understood as part of the brand equity of a range of different companies. For example, *Buffy the Vampire Slayer* is a co-production between 20th Century Fox Television, Mutant Enemy, Kuzui Enterprises and Sandollar Television. Brand logos for all four companies appear at the end of each episode. Meanwhile the series was initially transmitted on The WB network, where it was a central part of their re-branding strategy as the teen network in the mid-1990s (see Johnson 2005). However, the series later moved to the emergent UPN network, while 20th Century Fox distributed the series on DVD and video, and licensed its merchandise.

The financial rewards to be derived from ownership of particular brands, and the capacity to develop ancillary markets for copyrighted products, is one of the driving forces behind so many of the massive multimedia conglomerate corporate mergers. As Johnson (2007: 7) continues:

> However, the example of *Buffy the Vampire Slayer* suggests that the unique identity associated with a programme is one that can be exploited by the owner of the rights to the programme across a range of different media. While this does not necessarily place power in the hands of production companies such as Mutant Enemy, it does suggest that owning the rights to programming emerges as a potentially valuable way to make profits within the era of TVIII.

As the conditions in which a show would be aired were changing, so too were the technologies designed to allow for the repeated viewing of that show. While VHS videos had been available for over two decades, the quality was not good and the ability to easily find a section, rewind and still-frame were limited. Video certainly offered a film or television show a sense of permanence that had previously not existed, and as such had helped to begin the processes by which the assumed transience (and therefore unimportant and triviality) could be challenged and a greater sense of seriousness be afforded to, especially, television as an object of scholarly scrutiny. But it took the appearance of the DVD to fully realise the concept that a show could not only be repeatedly viewed, but that many additional layers of information could also be offered: screen shots, commentaries, scripts, interviews, overviews.

It is not coincidental that the year of *Buffy*'s television premier, on a new network, was also the year that DVDs were first test marketed in the USA (a year after Japan, and a year before Europe). This new technology allows, as Hills (2007) notes, the television text to be removed from the flow of TV scheduling, and instead allows it to stand in isolation, as a discrete aesthetic object. He rightly points out that only certain kinds of television texts can be isolated in this way, and that the text produced by this strategy of isolation also is related to questions of authorship.

Whedon's success cannot be attributed solely to the DVD, but it is certainly true that what DVD technology allows in terms of close analysis, bounded objects, textual valorisation and repeated viewing means that his whole career as a television producer of highly regarded television texts has coincided with a technology exactly designed to celebrate and analyse the kinds of texts he creates. As Hills (2007: 49) suggests:

> If DVD culture works, partly, on television to re-position many of its texts as symbolically bounded and isolatable 'objects' of value, then as a machinery of valorisation stressing the 'total system' of TV serials and series, it works to popularise 'close reading' and the artistic re-contextualisation of some TV content.

A show that benefitted from the possibility of this re-contextualisation was the popular Roseanne Barr vehicle, *Roseanne* (ABC 1988–97). Whedon's first credited contributions to a television show was on this sitcom in 1989. Hired to the writers' room, Whedon penned (and then had 're-written beyond recognition' [Bennett, 2011: n.p.]) five scripts. His first, 'The Little Sister' (R season 2, episode 2 [S2E2]) aired on 19 September 1989. Almost a decade to the day later, the second season of his hit *Buffy the Vampire Slayer* was airing on The WB – a network that had not existed at the time of his writing for *Roseanne*. This was followed by 'House of Grown-Ups' (R S2E5), 'Brain-Dead Poets' Society' (R S2E10), 'Chicken Hearts' (R S2E13) and 'Fathers and Daughters' (R S2E23). 'Fathers and Daughters' was broadcast the same year that Whedon was writing for the film-turned-television comedy, *Parenthood* (NBC 1990), a show produced by David Tyron King, which was cancelled after a very brief run. His two scripts, 'The Plague' (P S1E3) and 'Small Surprises' (P S1E8), along with his *Roseanne* work meant that Whedon was attracting attention as a talented and reliable comedy writer that would lead to a number of jobs writing loop lines for films. This involved a short dialogue or joke that would help connect one scene to another, and in this capacity he wrote lines for Kim Basinger and Alec Baldwin in *The Getaway* (1994, Roger Donaldson) and for Sharon Stone and Gene Hackman in *The Quick and the Dead* (1995, Sam Raimi) (Havens, 2003: 20). At the same time, he was awaiting news of the script for a feature film he hoped to get produced, called *Buffy the Vampire Slayer*. Optioned by Sandollar in 1988, it was finally offered to Fran and Kaz Rubel Kuzui in 1991 who agreed to make the film if Fran Kazui was to be the director. 20th Century Fox agreed to pay US$9 million to make the movie in exchange for worldwide rights. The film and its aftermath will be discussed in Chapter 1, but for now the important thing to note is that Whedon was a recognised television writer, had a film script in production and was also working as a script doctor on major Hollywood films, such as *Speed* and *Waterworld* (1995, Kevin Reynolds).

But outside of the industry, he was essentially unknown, like most television and film writers at the time (unlike film directors). Twenty years later he is a household name. The television industry has changed dramatically and Whedon remains as committed as ever to the importance of mass art's 'culture-changing' function. Declining to call his work political (I will, however maintain that his aesthetic strategy is praxis), Whedon said in early 2017:

> It's not useful for an artist, for their art, to be political … You kind of have to separate the art from the politics and do them one at a time. My politics are all over my shows. *Ultron* was basically bagging on The Avengers for being out-of-touch rich people. It's always a conflict for me. (O'Connell, 2017)

And it is a conflict that will animate much of the rest of this book.

Part I

Histories of Whedon's works: Politics, industry, art

'Buffy is the slayer. Don't tell anyone': Creating a cultural phenomenon 1

This chapter will look at the first three seasons of *Buffy*, and the ways in which Whedon was able to make the show, the character and himself a 'cultural phenomenon'. This was an explicit desire for Whedon in relation to his first show, 'I wanted her to be a cultural phenomenon. I wanted there to be dolls, Barbie with kung-fu grip' (Lavery and Burkhead, 2011: 28). The mention of Barbie speaks to the heart of one of the difficulties of talking about Whedon. The popular, genre-based mass appeal of his shows and the demand for secondary markets suggests a market-driven profit-based compulsion that obviates, if it does not destroy, the claims to art and progressive politics that this book is proposing. In response to this, it is important to recognise that television is a commercially driven medium and that artistic success can only be achieved if there is also commercial success. Equally, the creation of a television show (unlike a novel, for example) requires enormous investment from a wide range of people who will seek to recoup their investments and make a profit (economic or reputational) from them. To assert that this occludes the possibility of a televisual art is a common but stupid position. There have been recent efforts to recast notions of the aesthetic by insisting that art can never be entirely autonomous but yet still exists as something more than merely ideological symptom or blinker, and in the introduction to the most sustained engagement with this 'new aesthetics' we are told, 'it is impossible now to argue that aesthetics is anything other than thoroughly imbricated with politics and culture. And this without doubt is an entirely good thing' (Joughin and Malpas, 2003: 3). Additionally, art (or form as a function of art) is 'linked to new technologies, economic structures of exchange, social relations of production as well as intrinsic artistic formings of the always already historically shaped material' (Ziarek, 2003: 53).

Whedon's 'cultural phenomenon' is part of these technologies, structures of exchange and relations of production in very clear and explicit ways. His art is industrial, commercial (as indeed all art has always been) and, as such, political. Equally, its intrinsic artistic formings (the aspects mistaken for, or desired as being, autonomous) provide the aesthetic qualities that intersect with the 'political, cultural and industrial' to produce his version of television art. And his art is imbued with a democratic politics that attempts to offer progressive social liberal views while also being attentive to the dangers of the globalised economy that in some ways allows his vision to be seen at all: 'We are now in such a homogenized, globalized monopolized entertainment system ... Eventually there will just be Gap Films and McDonald's films. And that will be it' (Lavery and Burkhead, 2011: 178). His promotion of a feminist politics in a mass entertainment context, which arguably threatens that very politics, is one of the many contradictions and difficulties that his work has to engage with. But he does promote it, and the politics is not ancillary to the art, it is what the art is, formally textually, texturally.

Art and feminism, the two things in the world of which Whedon is most proud, are at the forefront of the opening of *Buffy*. The show's premise, derived from the original movie, is that the person who is routinely the victim in horror films – the blonde girl – becomes the hero. Whedon says, 'I want to see the movie where she walks into a dark alley, a monster attacks her, and she just wails on him' (Lavery and Burkhead, 2011: 53). Here, it is the artistic choices that are seen as irreducibly political: the casual murder of the young woman is both a generic trope and a political expression; it is lazy storytelling and misogyny. Whedon, in *Buffy*, refuses at every turn lazy storytelling, and insists on the inter-penetrating relationships between art and politics. However, the politics is presented as much as an affective aspect of the art as an intellectual one. The audience *feels* the politics as well as thinks it. In part, this is because of Whedon's commitment to the emotional realism of his shows, which shall be discussed presently, but also because he invests his characters (even those seemingly unlike him) with a sense of himself, his own frailties and needs. The blonde girl in the movies is a boring trope; the blonde girl Buffy is a character with whom, in part, Whedon 'identifies'. This identification derives in part from a sense of physical vulnerability ('I have been mugged a lot of times') but also because the pretty blonde frivolous girl that Buffy could appear to be was never expected to be able to 'take care of herself' in much the same way Whedon suggests he was not (Lavery and Burkhead, 2011: 53, 53, 53).

So, Whedon strives to create televisual art that is intrinsically political, but also seeks to ensure that the politics is usually a function of the characters' experience and/or a supposed audience's ability to identify with those characters. Allied with this, is a belief in the knowledge and intelligence of the audience and this is manifested in the opening scene of the pilot of *Buffy*. This scene is vital in establishing many of the moods and tones of the show, but what it also does is assert at the very beginning of the show that it is not only being attentive to horror conventions but also that it recognises and expects the audience to recognise the political challenge that generic rewriting poses. The initial set-up firmly locates the action within a horror context: night-time, low lighting, eerie music and sounds; we are in a high school science lab (the connections and conflicts between the claims for knowledge made by and on behalf of science – a version of Enlightenment rationalism – and the supernatural will be a key feature of the show as it progresses), and the camera provides partial, awkward views. As a window smashes and two characters appear, the audience can reasonably assume that the young man and the blonde girl are up to no good. The girl seems innocent and nervous, scared by sounds, worried about being there. The boy is confident, taking the lead. Horror conventions dictate that possibly both, but certainly she, will die (he might be the aggressor). Given the title of the show, we might as an audience assume that the girl will be Buffy, which would undermine the generic conventions but also be narratively simple. Instead, the girl morphs into a vampire and kills the boy. The usual victim is not the victim, nor is she the hero: she is a monster, able and willing to kill the boy. Generic convention has been held up, played with, subverted and undermined. The refusal to trade on tropes is both an artistic choice (the storytelling is more interesting, more textured, richer, more exciting) and a political one (the narrative laziness that sees the blonde girl die is also misogyny, refusing to be lazy is equivalent to challenging misogyny). We have not yet met Buffy, but *Buffy* has already set out its stall, and in the next three seasons will offer ever more subtle, complex, emotionally resonant stories using all the resources of myth fantasy and legend to offer a 'very real, emotional' (Lavery and Burkhead, 2011: 58) show that will propel televisual art forward. And it will do that, initially, in high school.

By discussing the first three (high school) seasons on *Buffy* in this chapter, I am not asserting any form of qualitative or thematic division between these seasons and the four later ones. But the high school years of Buffy and her friends, before their graduation and increasingly variegated trajectories, do provide a critical unity that does not occur again in the analysis of Whedon. The nature of Whedon's storytelling desires, especially his determination to have stories and characters grow, develop, have memory and exist as an organic whole across seasons, means that some aspect of this chapter will have to discuss episodes from the later seasons, but I will keep these excursions as brief as possible in order to focus on this period.

An obvious point about the first three seasons is that never again will there be the very first Whedon-created and executively produced show to confront. Allied to this is that for these three seasons, Whedon is in sole charge of his sole show. The oeuvre-to-come has not yet arrived, and there is a conceptual simplicity in considering Whedon's ideas and choices as they are (for the most part) only targeted at *Buffy*, although the ever restless energy and creativity means that even within this time frame, other ideas were percolating – not the least of which was *Angel*. Additionally, many of the writing and production staff so frequently associated with the Whedon stable (Marti Noxon, Jane Espenson, Doug Petrie) are on board by the end of season 3. Finally, the relationship with the network, The WB, in these years is largely good.

It is to the network, and the development of *Buffy* from big to small screen that the chapter will now turn, before moving on to describe the creation of the format and some of the central thematic and aesthetic characteristics that led to its critical centrality in the rebirth of Quality TV.[4]

At *Buffy*'s core is Whedon's well reported dissatisfaction with the traditional horror movie and its depiction of the vulnerable weak blonde girl, 'The idea for the film came from seeing too many blondes walking into dark alleyways and being killed ... I wanted, just once, for her to fight back when the monster attacked, and kick his ass' (Havens, 2003: 21). This was the motivation behind the script optioned by Sandollar in 1988 and sold to the Kazuis in 1991. Whedon's response to the final film is as well-known as his initial motivation, 'The director ruined it' (Havens, 2003: 23). His witty take on horror movie misogyny was intended to still be a horror movie, but Kazui chose to read and direct it as much more of a parody and as such the horror and suspense was sacrificed to over-stated comedy.

The disappointment in the film was one of a number of experiences that led Whedon to wish for much greater creative control. His work on

---

[4] Quality TV is a disputed and much debated term. Discussions of it tend to cite particular shows that are Quality TV (definition through example, a kind of recursive self-fulfilment); or, more helpfully deploy a series of thematic, artistic or methodological terms to indicate the characteristics of Quality TV. Among these terms, which will also be used in the current work, are generic hybridity, literary and cinematic ambition, complexity, sophisticated serialised narrative, and inter-series mythologies. This list is taken from the introduction to the excellent collection of essays on the subject in Janet McCabe and Kim Akass' *Quality TV: Contemporary American Television and Beyond* (2007), which I would recommend to anyone who wants to pursue the concept.

Roseanne and *Parenthood* had shown him how different writers' rooms could work, but also illustrated that as a writer he was unlikely to have his vision realised as he was always going to be subject to the executive producer. Similarly, his work in films either as script doctor or credited writer did not offer him the freedom to visualise the scripts he wrote. While he has claimed that writing provides him great 'happiness', that happiness could not sustain the succession of disappointments he endured either in having to compromise to studio conservatism (with some of his jokes for the co-written *Toy Story* script), creative invisibility (*Speed, Waterworld*) or, worse of all, seeing his own scripts badly directed. The mis-handling of his *Buffy* script was matched by what Whedon considers the dreadful direction on *Alien Resurrection*. With typical forthrightness, he accused the film of being 'as badly directed as a movie can be', and was so appalled by the director's cut, which he watched with studio executives, that he began to cry (Havens, 2003: 28–9).

The opportunity to have the creative control he sought came from the unlikely re-arrival of *Buffy*. While the film had been a camp parody, the script was well respected and Whedon's subsequent work was equally highly regarded, especially by Gail Berman who was an executive with Sandollar, the company who had optioned the original script in 1988. Clearly impressed by Whedon's writing, she was also aware of an emerging televisual opportunity. In the period between the *Buffy* film and *Alien Resurrection*, there had been a significant shift in popular culture output, emblematised by the Spice Girls. Girl Power as both a politics and an economic phenomenon had grown out of the more explicitly radical Riot Grrrl movement, and by the late 1990s it had become mainstream. Its presence as a contributor to music and to film was clear. *Scream* (1996, Wes Craven) provides an interesting recasting of the girl in the horror movie fighting back, but in television there was less evidence of the teenage girl who was seeking to assert her own autonomy. One exception to this was *My So-Called Life* (ABC 1994–95), but despite critical acclaim it was cancelled. A mass popular cultural phenomenon that was being readily accommodated in film and music did not have a televisual representative. *Buffy*, which Whedon himself has referred to as a cross between *My So-Called Life* and *The X-Files* (Fox 1993–2002) (Tracy, 1998: 22), would prove to be its champion.

Berman needed to persuade Whedon back into television, a medium he had not working in for many years, and Whedon himself needed to think through the possible format of the show as well as its rationale. Rejecting the idea of its being a children's show, a kind of 'girl power *Power Rangers*' (Havens, 2003: 32), Whedon wrote a script and directed a presentation film. This was Whedon's first attempt at directing, and it was a largely unpleasant experience as his own lack of knowledge was compounded by what he felt was an unhelpful and unresponsive production team. Anthony Stewart Head recalls the filming of the promo, and describes an 'us against them' feeling as well as recounting a conversation with Whedon in which Whedon is claimed to have said:

> This is going to be huge. No-one gets it. The suits are trying to bury it. They haven't the faintest idea what they've got here. This is going to be taken by fans and spread by word of mouth. (Golder, 2011: n.p.)

While Whedon would be proved spectacularly right, the making of the promotional film was difficult. The experience meant that he felt unwilling to direct an episode of the actual series until the finale of season 1. Whedon sees his desire to direct as an extension of his writing, 'I'm a storyteller. I want to tell stories. I want to direct ... I want to speak visually and writing is just a way of communicating visually' (Havens, 2003: 56). In one version of the genesis of *Buffy*, having a television show is just an excuse to use it as 'film school, and I'll teach myself to direct on TV' (Havens, 2003: 56).

While not favoured by Whedon, the as-yet unaired and commercially unavailable presentation (though readily available on the web) has all the hallmark wit and humour, largely excellent acting and, although lacking a soundtrack and good effects, implies the horror of the show. Nearly all the characters are there (except, notably, Angel, although David Boreanaz did film some scenes as an unnamed stranger, but these were cut due to time restrictions and story coherence [Pascale, 2014: 95]), and with the exception of Alyson Hannigan as Willow, the cast is effectively in place. The presentation was a success, and Whedon now had the task of collecting a writing staff and production crew together in order to finally get his own vision on screen in a way that was entirely in keeping with his own wants. I shall discuss the development of this team (Mutant Enemy, Whedon's production company) in Chapter 2.

Whedon's reputation as a skilled writer, and the presentation film, were sufficiently compelling for the still emerging The WB network to agree to a US$1.1 million per episode licensing fee for the Fox produced show. It is clear from a range of comments that relations between The WB and Mutant Enemy in the early years were cordial, bordering on warm (though inevitably occasionally sceptical, as Whedon's comments about 'the suits' above suggests). Jane Espenson has remarked how the Mutant Enemy writers were left 'remarkably alone', and Whedon has given a number of illustrations where potentially awkward content has been the discussion of editorial concern but was always allowed to remain. Most famously in this context was Buffy's use of the word 'slut' to describe how she might look in a particular dress in 'Welcome to the Hellmouth' (B S1E1), and in season 4's 'Hush' (B S4E10), Buffy's mistaken staking gesture and Anya's sign to Xander that she would like to have sex with him. Back in the first season, Jamie Keller, The WB CEO, had shown his delight in the show by declaring that '*Buffy* has all the ingredients. People are finally beginning to say that the show is cool' (Pope, 1997: B1).

Indeed, The WB put a lot of effort into advertising the show with full-page advertisements in publications such as *TV Guide*. Catherine Johnson has written about this campaign from the perspective of Whedon's authorship and the ways in which the Whedon trademark developed over the course of *Buffy*'s run. Initially, the adverts did not use any idea of authorship at all, focusing instead on the lead actor. As Johnson describes it, the advert was like this:

> Across the top is the series' trademark logo, which is replicated in the merchandising produced from the series. Underneath and dominating is a large image of Buffy Summers (Sarah Michelle Gellar) facing the camera and looking off to the right, with a smaller image of her friend Xander (Nicholas Brendon) behind and to her left. The image is accompanied by the text 'for each generation, there is only one slayer' offering a simplified premise for the series. (Johnson, 2005: 114)

Johnson's argument goes onto analyse the different ways in which Buffy is promoted *contra* Sarah Michelle Gellar, and it is a fascinating analysis. What I am interested in here, though, is The WB's efforts to promote the series, even if the promotion is inevitably restrictive. One point Johnson does not make is that at the bottom of the advert is The WB logo followed in large type by the phrase New Drama Series, thereby pigeon-holing a show whose very critical 'cool' appeal is in large at due to its cross-generic format. As has been described elsewhere, despite the network's support for the show, its title did provoke some disquiet. The WB seemed to find the name awkward, suggesting that 'Joss Whedon re-name it with some kind of pun such as *She Slays Me!* Later, the network marketed the show – without telling Whedon – to affiliates as just *Slayer*' (Miles, Pearson and Dickson, 2003: 29). The drama-comedy-horror admixture of the title and its generic multiplicity is ignored in the quite wonderful trailer that aired as a two-minute lead-in to the very first airing of the show. This followed in the wake of a series of promotional slots that had introduced previous slayers in the weeks before to the premiere, and this willingness to invest an as-yet unseen show with a depth of history and backstory is surely one of the reasons it was able to achieve such immediate resonance. A noticeable feature of this trailer is that, like the magazine advertising, it focuses on the drama and horror of the show at the expense of the humour. The early slayers are introduced via a powerful male voice over and documentary-style black and white photographs of open windows, church yards, a portrait of Lucy Hanover (the slayer in 1866), and then dead bodies, trains and city shots of Chicago and another portrait of an unnamed young woman, presumably the 1927 slayer who stops the murders at Union Station. We are then informed 'Now in 1997 it's starting all over again.' We have a shot of what we will come to know as Sunnydale High, which begins in black and white and then becomes colour and this, in turn, is followed by a montage of action shots from the series to come, accompanied by a frantic audio track that comprises dialogue, animal shrieks, discordant music and, as the cuts become more frenetic, a slicing-thumping sound accompanies each one. The overall effect is very exciting, and is a clear indication of The WB's commitment to promoting the show and trying hard to make it a hit.

And a hit it was. While early reviews were mixed and described the first few episodes of season 1 as 'oddball camp' (O'Connor, 1997) and 'unexceptional' (Mietkiewicz, 1997), the more common response of critics was to agree that it was 'one of the brightest shows of the season' (Gliatto, 1997). Whedon's assertion that word of mouth would build the show's fan base is demonstrated by the fact that by the season's end, Thomas Hine could not only claim it as a 'critical and cult favourite', but also did an early piece of web demographic research by telling us that there 'are more than 320 Web sites devoted to her every aspect' (Hine, 1997). Critical, cult, fan and commercial success had been achieved and a second season was ordered. In season 1, half of all episodes were credited as being written by either Whedon or David Greenwalt. Between them they wrote one-third of season 2 episodes, with Marti Noxon writing six. In season 3, Whedon, Greenwalt and Noxon together wrote 12 episodes (or half of all output) with a further third being offered by Jane Espenson, Doug Petrie and David Fury. These figures will be looked at more closely in Chapter 2, but one of the implications is that a very stable writing room, and a very clear sense of writerly knowledge and adherence to Whedon's vision, was possible by virtue of such an integrated team. In addition, it is worth noting that some of the episodes in the early season, while credited to other writers, were rewritten entirely by Whedon. This is important for two reasons: first, while we have to rely on credited contributions to get a sense of who does what, it is clear that in Whedon's case, his contribution is always well in excess of any simple notion of accreditation. And second, it means that he is able to respond to a claim made by Graham Yost, who was the original writer of *Speed* and who had Whedon's name taken off the final credits through arbitration, that Whedon would have done the same thing in his place. Commenting on his unaccredited writing contribution to *Buffy*, Whedon says, 'it means I finally have an answer [to Yost]. Which is, "No, I wouldn't"' (Lavery and Burkhead, 2011: 97).

The solidity of the writing room would never be quite matched by an equivalent directorial team, but, in addition to Whedon himself, a great many of the directors who would contribute many episodes to *Buffy* were in place – Bruce Seth Green, David Solomon (who helped Whedon edit the unaired presentation piece), James Whitmore Jr and David Semel among them. Just as Whedon rewrote parts of most, and occasionally all of a script, so too he oversaw the directors. Partly this was down to his being on set for almost the entirety of the first three seasons, 'because once you've written something you have to make sure it's actually shot the way it's written ... You can get a terrible hack or a really great guy who just missed one really important point' (Lavery and Burkhead, 2011: 106). The overseeing role is, for Whedon, a function of being executive producer who is 'basically the director [who] doesn't have to create anything but is responsible for everything' (Lavery and Burkhead, 2011: 105). Whedon expresses an understanding of the difficulty of being an itinerant director through a comment told to him by David Semel about the problem of entering into a new environment where everyone already knows each other, understands the executive producer and the director has to 'pretend that you're going to tell them what to do and that they're going to listen to you' – Whedon comments, 'It's tough' (Lavery and Burkhead, 2011: 105).

Despite the difficulty of being a director in this situation, Whedon was able to work with a changing but steady group of trusted colleagues who, along with the stable writer's room, provided the basis for the creation of the show's second and third seasons. By the end of season 3, the characters (and the viewers – 'the characters have to feel the way the audience does' (Lavery and Burkhead, 2011: 73)) have been taken on a very long and often harrowing journey. And it is a journey in which the emotional lives of the characters and viewers have been embroiled in the aesthetic-political structures of the show's stories, seasons and arcs.

The emphasis on the emotional lives of the characters is one of the defining principles of Whedon's work. As Glen Creeber (2004: 115) points out, Whedon is, himself, part of a tradition of writers and producers who seek to have emotional depth:

> Even TV serials like *Twin Peaks* (ABC 1990–91) ... could be said to have been influenced by this new style of drama, [the] interest in small-town life

> and close-knit communities and friends echoing the type of preoccupation with private existence more commonly associated with traditional TV soap operas ... Indeed much contemporary TV teen drama like *Buffy the Vampire Slayer* ..., *Dawson's Creek* (The WB 1998–2003) and *Charmed* (Spelling Television 1998–[2006]) addresses similar concerns ... always from the perspective of their private and emotional lives.

Whedon's main concern is to write stories, to tell tales, to create worlds inhabited by characters about whom the audience really cares. His desire to recast genre tropes (the blonde girl in horror movies) has obvious artistic intention, which is the re-invigoration and extension of a form; and it has clear political resonance, which is an attempt to provide different versions of masculinity and femininity with these, as Lorna Jowett (2005: 1) puts it, being neither conservative nor radical but 'a contradictory mixture of both'. However, both of these have to be subservient to the 'emotional realism [that] is the core of the show' and which, moreover, is 'the only thing I'm really interested in' (Lavery and Burkhead, 2011: 7). First and foremost, then, the early seasons of *Buffy* had to provide compelling stories that had deep emotional impact. The fact that these stories exist in a fantasy world of demons is a way of allowing the emotional realism its widest possible scope because you have 'great license' to take characters to 'very dark' places on a weekly basis without having to worry that your characters will look 'schizophrenic' as they would on a 'normal' (non-genre) show (Lavery and Burkhead, 2011: 7). At the same time, however, the viewer has to feel emotionally connected, drawn to the 'realism' in the sense of there being an identification on behalf of the viewer and his or her lived reality, and the reality of the characters.[5]

For Whedon, audience identification with his characters is not just an aspect of the show, it is its reason, it is the force that drives him to write.

---

[5] I am using 'identification' as a term that indicates the fact of a strong emotional response by a viewer to a character or show with which they see/feel/desire/invent some shared identity. It is not being used to offer an explanation as to how this identification occurs, beyond the suggestion that the televisual format (an approximation of mimesis) provides the conditions of such an identification. For a fuller and more developed account of identification, see Murray Smith's (1995) *Engaging Characters*, where he offers a careful discussion that actually rejects 'identification' as a critical term in favour of 'levels of engagement' that comprise a 'structure of sympathy'. A similar attempt to understand the emotional response and how individuals identify with characters and shows in the complex area of serial television and intermedial spectatorship is offered by Benjamin Brojakowski's (2015) 'Spoiler alert: understanding television enjoyment in the social media era'.

Often ignored or castigated as irrelevant or 'naive', identification is crucial in understanding the power of Whedon's show. The multiple identifications offered by *Buffy* and sought so strenuously by Whedon, are versions of a broader notion where identifications:

> are the source of some our most powerful, enduring and deeply felt pleasures ... the source of considerable emotional turmoil, capable of unsettling or unmooring the precarious groundings of our everyday identities ... Identifications are erotic, intellectual and emotional. They delight, fascinate, confuse, unnerve and sometimes terrify. (Fuss, 1995: 2)

Whedon writes about his effort to make *Buffy* a show with which everyone who has gone through adolescence can identify, and whose identification with the 'mythologised' process into adulthood makes them a hero. The exaggerated stories that *Buffy* allows through its horror-fantasy form creates a context for identification where the viewer loves the show 'in a way other shows can't be loved' (Lavery and Burkhead, 2011: 28).

Identification only happens, can only happen, through mimesis. For Phillippe Lacoue-Labarthe (1990: 82), we need the concept of identification because it is: 'ultimately the only one we possess to designate what is at stake in the mimetic process and, above all, because once eased out of its aesthetic-psychological context ... it can be drawn into the stronger network of the proper ... and appropriating, of appropriation and de-propriation or disappropriation etc.'. The intimate connection between identification, mimesis and forms of appropriation encourages Robert Eaglestone (2003: 159) to assert 'identification is the basis of politics ... What is at stake in the mimetic process is identification, which is what makes up the political.' One of the essential aspects that links the aesthetic to the political is identification, and this is at the heart of Whedon's artistic endeavour. The identification (whether erotic, intellectual or emotional, though for Whedon strongly directed to the emotional) is predicated on a mimetic process that impels emotional realism, though need not be based on a formal realism. In addition, we need to recognise that mimesis, both as a category and as a specific object of study, must not be understood ahistorically; to do so 'neglects not only the aesthetic process of production but also the changing historical forms of mimesis' (Ziarek, 2003: 53). Television drama is a perfect example of the changing forms and the absolute link between aesthetics and modes of production.

Buffy derives its emotional realism precisely from a format that espouses the fantastical. The world represented in *Buffy*, and established so securely in the first three seasons, is not imitative of a real one, or at least is not solely imitative of a real one. But emotional realism is not formal realism, and formal realism is only ever a technique anyway. In televisual terms, realism is the establishing of a format and then working *within* the boundaries of that format each episode to tell the stories. If the format includes vampires and high school students and sunshine and werewolves and arcane organisations and ancient rites and monsters in another dimension, then as long as those features are understood and kept in the narrative world, in the format, then the world will appear 'real' in the sense of textually self-similar.

Buffy's great achievement is to have created a format (a textually self-similar world) that is fantastical *and* recognisable (real-seeming), which allows these emotionally intense stories to be told, which urges identification not only with its characters, but with the world created by the show – which is the same as saying with the show as such. The identification with the show (intellectual and emotional) is created in part because the format becomes unstable, expands *beyond* the seemingly safe confines of its textual self-similarity thereby becoming less known, but *feeling* truer.

The first example of this occurs in the penultimate episode of season 1, 'Out of Mind, Out of Sight' (B S1E11). The season has typically offered us a set of episodes in which the monsters and demons act as metaphors and allegories for growing up in an American high school (Wilcox, 2001). The traumas of dating loom large, as do parental pressure, peer pressure, gangs, physical abuse, intractable authority and so on. The metaphors have been recognised as such by the audience by the wonderful imposition of the supernatural onto the real-seeming world of Sunnydale such that the representational conflict between realism and horror is resolved at the point of allegorical recognition. The world, then, remains understood and knowable; the demons are a threat to that world, are defeated, and the emotional metaphor is registered. However, in the episode, the affectively powerful but intellectually contained representations are massively subverted, and it is a subversion that marks the beginning of the audience's awareness that the realism that underpins the show (the textual self-similarity) and provides us with a 'real' Sunnydale is true only as technique and belies the fact that Sunnydale is in fact not what we thought we knew at all.

When the character Marcie Ross is so ignored by students and teachers at Sunnydale High that she becomes invisible, the metaphor is clear. Interestingly, the episode is one that under the name 'Invisible Girl' was part of Whedon's pitch for the show, and fleshed out his thesis that 'High school is a horror movie' (Lavery and Burkhead, 2011: 50).

More than that, Whedon's own sense of identification with his characters (as well as his determination to make the audience identify) is here very clear, being based as it is on 'when I was fifteen I actually drew a picture of myself becoming transparent' (Lavery and Burkhead, 2011: 50). In the episode, Buffy and friends chase down the mystery, uncover the cause and try to right the wrongs. As Scott Westerfield has discussed, the resolution of this sort of story, a 'trespass' story as he calls it, tends towards a restitution of the normal, the explanation of the event and the covering-up of the awkward supernatural elements. Most pertinently for *Buffy*, the gang of the original *Scooby Doo* (CBS/ABC/The WB/CW 1969–present), from whom the show's so-called Scoobies take their name, were always able to demonstrate that the supernatural was, in fact, simply a ruse created by a criminal, thereby normalising the events (Westerfield, 2003: 30–40).

Buffy has had its cover-up stories, the implication of which is that the residents of Sunnydale, and of the wider world are unaware of, and need to remain unaware of, the existence of the supernatural. The earliest of these is Cordelia Chase's explanation for the events in 'The Harvest' (B S1E2), which she reasons away as:

> Well, I heard it was rival gangs. You know, fighting for turf? But all I can tell you is they were an ugly way of looking. And Buffy, like, knew them! Which is just too weird. I mean, I don't even remember that much, but I'm telling you, it was a freak show!

Giles's (Rupert Giles, Buffy's watcher) response to the incredulous Scoobies is simply, 'People have a tendency to rationalise what they can and forget what they can't' (B S1E2). So, the show is playing with the notion of a normal town besieged by monsters, but which no-one except our heroes and the audience know about.

The case of Marcie Ross is different, however. Having figured out the cause of the attacks and discovered Marcie's condition we have a subversion of narrative expectation insofar as the discovery (knowledge) does not bring success (restitution) because Marcie cannot be saved by Buffy. Among other plausible reasons for this is Buffy's own assertion that Marcie is a 'thundering loon' (B E1S11). This pleasingly amusing undermining of expectations is then drastically amplified when we see Marcie being led into a classroom (or we see a seemingly empty classroom with books rustling, desks opening and chairs moving and infer from that that Marcie is there with other people [see Figure 1]) and discover that this is a spy training-class for the FBI and today's lesson is 'Assassination and infiltrations' to which invisible Marcie's response is 'cool' (B S1E11).

Figure 1 Marcie Ross enters her classroom, filled with other invisible would-be FBI agents. *Buffy the Vampire Slayer*, 'Out of Sight, Out of Mind', season 1, episode 11, first broadcast 19 May 1997. As we watch the agents open the door to a classroom, seemingly empty except for the teacher, it becomes clear that the world of the supernatural is known about well beyond the confines of the Scoobies and the Watchers' Council.

Suddenly the premise of the show, its expression of a sophisticated 'trespass' story is shifted. Trespass stories work by virtue of the secret, which is absolute. Yet here, the world in which Sunnydale is situated is now not one where only we and the Scoobies know of the supernatural, potentially demonic, aspect, but the FBI does too. Apart from being a nod to *The X-Files* (Fox 1993–2002), this causes the audience to shift its response to the world of the show. The textually self-similar has slipped and a seeming given (no-one knows about the monsters) has to give way to the knowledge that some, perhaps many, more people are aware of the monsters' presence.

The audience is never given an explanation for the fate of Marcie. We are simply presented with a fact and left to infer our own response. We are left in a state of unknowing. This is a ploy that the show uses on a number of occasions and it is one of the reasons for the sustaining interest in it. Unlike the simple restoration of order at the end of a trespass tale where the real is unproblematically maintained in a mythical state of sameness, the *Buffy*verse is malleable, changeable and unknowable in an absolute sense; it is conceptually monstrous such that the world itself is a constituent part of the potential for surprise and shock.

If the FBI can know about Marcie, then the secret is evidently less well kept than previously assumed. This can be accommodated in our experience of Sunnydale (and maybe even, as Giles suggests, forgotten about) only at the expense of foregoing the belief in the reality of Sunnydale as somehow equivalent to a world that we could plausibly inhabit. The fictionality of the world has been explicitly re-enforced through the expansion of the knowledge of the supernatural beyond Sunnydale but, importantly, beyond our ken, too. So, at the same time that show's fictional element has been re-asserted, it *feels* truer than ever because, like our own world, it refuses to explain aspects of itself. It is both familiar and strange, known and inscrutable. The audience may identify with Marcie by virtue of feeling unexceptional or ignored; it may identify with Buffy as the selfless saviour, it may identify with Cordelia and her realisation that her actions and words affect the world: but in addition, and the addition is vital, they will identify with the *world* presented in its growing strangeness, its resolute resistance to simplification and, as a consequence, its openness to both the terror of external change and unrecognised threat *and* the potential of the world not only to change but to *be* changed. The world of *Buffy* is a world that encourages identification through mimeses, but that also asserts the (difficult) possibility of political action – which is to say, refusing the ineluctable, the fated, the given, static and natural.

The first three seasons in different ways provide stories and characters who defy fate, refuse the given, and challenge both the world within the show, but also the world without to identify and as such to recognise both their own political potentiality, and the intersection of art and politics that the show enacts as much as illustrates.

Season 1 establishes the show's main characters, their environment, the production values, and the thematic and narrative concerns that will be the core around which the remaining season will circulate. The production values of *Buffy* are at least as important to its success and critical evaluation as the themes and characters. The growing fragmentation of the markets since the de-regulation of television in 1984 by the Reagan administration and the concomitant need for networks to differentiate themselves from each other and to market their brand identity meant that style (or as Catherine Johnson [2005: 98] puts it, 'the performance of style') became hugely important in the creation of a show. This is discussed in relation to the creation of formats in Chapter 7, but its importance for *Buffy* is clear. The shift from 'family' programming to 'teen' programming that The WB undertook and that *Buffy* helped to promote does not imply a demographic so much as an ideal. A teen show need not be watched only by a teen market, and the notion of 'teen' is as much a marker of a sensibility as an age group. Whedon's group of high school kids clearly offers a teen-related set of storylines with all of the possible teen-related advertising potential implied by that. Equally, however, Whedon wrote a horror-fantasy show, and creates a world that is as much cult as teen, with the necessary 'performed styles' that become transferable to secondary market merchandising. Whedon's unabashed celebration of the cult-related merchandising that opens this chapter indicates, once again, the absolute interconnectedness of the economic and the aesthetic. It also demonstrates that the style of *Buffy* did what it was meant to do: it helped to create a cult teen hit with which the audience identifies to a degree of almost 'slavish devotion', which receives entire 'respect' from Whedon because the show is 'designed to foster' that level of commitment, and Whedon shares it (Lavery and Burkhead, 2011: 16). The 'design' of the show is probably meant more generally than this, but it is clear that the production design, the visual style, contributes significantly to the show's success, and its identifications, precisely because this is where the *feel* of the show comes from. This feel of playfulness and foreboding, daytime lightness and night-time dark, teenage drama and gothic horror show, emotional anguish and comedy is not only written but also seen and heard. This will be discussed more fully in Chapters 4 and 6.

The opening season creates the format and establishes the main concerns. The mythology is given to the audience early on in an exposition scene that will be discussed in Chapter 4, but the idea of a girl who is singularly chosen (though by what mechanism remains a mystery expect that it is fated and irrefutable) to fight vampires and demons is clear. The notion that Sunnydale is over the mouth of hell, and therefore especially susceptible to supernatural phenomena, is also presented. Buffy is introduced as both slayer and teenager, and her friends Xander Harris and Willow Rosenberg are presented as typical high school students in an atypical high school by virtue of its provenance to the Hellmouth and the presence of a representative of the Watchers' Council, Rupert Giles, the librarian. Over the course of the season, we see Buffy struggle with the tensions produced by virtue of her trying to be a 'normal' girl and a mythical warrior, of trying to have friendships while needing to protect those friends from the apocalypse, of having her mother not know her secret. In the figure of Buffy, the show's themes of fate, responsibility, freedom, moral ambiguity, family, love and friendship are embodied. Her obligation to fight vampires places her in conflict with authority figures such as the school principal and her mother; the desire to protect her friends by fighting alone competes with the urge to have a community; her wish for the freedom to date is compromised by the need to keep secrets; and her moral duty to kill vampires is severely threatened by her falling in love with Angel, a vampire with a soul.

Seemingly simple aspects of the mythos (slayers kill vampires) produce extraordinarily complex storylines both in terms of narrative progressions, emotional intensity and interactions, and ethical and political questions. Buffy's love for Angel does not exist in a vacuum, and her desires and actions directly impinge on her friends and family. As do her friends' actions on her, though often in the sense of Buffy having to rescue them as result of their actions. Xander falls in love with a girl who is a mummy and a teacher who is a monster; Willow's online lover turns out to be an ancient demon; a cheerleader is, in fact, possessed by her over-bearing mother; and all the while Buffy is trying to find a way to defeat the Master, an old and very dangerous vampire, trapped under ground but on the verge of escape. His bullying, threatening, controlling role as head of his family is contrasted with the structures of emotional attachment Buffy finds herself in where negotiations of the hierarchy are constantly at play, whether it be the tutee/surrogate daughter/colleague relationship with Giles; the ever-fluctuating dynamics of the Scooby gang, or her relationship with her mother – Buffy's friendship and family groups are fraught but respectful places of discussion, disagreement, trust and responsibility. Jessica Prata Miller (2003: 40) convincingly argues for Buffy's (and by implication *Buffy*'s) refusal to accept abstract moral positions:

> Buffy frequently works through moral questions in context rather than trying to abstract away from details. And if this context includes people she knows well, then their unique attributes, situation and features also get taken into account.

The first season sets up a storytelling format that will be repeated throughout all of Whedon's shows. Each episode sets up a specific monster or demon to be fought. In the process of researching the demon, devising a strategy for defeating it, and enacting this strategy, the characters will interact with each other. These interactions will usually address both the particular story, but also the on-going stories that each of them is experiencing. Often, though not always, the characters' stories will reflect on the monster story, or vice versa. At the episode's end, the monster will have been defeated and there will be closure *of that story*, but the character stories will carry over to the next episode and the next. In this way, Whedon is able to offer satisfying, self-contained narratives of horror, suspense, drama and resolution. To this extent, he provides the financially desired format of the syndicated series, where unchanging 'flat' characters repeat each week a recognisable story that is different enough from the previous week's story to seem new or innovative, but similar enough to afford the pleasure of the same, the illusion of difference in the iterability of the actually invariable. Alongside this, however, with its derogation of the aesthetic, Whedon has these expansive character dramas that take place over the whole seven seasons. As with the expansion of the world discussed above, the characters change, develop, react and respond, remember, challenge. Whedon's frustrations with the unchanging character is well known and best summed up in his comments regarding *The X-Files*: 'After five years I just started yelling at Scully, "You're an idiot. It's a monster," and I couldn't take it anymore. I need people to grow, I need them to change, I need them to learn and explore, you know, and die and do all of the things that people do in real life' (Lavery and Burkhead, 2011: 4).

While it may be true that the above quotation and indeed the show itself can allow for claims such as this by Catherine Johnson (2005: 157): 'the primary emphasis in *Buffy* is on the development and growth of its characters over time', it is important to assert that not only the characters, but the show also grows, explores and has memory. Season 2 maintains a focus on the themes described above, but intensifies in quite some measure the love interests of the characters. And love is devastatingly unforgiving. Xander begins to go out with Cordelia, which breaks Willow's heart and alienates Cordelia from all her friends. Willow finds solace with Oz, but nearly dies at the season's end; Giles falls in love with computer teacher and techno-pagan Jenny Calendar only to first feel betrayed when it is clear she is a member of the gypsy clan who cursed Angel, and then to feel the unadulterated horror of discovering her dead body, laid out in a macabre, sadistic dumb show by Angelus. Spike and Drusilla, the resident evil in Sunnydale now that the Master has been defeated, find themselves in a bizarre love triangle with the newly de-souled Angelus, and Spike even goes so far as to team up with Buffy to get Drusilla away from Angel. Love is a horrifying, destructive, relentless source of pain, misery and confusion.

Love and its depredations is also a source of some of the deepest seams of aesthetic pleasure and identifications. Whedon worked with this knowledge in order to produce a season of stunning emotional rawness, but also (and just as importantly) to enable The WB to expand its broadcast provision. Love, sex, death and rebirth – all that happened in two exceptional episodes in January 1998. On Monday 19 January, after the Christmas hiatus, the episode 'Surprise' (B S2E13) had aired in which Buffy celebrates her birthday by finally consummating her relationship with Angel. Angel, over 250 years old, a vampire with a soul and Buffy's love interest, defender and champion for the previous season and a half was now her lover. Whedon has routinely stated that one of the reasons for the idea of *Buffy* was to refuse the notion that the pretty blonde must be punished for having sex, which seems to be the staple of many horror texts. However, having Buffy have sex with Angel presented a problem, namely: how to avoid them becoming like Sam and Diane[6] in *Cheers* (NBC 1982–93) (Whedon, 2001a: n.p.). His answer was to find 'the emotional horror of everything they go through' and this begins in 'Innocence' (B S2E14).

Effectively written as the second part of 'Surprise', 'Innocence' is notable for being the first episode that Whedon wrote and directed that was not a finale or premiere. It was the fourteenth episode of the season. However, in many respects it is exactly a premiere. In a very real sense it was The WB's premiere to its 'New Tuesday' line up, acting as the station's Tuesday flagship and lead-in for the new teen drama *Dawson's Creek*. It is a testament to the network's faith in the show, and in its developing identity as a young adult channel, that *Buffy* would be its standard bearer. The show that had more than any other established The WB as a critically lauded network would now launch its iconic night.

The co-ordination necessary between network and executive producer was considerable. The network needed to provide Whedon with enough time to create an episode that would drag the audience over from Monday to Tuesday, and compete with the comedies *Clueless* on UPN (1996–99) and *Mad About you* on NBC (1992–99), Fox's movie night, CBS's action thriller *JAG* (1995–2005) and *Soul Man* on ABC (1997–98). Not only that, the episode was also, of course, intended to create new audiences. In essence, Whedon was being asked to write a new pilot. It is a stunning episode. Whedon himself calls it 'the most important episode of *Buffy* that we did' (Whedon, 2001a: n.p.) and in the context of its launching a new night of the network and acting as a pilot to grab new viewers it is easy to see why.

The answer to the 'Sam and Diane' question is breathtaking in its audacity. Buffy's love interest, champion and friend for the previous year now, because of the curse that we have known about from the beginning, transforms into Angelus, the sadistic, appalling, ferocious vampire who will terrorise Buffy and her friends, kill school teacher,

---

6 The Sam and Diane question is how to maintain the dramatic conflict and narrative desire created by two people *not* being in a relationship when they end up in one – the particular reference is to the disappointment felt by many fans of *Cheers* after the pair became a couple and the subsequent inability to find storylines and character interaction that replicated the pre-couple episodes.

and Giles's love interest, Jenny Calendar, and who we see in the opening few seconds of the teaser murder a prostitute with lascivious relish. Whedon has produced a new show, which is so similar to the old one that it is both a pilot and a continuation, something frighteningly new and the completion of a two-parter: it is the premiere to The WB's 'New Tuesday' and to a new-*Buffy*, a show that literally overnight became darker, crueller, more painful, more adult.

Season 2 had already expanded the world of the *Buffy* by introducing a second slayer, Kendra, called when Buffy had died fighting the Master at the end of season 1, a death that seemed to assert prophecy and fate, but which refuted it by virtue of Xander's administering of CPR, an intervention at once narratively and emotionally compelling, but politically important as it affirms the world than can change and can *be* changed by human intervention. In addition, we discover the complex and unexpectedly vicious parts of Giles's character, and witness a careful, subtle, tender grown up love affair between him and Jenny. But it, and all the love affairs, produces pain. Most of all, Buffy's. The season's end is a two-parter that could be the subject of a book on its own. Angelus is trying to release an ancient demon called Acathla to bring about hell on earth. During the episodes, we see Angel's history in flashback; the mythology is extended through the character of Whistler, a mysterious demon who offers gnomic advice and is an intermediary for some higher powers; Buffy's mother discovers her secret and kicks her out of home; she is expelled from school; Spike teams up with Buffy; Willow's increasing capacity as a witch is seen; Kendra is killed; and Buffy's only way of saving the world is to kill Angelus, which she does but only after the spell Willow performs to give Angel his soul back works, and Buffy realises that she is in fact killing her lover, her friend, her heart's desire and not the sadistic monster who has been inhabiting him. It is a devastating scene. Along the way we have been offered historical drama, police procedural, hospital drama, action, and a moment of exquisite mordant comedy when Spike and Joyce, Buffy's mother, sit silently in the lounge.

As mentioned, the story revolves around trying to stop Angelus discovering the spell that will release the sword from Acathla and thus herald in the end of the world, and also around Willow trying to recreate the initial curse that gave Angelus his soul to make him Angel in the first place. This curse was discovered on a floppy disk at the side of Jenny Calendar's desk and demonstrates that Ms Calendar had been trying to rectify the wrong she is deemed to have done by not telling Giles and Buffy that she knew of Angel's curse. As Angelus, Drusilla and a duplicitous Spike torture Giles in order to gain the information they need, Willow in her hospital bed tries to summon the magical power necessary to make her spell successful. The police are after Buffy because they suspect her of killing Kendra. Willow sends Xander off with a specific purpose – he is to find Buffy and tell her that she needs to stall for time in order to give Willow the opportunity to let the spell work. When he does catch up with her, all he says is that Willow wants Buffy to 'kick his ass' (B S2E22). This will be discussed briefly below.

As Buffy enters the old factory that has been Angelus's base, she has been expelled, accused of murder, kicked out of home and is about to kill the man who was her true love and who is responsible for the murder of her watcher's lover. Her position is, to say the least, bleak. Xander helps rescue Giles, Spike grabs Drusilla and the fight between Buffy and Angelus gathers pace. At one point, Buffy stumbles. The stage directions from the shooting script have this:

> Angel approaches Buffy. She tries to move from the corner, but he moves with her. She's boxed in.
>
> He plays the sword near her face, loving this.
>
> ANGEL
> That's everything, huh? No weapons, no friends.
> No hope. Take all that away and what's left?
>
> Buffy stares at him, his words hitting home. She looks exhausted, and terribly sad. She shuts her eyes.
>
> He lunges, shooting his arm out, the sword straight at her face.
>
> Without opening her eyes she slams her palms together over the blade, stopping it an inch from her face.
>
> She opens her eyes.
>
> BUFFY
> Me.

The 'terribly sad' Buffy of the script is rendered with astonishing pathos by Sarah Michelle Gellar in the aired episode, but she is also exceptionally well helped by Michael Gershman the director of photography who creates frames and lighting effects that augment Buffy's sense of isolation and abandonment perfectly. The scene occurs in the garden of Angel's mansion, a space designed explicitly to 'stay away from Gothic' (Meyer, 2001), and which, further, had a 'modern, sterile look' (Landau, 2001). Contextualised outside of the easy stereotypes of horror anthology shows, and also well away from the plush domestic spaces of soap operas, this battle (the slayer versus the evil Angelus; the young girl confronting her tormentor; the lover seeing her past love) pits two evenly matched but emotionally opposite characters. Angelus is confident, cocky, sure of his success, thrilled by his ability. Buffy is in the midst of a personal crisis that will culminate either in the end of the world, or in her killing her ex-lover. As the fight progresses, we see Angelus in the ascendancy. Spike has the unconscious Drusilla in his arms, sees Buffy's plights, comments on her imminent demise, shrugs and leaves.

This brings Angelus into shot, through the doorway of the garden and into the courtyard. He is in medium close up with seeming-natural light coming from behind him and to his right. His cheek is softly lit, and there is a shadow over the rest of his face. Over his right shoulder a branch of a creeper and its foliage and flowers are simply and naturally lit, and the space behind him offers him a sense of purpose and confidence.

Buffy, by contrast, is crouched against a wall, she has no space, nowhere to go: Angelus is in front of her, wielding a sword, and the wall blocks off any escape. It is dark, the creepers are not lit, the foliage barely visible. She is lit by a wall-mounted lantern (now out of shot) that hangs directly above her and slightly to her right and emits a bright yellow-white light that works against the otherwise blueish lighting of her in the scene. We see her in full close up and the downlight from the slight angle places her left eye, the left side of her nose, and her left cheek in shadow. Her lips are pale. The other side of her face is lit brightly and appears to actually reflect the light in an unhealthy fashion. This lighting choice is in stark contrast to more usual representations of heroes:

> As with film lighting, in television drama there is often a conventional link between 'clean lighting' – lighting which throws little or no shadow onto the face, so the features seem less harsh and the face more beatific – and the implied 'pureness' of the character and apparent prettiness of the actor. (Lury, 2005: 39)

There is a cut to Angelus, swaggering and taunting, and then a cut back to Buffy. In the previous shot we were sitting at roughly six o'clock to her twelve o'clock; now we are situated somewhere between seven and eight o'clock but still in a very full close up of her face. This slight angle of our vision places even more of Buffy's face in shadow but means that the remaining skin appears to be even more reflective, even sallower. She shuts her eyes and as Angelus thrusts the sword to her face her

Figure 2 Buffy, finding her strength and asserting that what is left after everything else is taken away is, 'Me'. *Buffy the Vampire Slayer*, 'Becoming (part two)', season 2, episode 22, first broadcast 19 May 1998. The lighting, composition, make-up, set design, choreography, music and Gellar's acting provide a moment of heightened televisual drama and dense characterisation.

hands shoot up and grasp the blade between her two thumbs. Alone, crouching, seemingly defeated, Buffy draws strength from herself and deflects the attack.

We cut back to Angelus, surprised by the rebuttal of his thrust. And we then cut straight back to Buffy. We are now between six and seven o'clock. Her face is reflecting even more light, her skin is clear and her demeanour is calm. She opens her eyes wide and says in response to Angelus's earlier question, '... what's left?' by saying simply, 'Me' (see Figure 2).

The scene from Angelus's entrance to Buffy's affirmation of herself has taken 18 seconds. In that time we have seen a physical fight scene transmute into a psychological victory. Buffy's transformation has been achieved through three cuts each of which has slightly shifted our perspective and each of which has amplified the lighting effect on her face. The odd reflective nature of her face changes meaning as it moves from seemingly implying illness, vulnerability to actually expressing sureness of purpose and self-belief.

Storytelling here, narrative, is absolutely created through cinematography, lighting and editing, and they combine to provide a particular lighting effect that serves to significantly amplify the sense of Buffy at her most stripped down, emotionally and physically vulnerable in order that the sheer fact of her being the Slayer is magnified. The young girl might be at breaking point, but the Slayer finds her centre and strength. It is a marvellous piece of televisual storytelling, and the fact that it acts as a precursor to Buffy having to kill the newly re-ensouled Angel only minutes later makes it all the more memorable. And, as Arnie Cox and Rebecca Fülöp (2010: 70) also make clear, the score works incredibly hard to add further emotional intensity, in part because of its familiarity, 'only a theme that has accrued so many associations could generate such pathos'.

Buffy's strength, though, is matched by her grief – she has killed her lover, been expelled from her school, and been exiled by her mother. She leaves Sunnydale on a bus headed for we know not where, until season 3.

The third season has two major new additions. The first is 32 mm film stock. The first 36 episodes had all been filmed on 16 mm. As Michael Gershman, the director of photography, says, 'it is hard to get depth from 16 mm' (Oppenheimer, 1999: 91) and his solution was to use two different kinds of light in a frame, with different colours, to provide the illusion of depth. This became a signature part of *Buffy*'s look, and is part of what contributed to its distinctive style, but the move to 32 mm allowed for greater clarity and depth. This improvement in the visuality of the show was used to tell the story of Buffy's return, her efforts to regain the trust of her mother, watcher and friends, and the arrival of new slayer Faith who had been called after Kendra's death. Angel mysteriously arrives back from the Hell dimension where he had been suffering agonies, and Buffy keeps his presence secret, thereby breaking her friends' trust once again. Willow is jealous of a burgeoning closeness between Buffy and Faith. Faith, though, is unstable and she betrays the Scoobies by joining forces with the season's major bad guy, Mayor Wilkins who is a demon worshipper seeking to 'ascend' to the realm of demon himself. Xander and Willow each betray their lovers by giving in to their sexual desires for each other just as Cordelia and Oz come to rescue them. Giles betrays Buffy by performing an ancient rite of passage as demanded by the Watchers' Council. Cordelia, humiliated and heartbroken, conjures an alternative Sunnydale to which Buffy had never come and we see the devastation of a world without Buffy, and importantly, the cold nihilistic killer that Buffy would be without her friends whose trust she so flagrantly abuses. It is a season of doubles, doubt and deception.

If love wreaked havoc and destruction in season 2, it is the gruelling work of friendship and trust that is at the heart of season 3. And Buffy does, again, prove her loyalty and responsibility. At the point at which she, her friends and her classmates are about to graduate and leave school, she is awarded a new 'Class Protector' award, and she galvanises everyone into an army to defeat the mayor. At the point of its passing, the community coheres and trust is rewarded with victory. The high school is destroyed in the huge explosion needed to kill the ascended Mayor. Angel leaves in a selfless, if painful, gesture; Xander buys a newly destitute Cordelia her prom dress that she, graciously, accepts; Willow and Oz reconcile and Giles's expulsion from the Watchers' Council for showing too much love to Buffy proves to her his genuine commitment. Less emotionally intense, perhaps, than season 2, season 3 is more emotionally nuanced as one might expect from a show in which the characters are growing up.

The third season is also the first in which there was public disagreement between Whedon and the network. The cause of the disagreement lay initially outside of the control of either and was the Columbine High School massacre. Eric Harris and Dylan Klebold's murderous rampage led to a number of responses in the USA, one of which was a predictable attempt to find an aspect of the media somehow culpable. Jamie Keller, The WB CEO, decided that the episodes 'Earshot' (B S3E18) and 'Graduation Day II' (B S3E22) would be postponed out 'of sympathy for the people in those ... communities' (Stafford, 2007: 11). The tacit acceptance in this move of the thesis that there is a causal relationship between media representation of violence and acts of violence in the real world prompted Sarah Michelle Gellar to issue a statement that said, 'By cancelling intelligent programming like *Buffy*, corporate entertainment is not addressing the problem' (Topping, 2002: 229). Whedon's response was more in line with The WB's but he still clearly expressed his disappointment in any claim that the media was responsible. In relation to 'Earshot', Whedon (2001b) wrote this on a posting wall:

> On the inevitable subject, as far as pre-empting the ep, I agreed with the decision and when you see it you'll agree, I think, that it was just badly timed. But it WILL air. I'm proud of it. It comments on that type of sitch, and obviously we come down AGAINST massacring people, but ANY comment after so desperate a tragedy would be offensively trite. Needless to type, this BLAME THE MEDIA thing makes me crazy. Remember when Dan Quayle blamed the LA riots on Murphy Brown? Everybody laffed, but NOBODY TALKED ABOUT THE RIOTS ANYMORE. It's just a way of avoiding the subject – and of making sense of something to ugly to deal with by latching onto a scapegoat. Sigh. (But it is Marilyn Manson's fault.)

Notwithstanding the trademark irony of the final comment, Whedon shows a sensible response that insists on his show's sincerity and commitment, but also suggests that a boy up a tower with a gun might be less than sensitive at the particular time it was due to air.

He is less sanguine about the postponement of 'Graduation Day II'. While expressing understanding at The WB's decision, Whedon (2001b) is clear that he does not agree with it:

> Controversy. Not my fave. For the record, I don't think The WB had to pre-empt the ep, but I understand why they did. When those of you who haven't seen it do, you'll wonder what all the fuss was about. But one violent graduation incident and The WB and I would feel like collective @$#%. So. July. Hey, at least we won't be up against the final *Home Improvement*.
>
> Crazy people with guns bother me. They just do.

Whedon's assertion that it is 'crazy people with guns' who are the problem, and not his show, is important, although his concerns about 'violent graduation incident' also demonstrate his realisation of the possible correlations that could be, however erroneously, drawn. The emphasis on the media's culpability as opposed to, for example, ease of access to guns, led to the Center for Media and Public Affairs in Washington, DC to publish 'Marketing Mayhem: Violence and Popular Culture' in September of the same year. This document 'ranked *Buffy* the seventh most violent show on TV with an average of fifty-nine violent acts per episode [compared to number one, *Walker Texas Ranger* which had 112]' (Parks, 2003: 120).

These two episodes, and the responses to them, provide an explicit example of the question of responsibility that is so central to many discussions of art and artists. An assumption central to a humanist tradition of and promotion of art is that it humanises us, makes us *better*. It does this through showing us the most beautiful, the most perfect, the aesthetically perfect. This is good art. Conversely, bad art (or non-art) is that which shows us the worse, that tends to degrade, horrify, lessen. Jonathan Dollimore (2003: 43) ventriloquises a similar position when he says, 'those who love art ... promulgate well intentioned lies, telling us that great art and the high culture it serves can only enhance the lives of those who truly appreciate them; that such art – unlike say, propaganda, popular culture or pornography – is incapable of damaging or "corrupting" us.' While Dollimore seems to tacitly accept a division between high art and popular culture (and would therefore be unconvinced by Whedon's output as art), his claims about the supposed *safety* of high art, its humanising/humanitarian capacity are pertinent indeed for

Whedon. Dollimore proposes an aesthetic that maintains its cognitive aspect, and alerts us to the fact that character – the most significant part of identification for many readers and viewers – has routinely been daemonic in many of the most celebrated texts. The aesthetic he (2003: 48) is exploring:

> confronts us with what we are not; or rather it confronts us with the psychological cost of being who we are, or perhaps the social cost of becoming what we would like to be, had we but courage equal to desire. It means we can never be complacent about the benign influence of art, any more that we can about knowledge per se. To take art seriously is to know it comes without the humanitarian guarantees that currently smother it.

Whedon's position as an artist whose works are seen by millions, many of who identify very strongly with the show and its characters (characters who are rarely straightforwardly daemonic but who each have demons of their own to battle) would seem to share Dollimore's view. Responding to a question about Columbine, and whether he feels a particular responsibility about representing violence, Whedon begins by saying that he has felt a responsibility about representing violence the first time he picked up a pen (Lavery and Burkhead, 2011: 29) but then continues like this:

> A writer has a responsibility to tell stories that are dark and sexy and violent where characters that you love do stupid, wrong things and get away with it ... that's what makes stories resonate, that thing, that dark place that we all want to go to on some level or another.

In a similar vein, and in response to a similar question, he says he has always 'worried about how much I needed to mix my political beliefs ... with the story I wanted to tell. How much I needed to protect good role models ... At the same time I feel strongly ... that we have a responsibility to be irresponsible' (Lavery and Burkhead, 2011: 56–7). Whedon's art is not polemical or didactic, nor is it oblivious to its inter-connectedness with the culture that co-creates and co-responds to it (the 'Earshot' episode needed to be broadcast on a different date because although not written as a response to that event – how could it have been – the fact that it is a response to similar events would have made its scheduling offensively trite), but more than anything, Whedon's art is responsible to the purpose of art of narrative: 'stories come from violence, they come from sex. They come from death ... and I think that stories are sacred ... and it has to come from this place to be pure to be art to be anything other than a polemic' (Lavery and Burkhead, 2011: 57).

The first three seasons of *Buffy* have given us these stories, and through them the characters with whom the audience identified. An irresponsible responsibility; a work of art that confronts us with the psychological cost of being who we are, makes us identify with that cost, with those characters; a complex creation built on finance, mass media, global institutions; marketed, distributed exploited for full commercial value. Art and commodity; cult and franchise; character and figurine – Buffy had her kung fu grip, and Whedon's success as a television producer was just beginning.

'How do you know what this guy's gonna do?': Producing worlds, changing worlds 2

With the airing of *Angel* on 5 October 1999, Whedon was now the executive producer of two hours' worth of television every Tuesday night. The five seasons that *Angel* ran for (1999–2004) coincide with the final four seasons of *Buffy* (1999–2003) and the only season of *Firefly* (2002). This chapter will look at the development of each of the shows, and their respective production histories and contribution to the notion of Whedon as writer, director and producer, especially in the context of managing a production company (Mutant Enemy) and engaging closely with the fortunes and otherwise of three of the American television networks.

The last four seasons of *Buffy* are interesting not just for the stories told, character developments and extension of the mythos, but also because of the ways the show's production history had such a huge impact on American network television. This chapter will begin by describing the gradual decline of trust and goodwill between Whedon and the controllers of the network *Buffy* was on (The WB) and the show's move from The WB to UPN. I will then assess the ways in which the seasons deepen the complex political and philosophical engagements the show has.

Buffy and the networks

As described in Chapter 1, *Buffy* was incredibly well supported by The WB in its early years. It was given high levels of pre-publicity, was invested in well, was used as the vehicle through which to launch its new night, and then it approved *Angel*. Whedon was given creative control of two hours of television every Tuesday night for 22 weeks of the year. Obviously, The WB gained enormously from this arrangement, but it is important that the later differences do not overshadow much of the very positive synergies of the first three seasons. Even season 4 kept both partners more or less happy, although the decision of Seth Green to leave the show to pursue a film career gave rise to the character of Tara who, as Willow's lesbian love interest was the cause of more controversy than almost any other aspect of the series. In season 5, the pair would kiss, unobtrusively in 'The Body' (B S5E16). The network was unhappy. Whedon reports that they said, 'We have gay characters in all our shows. Why didn't you tell us you were making characters gay' (Lavery and Burkhead, 2011: 30). The studio reservation is less a moral one (those came from many different sources) but industrial. Too many gay characters on too many shows takes away from the 'shock' value, a shock value Whedon was never aiming at. Be that as it may, season 4's main concerns were with figuring out a way for Buffy to be without Angel and of figuring out ways to make *Buffy* and *Angel* work as occasional cross-over shows (see Chapter 5). The network assisted in this by having them back to back, which clearly enabled certain kinds of storytelling to occur that would otherwise have not been possible.

It was in season 5 that the tensions began to show, and the bitter arguments between Whedon and The WB became an industry changing event. Fox said it was increasing the licensing fee of *Buffy*, and relations were suddenly fraught.

Fox's decision was not surprising. As Lynette Rice (2001: n.p.) reported at the time:

> It's not like the studio expected to make money before now. Producers routinely lose millions in a show's first five years – and that's assuming there is a first five. Up until then, the network pays a nominal licensing fee – anywhere between $900,000 and $1.1 million for a drama – and the studio swallows the deficit. (The WB currently pays $1 million to air an episode of *Buffy*, less than half of what it costs to make.)

However, Jamie Kellner, The WB founder and soon-to-be CEO of Turner Broadcasting, did not accept that this traditional structure should obtain for emerging networks such as The WB as it was still looking to make a profit for the first time. Kellner was prepared to offer US$1.6 million per episode, but the Fox studio was insisting on over US$2 million. Not only, though, did Kellner, feel that different business models should be available for The WB, but he was also critical of the value of *Buffy* itself. He made the point that, 'It's not our No. 1 show, ... It's not a show like *ER* that stands above the pack' (Rice, 2001: n.p.). He continued his defence of refusing to pay the renewal fee by saying that *Buffy* was failing to bring in The WB's desired demographic. One of Kellner's biggest arguments for keeping *Buffy*'s licensing down was its fans. He argued that rather than sucking in new teens, which were the lifeblood of The WB, the show attracted increasingly older viewers. When the drama moved to Tuesdays in 1998, it averaged a 19% share among 12 to 17 year olds whereas by season 5 it was nearer a 12. Conversely, *Seventh Heaven* (The WB/CW 1996–2007) was averaging a hefty 18 share. 'Our audience is a younger audience,' said Kellner. 'Maybe what we should be doing is to not stay with the same show for many years, and refresh our lineup' (Rice, 2001: n.p.).

Unsurprisingly, Whedon was unimpressed by his own network's lack of enthusiasm for the show that 'put The WB on map critically'. He continues, 'For [The WB] to be scrambling to explain why it's not cost efficient – it's their second highest rated show, ... They need to step up and acknowledge that financially' (Rice, 2001: n.p.).

In response to Kellner's claims regarding demographics, Whedon was equally clear in his position, 'the idea that [*Buffy* viewers] are getting too old now is a spurious argument for not paying for a show that has as much to do with The WB being The WB as anything else ... We were told the median age of [our viewers] was 26 to 29 years old in year 2 of the show' (Rice, 2001: n.p.). While Whedon was both furious at The WB's position and worried about the future of his show, industry analysts were fascinated by what the stand-off might mean for the future of US television production. David Bauder of the Associated Press wrote about the dispute between Fox and The WB, and especially the ways in which The WB's stance angered Fox Television's Chairman Sandy Grushow. Bauder (2001: n.p.) writes:

> Although Kellner wouldn't give specific figures, he estimated that the *Buffy* producers would see 50 percent more money through his proposal than they're getting now under the licensing deal. He said he's never made such an offer to keep a show. The dispute led Fox's chair to state that it was possible that the show might end up on Fox itself, and derided Kellner's claim of relative poverty by pointing out that the network was owned by AOL Time Warner with, as he said, a division that transformed the TV industry by demanding an expensive licensing deal for *ER* from NBC.

The major concern for analysts was not simply that licenses become more expensive after a fifth season, but that in this instance, there might was a sense of 'self-dealing'. Given *Buffy*'s Nielsen ratings, there was little chance that ABC, CBS or NBC would seriously consider buying the show (even though different rumours did suggest some interest, especially from ABC), which left UPN – which, it was felt, would not be in the running – or Fox itself. The idea that the company that owned the production could then pull the show and put it on its own network provoked consternation in some quarters:

> 'It's the worst thing that could happen', says Marty Adelstein, a partner in the talent agency Endeavor. 'Fox [the studio] has a lot of shows on other networks and they do a lot of shows for their own network. They're good at spreading it around. But this would send the sign: Why pick up a show from a studio if it's going to eventually end up on its own network? It's bad for business.' (Rice, 2001: n.p.)

Not everyone agreed, however, and the battle lines for an industry shaking argument were being drawn:

> 'If Fox [the studio] did this in the old days, it would be out of business with one third of its clients,' says Pax TV CEO Jeff Sagansky, former head of Entertainment at CBS. 'Now there are so many networks. Even if the studio were to lose The WB as a client, there are plenty of other places to sell shows.' Adds another studio head: 'Why not let Fox put it on their own network and reap the benefits of the advertising revenue?' (Rice, 2001: n.p.)

In the event, concerns regarding self-dealing proved unfounded in terms of Fox Television buying the show, as UPN, to the surprise of many, bid substantially more than The WB was willing to and got the show. Reuters announced the news on 23 April 2001. Two factors were deemed noteworthy. First, as reported in news outlets as various as BBC television and *Variety* magazine, was the fact that the decision to move networks on purely financial grounds was the first time this had happened in modern TV history (see, for example, Adalian, 2001).

The second notable aspect was the cost of those financial grounds. UPN agreed to pay US$2.33 million per episode in a forty-four-episode deal. This was US$500,000 more than The WB's final offer of US$1.8 million. Whedon was, understandably, excited and commented that, 'I've been dumped by my fat old ex and Prince Charming has come and swept me off my feet ... 'I'm mostly very excited because I now have a network that cares about my show as opposed to one that insults it' (Adalian, 2001: n.p.). His continuing irritation with The WB was also evident: 'As long as I live, I'll never understand why Jamie Kellner said the things he said ... I know he's a businessman, but to insult your best show ... is unfathomable. They didn't exist (before *Buffy*). It sounds wicked braggy, 'cause it is, but it's not entirely untrue' (Adalian, 2001: n.p.).

The WB was no less angered by Whedon's position and responded to Whedon's comments by pointing out that it bought the scripts for *Buffy* when no other network was interested; found a partner in 20th

Century Fox Television; shot two pilots; redeveloped the show; and gave it a prime slot on the schedule. In a statement, the corporation said it:

> gave (*Buffy*) our strongest promotional and publicity efforts, established it as a hit and moved it to Tuesday with *Dawson's Creek* only to make it the company's promotional focus once again. [We] bought a spinoff show, *Angel, and* scheduled it exactly where Mr. Whedon wanted it scheduled, promoted that night heavily, and offered to buy two more years of both shows … and finally offered the highest license fee in our history to renew the program. … We're sorry that this didn't demonstrate to Mr. Whedon our utmost respect and commitment to the show. (Littleton, 2001: 26)

Away from the bitter exchanges, however, the move prompted a number of questions. These included concerns about what might happen to *Buffy* on UPN; concerns about what the impact on *Angel* would be; and also what the implications for the television industry and especially The WB and UPN were. Concerns regarding the industry were expressed by Jamie Kellner. While it may be assumed that he would be smarting from the battle with Fox, he was not alone in making the following observation that is, in effect, a worry that Fox is self-dealing by a different route. The accusation was that '20th Television has made an inauspicious decision for the television industry by taking one of their own programs off of a nonaffiliated network and placing it on a network in which they have a large vested interest, through their acquisition of Chris-Craft and public comments that Fox and UPN are discussing ways to merge' (Rutenberg, 2001: n.p.).

The chair of Fox Television, Sandy Grushow, rebutted this claim and insisted that if, 'News Corp. didn't own a single UPN station, we would've made the exact same deal.' He continued by asserting that Fox's:

> goal was to protect Joss Whedon's vision by enabling him to make the show we felt he had earned the right to make while at the same time covering the cost of production of that show in its sixth and seventh seasons. Unfortunately, The WB didn't see fit to value the show at anything close to that level, which is certainly their prerogative. (Littleton, 2001: 26)

Whatever the rights and wrongs of Fox's move it meant that Whedon had two Fox produced programmes with one each on the newest and most vulnerable networks: *Angel* on The WB and *Buffy* now on UPN. The impact on the shows will be discussed below, but the impact on the networks was, in one version of the story, calamitous. Two years before, Dean Valentine, CEO of UPN had commented to the *Hollywood Reporter* about the new show *Dilbert* (UPN 1999–2000) that was to be produced by Columbia TriSytar TV and was being executively produced by the cartoon strip creator Scott Adams, and the supremely successful

Larry Charles, who was at the time best known for his work on *Seinfeld* (NBC 1989–98) and *Mad About You*. The show's acquisition was seen by some insiders as an effort for UPN to try and emulate The WB's success with *Buffy*, both in terms of increasing ratings, but also defining a network identity and, therefore, audience. Valentine, however, was cautious about a single show being able to secure a viable audience, saying, 'I don't believe that one narrow audience can sustain one broadcast network in the long run' (Marder, 1999: n.p.). Just over two years later, and talking after the deal to show *Buffy* had been successful, Valentine was sounding more optimistic about a single show, 'This deal makes financial sense for us ... It will help us re-establish ourselves as a home of quality programming for a younger audience, and how do you not want to be able to put on a show that is that good?' (Littleton, 2001: 26).

The problem with this position is that UPN, in seeking not only to emulate The WB's strategy but also its specific tactics, is that the two networks now have to fight for the same audience whereas before they were fighting for a different share. As Holt (2003: 25) describes, 'WB, for instance, has conceived a strategy based on the eighteen- to twenty-five-year-old audience, while UPN caters more to a younger, more urban viewer'. Apart from the sheer expense of the licence and the money-losing nature of the deal, the longer-term effects on both The WB and UPN were that neither was able to achieve market supremacy. This meant both failed. On Monday, 18 September 2006, a new channel started operations, CW. It was effectively a merger of The WB and UPN and the initials stood for the parent companies CBS and Warner Brothers. The day before, both The WB and UPN finished broadcasting. The WB's final night line-up included re-runs of the *Buffy* and *Angel* pilots, indicating just how central to the success and identity of the network they had been. UPN's decision to show a block of their pilots from the first year of operation was unsuccessful. Their not showing *Buffy* is also instructive as Valentine's hesitation about Dilbert was proven right with *Buffy*. UPN gained ground on The WB after 2001, but both networks lost actual points, dropping from just below 3 in 2001 to a little over 2 by 2006. By selling *Buffy*, The WB had lost a critical hit, a fan favourite and part of its identity; by buying *Buffy*, UPN had spent more than it could afford, had entered into an unwinnable direct competition with its clearest competitor, and was basing its identity on someone else's. Both decisions, in hindsight, seem poor. While many other factors are also clearly responsible, the CW initials could quite easily be thought of as representing Cause: Whedon.

Helen Wheatley (2006) provides a useful immediate pre-history to the battle over *Buffy*. She discusses *Twin Peaks*, *Millennium* (Fox 1996–99) and *American Gothic* (CBS 1995–96) and asserts that their 'cinematically televisual' and 'highly complex visual' style is a direct response to being in a 'period of intensifying competition'. The technological improvements provided both opportunity and challenge for programme makers, which was further aided by 'relatively large budgets for serial shows' (Wheatley, 2006: 175). These budgets and complex styles were the financial and artistic response to 'increased competition' which required a 'strategy of niche marketing' leading to 'new audience segments and taste markets' as 'prime targets for the new networks' (Johnson, 2005: 107).

Differently organised and conducted, a similar battle for new markets was taking place in the UK. The place of Whedon products in this is central. Scheduling of *Buffy* and *Angel* in the UK has been discussed by Annette Hill and Ian Calcutt. They describe how the mixture of the shows being shown on 'minority' channels (BBC2, Channel 4 and Sky), the terrestrial channels having already well established demographics, and UK regulations that 'ensure that programming before the nine o'clock watershed should not contain material that could be considered offensive to a family audience', all conspired to produce a very uneven experience for viewers (Hill and Calcutt, 2007: 56–73). Scheduled in the tea time slot usually reserved for children's programmers or the news, the shows had to be heavily edited to ensure they did not fall foul of the law, and in so doing had significant deleterious impact on the episodes' coherence and meaning. Even with this, there were complaints about unsuitable material. Both the BBC and Channel 4 had complaints against them upheld by the Broadcasting Standards Commission (BSC). In the case of *Angel*, one episode that was chastised was 'In the Dark' (A S1E3). It is instructive to quote in full from the BSC bulletin from 31 January 2001:

> ANGEL
> Channel 4, 29 September 2000, 1800–1900
>
> *The Complaint*
> Six viewers complained about the level of violence and references to paedophilia in this episode, at a time when young children were likely to be watching.
>
> *The Broadcaster's Statement*
> Channel 4 said that a significant number of viewers would have watched the related series 'Buffy', which was broadcast in a similar time slot. The view was taken that subject to prudent editing, the material was acceptable for transmission at this time. The broadcaster said that the underlying theme in each episode was the triumph of good over evil and that the programmes had a very simple, moral message. The 'action style' violence was consistent with the style of certain adventure films and programmes shown during the daytime.

> *The Commission's Finding*
> A Standards Panel watched this episode of the drama series. It took the view that both the level of violence, including the use of hot metal pokers to repeatedly stab the lead character and the references to paedophilia, had exceeded acceptable boundaries for a programme aimed at a young audience and broadcast pre-Watershed. The complaints were upheld.
> *Upheld* CN 5446.6. (Broadcasting Standards Commission, 2001: 5)

A mere six people complained but the commission upheld the complaint, and in terms of time slot and possible audience, and the clear rules about family friendly viewing, it is perhaps understandable. Inevitably, the rules and regulations reflect public taste and values, and the complaint against the BBC and Sky One for *Buffy* season 6 'Entropy' (B S6E19) illustrate a reluctance to allow even mild and loving sexual relations. The judgement against the two corporations were similar. The BBC's was:

> A Standards Panel watched this episode in this well-established series. The Panel noted that the lesbian kiss was extended and that the encounter between the young man and woman, depicted the preliminaries to sexual intercourse on a table. It considered that the cumulative effect of these portrayals of sexual contact had exceeded acceptable boundaries for this programme aimed at a young adult audience and broadcast in the early evening.
> The complaints were upheld CN 11266.4. (Broadcasting Standards Commission, 2003a: 7)

The episode 'Seeing Red' (B S6E19), which includes the pre-mediated cold-blooded shooting of Buffy and death of Tara, as well as Spike's attempted rape of Buffy, also received complaints after being aired at 6.45 p.m. What is intriguing is that of the ten complaints, seven were about Willow and Tara's relationship (or homosexuality), only two were about the attempted rape of Buffy by Spike and one was about the shooting of Tara by Warren. The complaints panel issued the following:

> A Standards Panel watched this episode of the well-established fantasy series. It noted the opening sequences which contained brief homosexual scenes and references throughout the episode. It also noted violent sequences, predominantly between the two main characters, Buffy and Spike. The Panel took the view that the cumulative effect of homosexual references and violent sequences which including fighting, an attempted rape, and a shooting had meant that the episode strayed from the fantasy element that audiences would have expected and had gone beyond acceptable boundaries for the time of transmission.
> The complaints were upheld CN 11437.7. (Broadcasting Standards Commission, 2003b: 14)

While it may be true that the complainants cannot be taken to be representative of the UK population as a whole, it is instructive that a loving relationship creates more outrage than rape and murder. Other viewers were annoyed about the cuts required to allow the show to be aired at that time at all, and (in relation to the BBC and Channel 4) that the shows were on separate channels so the cross-over capacity (see Chapter 5) was destroyed. As Jowett and Abbott (2013: 9–10) explain, Sky avoided the latter concern as it 'aired *Buffy* and *Angel* back-to-back in primetime slots for their first run, and acquirers of subsequent TV horror followed this lead in scheduling'.

Despite viewer complaints to the BSC about the images shown, and fan complaints to the channels about sequences cut, the shows were part of a clear and successful strategy to develop new audiences. As Paul Rixon (2003: 54) states:

> In the 1990s, while American programmes were increasingly banished on the two main terrestrial channels, ITV and BBC1, to afternoons, early morning and late-night slots, on BBC2 and Channel 4 American programmes continued to play a small but important role, supporting the schedule and attracting sought-after audiences. For example, *The Simpsons, Star Trek Voyager* and *Buffy the Vampire Slayer* were often the most viewed programmes for BBC2.

Back in America in 2001, *Buffy*'s immediate future was secure (the forty-four-episode deal guaranteed two further seasons), but there was some fan disquiet about what a move to UPN might mean. First consideration was coverage, as UPN did not have quite the same national coverage as The WB. But there were also worries about editorial policy. Whedon sought to allay fan fears. Writing on a bulletin board the day after the final episode of season 5 'The Gift' (B S5E22) had aired, he said: 'Different network. But we've never been controlled by the network – WB was great about that, UPN has already shown they will be too' (Whedon 2001b). And although many critics see a shift in *Buffy* in seasons 6 and 7 (the UPN seasons), it is obvious that this was as a consequence entirely of creative decisions made by Mutant Enemy. Indeed, in a slightly earlier post, Whedon makes the very clear point that much of season 6 was already planned before 'The Gift' was even shot. More specifically, he mentions, along with the move to UPN, the forthcoming musical, 'UPN will be a good home for us. 'Cause the show won't change – except inasmuch as it's always changing. Next year is going to be intense. INTENSE. And the musical ... the musical ... could be the worst hour of TV ever made, but you won't be able to say we didn't go there' (Whedon, 2001c: n.p.).

The reference to the musical is instructive, because it makes very explicit just how little the move to UPN influenced storyline or editorial decisions. As Whedon mentions in *Script Book* of the musical, 'When I started writing the musical I knew exactly where everybody was emotionally and what had to break ... I knew this would be the episode where Buffy told her friends that she'd been in heaven and all the other truths would come out' (Whedon, 2002: 64). That such a detailed knowledge of the episode and its place in the arc was known before Whedon went on holiday just after season 5 ended shows how far advanced the planning for the next season, UPN's first, was. It also provided some special challenges for the writing staff. As Espenson (personal correspondence, 24 January 2008)[7] notes:

> The most extreme example of this was the musical. Joss wrote it long before we wrote all the episodes leading up to it. So we had to make sure that everything led up to it perfectly ... Buffy, Willow, Giles ... everyone had to be in the exact right place to launch into that episode. I remember that being very tricky. Marti [Noxon] was our leader during those episodes (because Joss was off writing songs, etc.), and she did a great job. See, usually, you can move stuff around a bit, and pull an event forward if you need it, but we couldn't pull anything out of the musical and use it before we got there. Very difficult.

In addition to the planning difficulty in writing the episodes up to the musical, Espenson mentions Marti Noxon as being 'our leader'. Whedon had let it be known that Noxon would be made executive producer, commenting that the move to UPN would have no influence on the show, 'the only difference is that Marti will share exec prod credit with me, and it's about time she did', although he does ad the caveat 'I'm in charge' (Whedon, 2001b: n.p.). Noxon herself affirmed her promotion in an interview with SciFi Wire:

> In the meantime, Noxon said that she will take over much of the day-to-day production chores on Buffy next year, as Whedon spends more time developing a proposed *Buffy* animated series, comic books and other projects. 'I'll be co-running *Buffy* with Joss,' Noxon said. 'Now, I'm sort of second in the chain of command. But next year, we're going to be more equals, although there is no equal to Joss [laughs]. But in title, we're going to be more equal.' (Noxon, 2001)

---

7 The full correspondence with Espenson, from which numerous extracts are presented, is available in Appendix 1.

Whedon's assertion of retaining overall control is important in a season that sees him for the first time relinquish sole executive producer status of *Buffy*, and which also sees his credited contributions in terms of writing and directing diminish to just one episode, the musical with, for the first time, neither the season premier nor the season finale written or directed by him. But whoever ran the show from day to day, it is clear that the move to UPN was not instrumental in determining the direction of *Buffy*. Indeed, despite significant fan and scholarly criticism of seasons 6 and 7, the production team were assured in their show. Doug Petrie said, 'I don't see any change at all. I think the good news for *Buffy* fans is that we're doing exactly the show we wanted to be doing all along' (Edwards *et al.*, 2009: 6). Response to the seasons has been mixed with concerns ranging from 'how grim' they are, the absence of Giles, the seeming loss of the puns and humour, the themes of addiction and abuse, the big bad as life itself and the sense of Buffy as victim. Sarah Michelle Gellar herself was also unhappy with the direction her character took, saying, 'It didn't feel like the character that I loved ... I felt like Buffy's spirit was missing' (Pascale, 2014: 192). One response, which is related to the loss of humour but implies much more, is given by Ira and Anne Shull (2009: 85), and strongly asserts the fact that both the characters and the show were growing up, becoming adult:

> In any event, none of us was wrong to claim that verbal style is a fundamental attribute of the Slayer's life and work ... we just didn't realise that the terms of engagement would change fundamentally after Buffy's resurrection, and that the balance of verbal style and metaphysical purpose would shift in favor of the latter in favor of clear-sighted adulthood.

In 2004, Whedon castigated The WB for its treatment of *Angel* saying, 'I believe the reason *Angel* had trouble on The WB was that it was the only show on the network that wasn't trying to be *Buffy*. It was a show about grown-ups' (Jensen, 2004: n.p.). What Shull and Shull (2009) convincingly argue is that during its UPN years (if not before), so was *Buffy*.

Producing *Angel*

This section will analyse *Angel* in the context of its production history. This will allow us then to provide a brief history of Mutant Enemy, Whedon's production company, as it grew and developed over the period from 1997 to 2004. The purpose of this section will be to affirm the absolute centrality of the creative team that Whedon built around him, and the industrial restrictions and opportunities afforded this team.

Angel the series was premiered on The WB on 5 October 1999, a little over two and half years after Buffy's premiere. It immediately followed the opening episode of season 4 of *Buffy*, and for the first two seasons of its existence (October 1999–May 2001) it would be the second half of two hours of Whedon-inspired television on The WB on Tuesday from 8.00 until 10.00 p.m. The opening episode of *Angel*, 'City of' (A S1E1), was directed and co-written by Whedon (with David Greenwalt), and its immediate precursor on *Buffy*, season 4's opener, 'The Freshman' (B S4E1) was directed and entirely written by Whedon. However, it would be wrong to assert quite so easily that *Angel* is a Whedon show in the same way that the first three seasons of *Buffy* are. The sections on the earlier seasons of *Buffy* in this book have suggested that even those episodes seemingly outside of Whedon's credited involvement usually had a significant level of his creative input, that seasons 1–3 of *Buffy* can be read in almost all its expression as Whedon's work (Whedon as television auteur). In later *Buffy* and in *Angel* the picture is slightly different, and this is an important distinction to make. It does nothing to undermine or diminish the quality of both; rather it is keen to place later *Buffy* and *Angel* in the context of a rapidly changing production environment which alters Whedon's involvement and in so doing provides a slightly different model of assessment than the auteur-related one of early *Buffy* scholarship.

On the first three seasons of *Buffy*, Whedon was 'up to my eyeballs' (Lavery and Burkhead, 2011: 103) in the writing, rewriting, polishing and show running aspect of the show. Heavily reliant on David Greenwalt, Whedon was still in charge and on set all the time. With Greenwalt, initially anyway, helming *Angel*, Whedon was less involved in the polishing, though still hugely involved in breaking the stories and 'thickly' involved in the show. However, with the additional show to produce Whedon 'couldn't be on set' and this is not just true of *Angel*, but *Buffy* also, 'I was literally on set for three years on *Buffy*. And then all of a sudden I couldn't be on either set that much' (Lavery and Burkhead, 2011: 103–4). Whedon's ability to control all aspects of production, including direction, became diluted. The fact that both *Angel* and *Buffy* in this period retained – even exceeded in some ways – the quality of early *Buffy* is a strong testament to Whedon's skills not just as a writer, director and producer, but also as a spotter of great talent.

Whedon is still ultimately responsible for both shows, and there is nothing that goes on screen 'that I had nothing to do with', and he is emphatic that they are 'my' shows and that he 'runs' them (Lavery and Burkhead, 2011: 104, 105). But the nature of the 'running' and the meaning of 'my' are different than on early *Buffy*. In the commentary to another season three *Angel* episode, 'Birthday' (A S3E11) (or, more precisely, the commentary to a deleted scene from the episode), Tim Minear and the episode's writer Mere Smith are discussing why the scene was cut. An initial point of discussion might be, why Tim Minear? He did not direct or write the episode, he is not the series creator. A second point of discussion might be about the genesis of the episode. Minear describes how Smith broke the story. This process, we know from Jane Espenson among others (see Appendix 1) would have always included Whedon on any The WB *Buffy* episode. In this case, the story was broken by Smith and David Greenwalt. Greenwalt's, most noticeable presence (and Whedon's most noticeable absence) is in some ways on the season one and season two overview featurettes on the region two DVDs. In both of these Greenwalt is the first speaker. He is joined by a range of others including Minear, most of the actors, a director. But no Whedon. It is a false analogy to suggest that the season overview functions like a preface to a book, but there is some sense in which the overview and the preface provide declaration of ownership or control. Whedon's absence may have many different explanations including something as banal as being somewhere else on the day it was shot, but his absence from the commentary, on the one hand, and the featurette, on the other, does imply a different relationship with *Angel* than with *Buffy* where his presence is absolute.

Angel as a character, of course, first appears in the televised premiere of *Buffy*. In this he is a handsome brooding mysterious stranger who offers Buffy gnomic advice and sets her heart aflutter. We go on to discover he is a vampire cursed to have a soul and to remember and seek atonement for his horrific sins. We see him and Buffy become lovers, mortal enemies, tragic heroes and ultimately we witness Angel leave Sunnydale at the end of season 3 of *Buffy* before heading to Los Angeles and his own series. What is noticeable about this brief history is that it does not mention what came before the televised pilot, which was the unaired pilot that acted as Whedon's pitch for the show. As described above, this pilot featured most of the finally assembled cast, except Alyson Hannigan who took over as Willow. But not only was David Boreanaz not cast as Angel, there was no character of Angel, nor even a character like Angel. Obviously, in a relatively short time frame not all the aspects that Whedon may have wanted to include would be in this pitch, but the lack of Angel is notable. What is equally notable is just how interesting Angel is in the opening episode of *Buffy*, and his good looks, mystery and intrigue are complemented by great lines such as his retort to Buffy who rebuffs his seeming declaration of friendship by saying, 'I didn't say I was yours' (B S1E1). But he is still very much an ancillary character, with Boreanaz billed as a guest star rather than as a member of the main cast. The character gets his own episode ('Angel' B S1E7) and in this we discover his two-fold secret: that he is a vampire and that he has been cursed with a soul. In light of how Angel develops, it is interesting that this episode was written by David Greenwalt, although not too much, perhaps, should be read into this as between them, Greenwalt and Whedon wrote half of all season one episodes of *Buffy* due in large part to the newness of the show and its Production Company, Mutant Enemy whose history will be discussed presently.

By *Buffy*'s season 2 start, Angel is a main character and Boreanaz is in the opening credits. As mentioned in Chapter 1, the relationship between Angel and Buffy is so central to the drama of the show that it is used as the pivot to change nights and launch The WB Tuesday on 20 January 1998. The episode 'Innocence' (B S2E14) unleashes Angelus, the un-ensouled vampire version of Angel, and television has a new, and utterly compelling, villain to endure. Whedon wrote the script and directed the episode and in the process set a tone for this darker, harsher, meaner character. Five episodes later and the tragic love of Buffy and Angel is played out against the backdrop of a poltergeist who re-enacts a tragic love and death 50 years earlier. In this episode, 'I Only Have Eyes For You' (B S2E19), Marti Noxon's script has Angelus inhabited by the spirit of a female school teacher. Nikki Stafford (2007: 177–8) describes a well-deserved common response to the episode's love scenes when she describes Boreanaz's acting as 'beautiful' and as displaying 'feminine gestures without ever playing it over the top'. And Whedon shared this feeling. In interview, he said, 'seeing David open himself up to playing this really emotional female role and doing it excellently – without overdoing it or being silly, without shying away from it as a lot of male action stars might have – was extraordinary. That was when I thought, "This guy could carry his own show"' (Francis, 2000: 72).

Whedon's belief that Angel could carry his own show was predicated on his conviction that Boreanaz could do the same. This is entirely different from the notion of a *Buffy* television show where the character led the creative drive and the actress would have to be found to make this happen. Boreanaz recalls that his first response to Whedon's idea was less than committed because he was 'focused on the season finale we were shooting' ('Becoming Parts 1 and 2') although the idea of extending the character did begin to appeal as he realised he 'really didn't have much place to go in Sunnydale' (Stafford, 2007: 60). Whedon had also posed the question to David Greenwalt. Greenwalt offers this recollection in the 'Season 1 Featurette' on the season 1 box set region 2 DVD release: 'one day Joss Whedon came to me and said, "What d'you think about making our own show with David Boreanaz as Angel?" and I said, "I think it's a fabulous idea and we should team him up with Charisma Carpenter who plays Cordelia"' (Greenwalt, 2001 – DVD commentary). In addition to the actor informing the decision to spin off the character, Greenwalt's contribution to the process is clear and undisputed. Indeed, he is credited as being co-creator of the show at the beginning of each episode and we can see from this brief quotation that part of the initial organisation of the show was his idea – the presence of Cordelia.

Throughout season 3 of *Buffy*, Greenwalt and Whedon were developing the idea for *Angel* and a presentation reel was created to publicise the show. The WB was broadly supportive of the idea, and well they might have been. The year during which season two of *Buffy* aired had seen their market share rise by about 20 per cent. This took The WB to about 3.1, which, while small in comparison to the so-called big four, had the effect of pushing it beyond its main competitor, UPN (Carman, 1998; Furman, 1998). A large part of the growth had been in the key teen demographic and this had been largely due to the success of The WB Tuesday night of *Buffy* and *Dawson's Creek*. During season 3 of *Buffy*, The WB added two more teen-focused programmes, *Felicity* (The WB 1998–2002) and *Roswell* (The WB 1999–2002). *Roswell*, like *Buffy* was a television adaptation of an existing franchise, in this case a series of young adult novels called *Roswell High*. Andy W. Smith highlights the preponderance of 'American high school drama with fantasy/horror/science fiction/comedy formats' that were adapted from other media in the mid to late 1990s. The WB added to canon with *Smallville* (The WB/CW 2001–10) (Smith, 2007: 90).

Between the end of season 2 and the start of season 3 of *Buffy*, a thirteen-episode order for *Angel* was agreed for the season following (Hontz and Petrikin, 1998: 1). A show that could harness that creative energy and quality, continue the expansion of the teen market and, therefore, entice more advertising revenue was going to be encouraged. The reel was created from a mixture of *Buffy* footage and newly shot scenes of *Angel* with an explanatory voice-over and impressive musical support. Shown to an audience of industry analysts and advertising consultants, the reel was clearly deemed successful enough to encourage The WB to extend the order. A character absent in the very first pitch for *Buffy*, who had developed in season 1 of that show, become established in season 2 and fulfilled his potential in season 3, was now in a position to lead his own show. *Angel* the series was up and running.

The fans' joy at a new Whedon show on their televisions, and Whedon's clear delight as well, cannot mask the fact that having two shows running at the same time presented Whedon with some difficulties.

When *Buffy* had begun, a writing and production staff was required to create twelve episodes in a very generous time frame. Now a writing staff had to be found that could produce – across the two Mutant Enemy shows – forty-four episodes in a much more restricted time frame as both shows were being shot as the season was underway, as opposed to being created ahead of time as had been the case with the first season of *Buffy*. Not only that, but *Angel* would need someone to take over control of the day-to-day business of ensuring its direction and quality: while Joss Whedon is widely recognised as both extremely talented and astoundingly energetic, running two shows simultaneously was not an option.

The question of who would run *Angel*, and, as we shall see, who would take over responsibility for *Buffy* in its later seasons, has an impact on the question of who is credited with writing and directing particular episodes. It is relatively easy to assert that an episode is a Whedon episode when he is the writer of that episode, its director and also the show runner of the season from which the episode has come. The extent to which an episode can be attributed to Whedon in an instance where he is not the show runner and he neither directs nor writes the episode is less obvious. Being less obvious does not make it less true, but it does imply a relational difference, and suggests that the 'is' in the phrase 'this is a Whedon show/episode' is open to some variety of interpretation. Whedon was emphatic about his ownership of every *Buffy* episode, but it is less clear that the following quotation would still be as true of *Angel*:

> I'm responsible for all the shows. That means that I break the stories. I often come up with the ideas and I certainly break the stories with the writers so that we all know what's going to happen. Then once the writers are done, I rewrite every script ... Then I oversee production and edit every show, work with the composers and sound mixers. Inevitably every single show has my name on it somewhere and it is my responsibility to make it good ... Every week that show is on, I'm standing in the back row, biting my nails, hoping people like it, so I feel a great responsibility. The good thing is that I'm surrounded by people who are much smarter than I am. So gradually I have been able to let certain things take care of themselves, because my crew, my writers, my post-production crew, everybody is so competent, that I don't have to run around quite as much as I used to. (Lavery, 2014a: 97)

In addition to asking the question of whether an episode (or all episodes) of a Whedon produced show that does not directly credit him with control (beyond the very important fact of being executive producer) 'is' a Whedon episode, we should also be asking of the contributions made by the writers and the directors who seek to manifest the vision we attribute to Whedon.

Statistics can often obscure more then they reveal, but there is an interesting pattern to be seen below. What I am trying to demonstrate in the following list is the relative frequency of credited contribution to any given season by Whedon and the relative frequency of credited contribution made by Greenwalt and others. The method is as follows. Each episode has a credit for writer and a credit for director. A value of 2 is given for each credit as director and each credit as writer, with a value of 1 being given where the writing credit is shared. This latter distinction is problematic where a specific credit is given for the writing of the story and a different one for the teleplay, especially as Whedon is seen to be so instrumental in the creation of stories on Buffy. This is why I am trying to establish a method for assessing the relative frequency of *credited* contribution. Each person will have their total values added up and these will be used to determine a percentage (for example, in season 1 of *Buffy*, Whedon has a total value of ten out of a theoretically possible forty-eight – had he written and directed every one of the twelve episodes – which gives him a percentage value of 21 per cent).

The purpose of the list is simply to illustrate in crude numerical values the shifting credited contributions made by certain individuals across the seven seasons of *Buffy*, the five seasons of *Angel* and the half season of *Firefly*. These will then be used to offer a narrative of the shifting personnel in Mutant Enemy and the effect this can be argued to have had on the shows. I am *not* claiming that this list offers a 'true' version of events. Whedon's ownership of the finished products is central, but there is an interesting story to be told about distributing a writing team, developing people to become show runners, negotiating roles and ultimately running three shows simultaneously on prime-time American television: an achievement of quite astonishing and bewildering magnitude. Whedon's ownership of the material is matched by his generosity, as described in relation to the arbitration of the *Speed* credit in Chapter 1. David Lavery enumerates a series of sections of episodes that are credited to other writers that were actually penned by Whedon but to which he makes no legal claim. The actual details are fascinating and well worth a read, but simply in terms of volume, the list is astonishing, including as it does: 'What's my line' Part I (B S2E9); 'Helpless' (B S3E12); 'Bad Girls' (B S3E14); 'Earshot' (B S3E18); 'Superstar' (B S4E17); 'Real Me' (B S5E2); 'I Was Made to Love You' (B S5E15); 'Bargaining' (B S6E1); 'Grave' (B S6E22); 'Selfless' (B S7E5); 'Conversations with Dead People' (B S7E7); 'The Killer in Me' (B S7E13); 'Dirty Girls' (B S7E18); 'Rm W/A Vu' (A S1A5); 'Are You Now or Have You Ever Been'

(A S2E2); 'Over the Rainbow', 'Through the Looking Glass' and 'There's no Place like Plrtz Glrb' (A S2E20–22); 'Billy' (A S3E6); 'The House Always Wins' (A S4E3); 'Home' (A S4E22); 'Destiny' (A S5E8); 'You're Welcome' (A S5E12); 'Jaynestown' (F S1E4); 'Safe' (F S1E7); 'Out of Gas' (F S1E8) (Lavery, 2014a: 140–5).

To take just the first of these as an example, Marti Noxon says of 'What's My Line?', 'Mr Pfister and all the monsters ... were pretty much all Joss pitches' (Golden *et al.*, 2000: 17). Despite this, there is value to be derived from assessing the credited contributions. What I am looking at is writing and directing credits, not at, for example, producer credits, although it is worth having a sense of what these can mean in the context of US television. Jane Espenson writes:

> To complete the confusion, 'Producer' is also one of the levels of titles given to writers employed on the staff of a show. You start out as 'Staff writer.' Your contract specifies that if you're brought back for a second year, you're automatically bumped up one level to 'Story editor.' There is no editing of stories involved – it's just the next title up for a writer on staff. Same duties: write scripts. Next level: Executive Story Editor. Same duties. Then Co-Producer. Then Producer. Then Supervising Producer. Then Co-Executive Producer. New responsibilities may or may not be added as you rise up this inevitable (and contractually specified) ladder ... you may start to go to editing sessions or get more involved on stage, or you might sometimes be asked to rewrite your colleagues' work. But generally, you're just a script-writin' machine! (Yay!). (Personal correspondence, 21 January 2008)

Table 1 presents an analysis of the writing and directing credits for the Mutant Enemy team over the course of *Buffy*, *Angel* and *Firefly* seasons. The table notes explain its composition. Seeming discrepancies can be explained by the fact that someone with four writing credits may in fact have co-written two of those while another person with four writing credits may have sole credit for each of their episodes.

I am first going to highlight some of the most interesting statistics without offering much in the way of explanation or analysis, and this will develop into an account of some of the movements within Mutant Enemy and the ways in which these had an impact on the creative processes relating to *Angel*.

The first statistic is that Whedon never had more credited input into *Angel* than into *Buffy* while they were both on air (the amounts are equal for season 6 of *Buffy* and season 3 of *Angel*). Season 5 of *Angel* sees a greater contribution by Whedon than to the final two seasons of *Buffy* (11 per cent compared with 5 per cent and 7 per cent), though during *Buffy*'s last season Whedon also contributed 25 per cent to *Firefly*,

Table 1 Mutant Enemy employees and a statistical assessment of their credited contributions as writer or director of episodes on *Buffy*, *Angel* and *Firefly*

		B1	B2	B3	B4	A1	B5	A2	B6	A3	B7	A4	F	A5
Whedon, Joss	W/D	4/0	1/0	0/0	0/0	2/0	0/0	2/1	0/0	0/0	1/0	0/0	3/0	2/0
	W&D	1	5	5	4	1	3	0	1	1	1	1	3	2
	%	21	24	23	18	5	14	3	5	5	7	5	25	11
Greenwalt, David	W/D	3/0	3/0	1/1		5/0		4/0		2/0				0/1
	W&D	0	1	1		2		2		2				0
	%	10	10	9		13		16		14				2
Noxon, Marti	W/D		6/0	5/0	5/0	1/0	1/0		4/0		2/0			
	W&D		0	0	0	0	2		0		1			
	%		12	11	10	1	11		6		8			
Petrie, Doug	W/D			3/0	3/0	1/0	0/0	1/0	1/0		1/0			
	W&D			0	0	0	4	0	2		1			
	%			7	7	2	8	1	10		7			
Espenson, Jane	W/D			3/0	5/0	1/0	0/0	1/0	4/0		6/0		1/0	
	W&D			0	0	0	5	0	0		0		0	
	%			6	10	1	10	2	7		10		4	
Fury, David	W/D			2/0	4/0	2/0	2/0	1/0	3/0	1/0	2/0	4/0		3/0
	W&D			0	0	0	0	0	1	0	1	0		1
	%			5	8	2	5	2	10	2	7	8		6
Minear, Tim	W/D					5/0		5/0		3/1		0/0	2/0	
	W&D					0		2		2		1	2	
	%					9		18		18		5	18	
DeKnight, Stephen S.	W/D						2/0		3/0			5/0		4/0
	W&D						0		0			1		2
	%						5		7			12		14

Table 1 Mutant Enemy employees and a statistical assessment of their credited contributions as writer or director of episodes on *Buffy*, *Angel* and *Firefly* (Continued)

		B1	B2	B3	B4	A1	B5	A2	B6	A3	B7	A4	F	A5
Smith, Mere	W/D							4/0		3/0		4/0		
	W&D							0		0		0		
	%							7		7		8		
Goddard, Drew	W/D										5/0			5/0
	W&D										0			0
	%										9			8
Edlund, Ben	W/D											1/0	2/0	5/0
	W&D											0	0	0
	%											2	5	10
Fain, Sarah and Craft, Elizabeth	W/D											5/0		2/0
	W&D											0		0
	%											9		7
Bell, Jeffrey	W/D									6/0		4/0		0/0
	W&D									0		1		2
	%									11		11		8
Seth Green, Bruce	D	13	11			5		2						
Contner, James A.	D			9	14	9	7	7	7	5	7	5		5
Grossman, David	D				9		7	2	7	7	7	5		
Solomon, David	D						9		11		10			

Notes: Column heads are seasons of the three shows, e.g. B1, Buffy season 1. W/D, first number is the amount of individual episodes the person is credited as having written during the season whether as sole writer, joint writer, teleplay writer or story writer; second number is the amount of episodes directed. W&D, number of episodes both written and directed. %, the percentage value derived from each of the previous figures. D, director only.

which is a greater contribution than to any season of either *Buffy* or *Angel*. For the first four seasons of *Buffy* and the only season of *Firefly*, Whedon provided between 18–25 per cent of all credited contribution. His highest on *Angel* is 11 per cent. It is also interesting that *Angel* is the one series in which Whedon directs an episode he did not write, and has a whole season during which he does not both write and direct at least one episode (season 2).

Greenwalt's contribution to *Buffy*'s first three seasons is fairly constant at about 10 per cent. After season 3, he has no further contribution to *Buffy*. His contribution to *Angel*'s first three seasons is also fairly constant at about 14 per cent, and he both writes and directs the same number of episodes in each of these three seasons. After season 3, his only credited contribution (beyond, of course, co-creator) is to direct one episode in season 5.

Noxon is noticeable for having writing credits on six of *Buffy* season 2's episodes. This was her first year on the show and no-one has ever written more in his or her debut season, and no-one except Whedon and Espenson can claim as many episodes in a season of *Buffy*. She was never credited with as many again, although, like Whedon and Greenwalt she undertook responsibility for directing some episodes that she did write. Noxon has one writing credit on *Angel* and none on *Firefly*.

Petrie has contributions to both *Buffy* and *Angel*, though with significantly greater amounts to *Buffy*. With one writer credit in each of *Angel*'s first two seasons set against three writing credits in each of his first two seasons on *Buffy* and a mixture of writer and writer-director credits thereafter, it is clear that his work on *Angel* was a very occasional – indeed, his entire contribution to *Angel* amounts to less than one-half of his lowest contribution to a season on *Buffy*.

Espenson, unlike Whedon, Greenwalt, Noxon, Petrie, Fury, Minear or Stephen S. DeKnight, never directed an episode but she did write for each of the three series (unlike all those listed except Whedon), and her contribution in terms of credits on individual seasons exceeds everyone save Whedon and Fury. Her six episodes in season 7 of *Buffy* equals Noxon and Whedon in terms of most for one season on *Buffy*.

Fury joined the staff in season 3 of *Buffy* and remains there on each of the remaining seasons of *Buffy* and all seasons of *Angel*. In no one season does he contribute more than 10 per cent of the total credited value but his consistent presence on both shows from the time of his entry is unique for all pre-*Angel* Mutant Enemy writers.

Minear comes in as the first major new recruit to *Angel* having had no previous contribution to *Buffy* at all. He is credited with 9 per cent of season one *Angel*, and 18 per cent of seasons 2 and 3 and for the season of *Firefly*. It is clear that the first season of *Angel* was fraught, with the Mutant Enemy writers' rooms feeling very different levels of respect. Minear says of that first season on the *Angel* staff:

> We're the new class coming in and David [Greenwalt] felt way more comfortable with the old class [*Buffy* writers]. So while we were his writing staff for *Angel*, for the first several episodes of the show, they had *Buffy* writers writing those scripts. (Pascale, 2014: 145)

The sense of isolation and being an outsider (a sense that Whedon's professional ethos and artistic creations had sought to combat and resist) was manifest for the *Angel* writers, and Whedon himself did nothing to allay it:

> As gregarious, entertaining and as brilliantly as he can hold a room full of people's attention, he's also oddly shy ... He didn't really know us, and there was a whole bunch of people there, which were the *Buffy* people, so I think it took a while for him to warm up to us. (Pascale, 2014: 148)

Minear almost quit, and when it was discovered by the *Angel* writers that there was a party at Whedon's house to celebrate the premiere of the two shows on 5 October 1999 but that not one *Angel* writer was invited, while all the *Buffy* ones were, there was a confrontation. The ensuing discussion led to a shift in the way that the *Angel* writers were treated and eventually Whedon and Minear became incredibly close working partners, with Whedon later saying, 'if there's no Tim Minear there would be no *Angel*. He's the unsung and unbelievably necessary hero of the show' (Pascale, 2014: 156). And, as mentioned previously, he became central to the production of *Firefly* too during *Angel*'s fourth season.

Minear's all-but disappearance from *Angel* after season 3 (there is a writer-director credit during season 4) mirrors many of the other contributors to *Angel* at this time. As a credited writer, Whedon's presence is always quite limited; Greenwalt disappears after season 3, Noxon does not write for it again after season 1, Espenson leaves after season 2, as does Petrie. As the substantial new appointments to *Buffy* dwindle (DeKnight in season 5 and Goddard in season 7 being the two most conspicuous), those to *Angel* increase significantly. Not only DeKnight and Goddard who join *Angel* in seasons 4 and 5, respectively, but also Smith in season 2, Jeffrey Bell in season 3, and also in season 4, Ben Edlund, and the team of Sarah Fain and Elizabeth Craft who will go on to have an important role in *Dollhouse*, as discussed in the next chapter.

The final season of *Angel*, then, has as its main writers the following: Whedon, Fury, DeKnight, Goddard, Edlund, Fain and Craft, and Bell.

Many of the names that one associates with Whedon's works and Mutant Enemy (Noxon, Espenson, Greenwalt, Petrie) are missing. In order to get a greater sense of how the shifts in writing staff (and the as yet unmentioned changes in show runner) are to be accounted for it will be helpful to place the previous bald descriptors of the statistics into some kind of narrative.

As discussed in Chapter 1, Gail Berman's production company had been responsible for funding the *Buffy* movie and held the rights for any future television show. She offered it to Whedon who took it on and created Mutant Enemy as his production company. Given his inexperience, Whedon would need a team well versed in television production, and he would also need a writing team. Fox was happy with the writers Whedon brought on for season 1 of *Buffy* but felt, understandably, that Whedon would still need an experienced colleague to help run the show. It was over six years since Whedon's work on *Roseanne,* and although he had accrued decent sitcom script credits, the experience was long past and his subsequent work had all been as a writer of film scripts, not as a producer and writer of a television show. It was perhaps unexpected that a figure of David Greenwalt's stature would apply. Greenwalt, along with John McNamara, had created *Profit* (Fox 1996), a dark and deeply disturbing show that had been scrapped after four episodes. Not only its edgy subject matter (the main character's explicit amorality and its implicit attack on corporate America; his affair with his step-mother), but also the interesting production techniques such as *Profit*'s brief monologue to the audience at the end of each episode, mean that the show was an astonishing precursor to later hits such as *Mad Men* (AMC 2007–15) or *Dexter* (Showtime 2006–13). It also meant that Greenwalt would blaze a trail for Whedon to follow in having literate, edgy, formally inventive shows cancelled by Fox. However, in 1996, the show had gained Greenwalt great acclaim and there was every expectation that he would be able to enter Hollywood or have the pick of any of the new crop of television shows. *Buffy*, in retrospect, was an obvious choice. At the time it was more of a gamble. However, he came on board as co-executive producer and the Mutant Enemy team was ready.

The period between September 1996 and January 1997 saw most of *Buffy* season 1 produced. The facts of its being a midseason replacement has been much mentioned, but the practical impact of this for Mutant Enemy was enormous. After production wrapped it would be a further two months before the first episode aired. Given the investment in the show, and The WB's balance book, it was always going to air. However, it was far from clear that it would return and the writers could not be guaranteed any more work. Many, for very obvious reasons, went elsewhere, including Greenwalt who went to join *The X-Files* as co-executive producer.

Buffy's premiere gained The WB its highest ever drama audience rating (3.4) and the show was renewed. Only three of the previous season's eight writers remained, and given that one of these was Whedon and the other two were a team who only ever wrote together (Dean Batali and Rob Des Hotel), more writers were desperately needed. The show's success enticed Greenwalt back and he brought with him from *The X-Files* Howard Gordon. Gordon, along with writing partner Alex Gansa, achieved industry recognition for their work on *Spenser: For Hire* (ABC 1985–88) and *Beauty and the Beast* (CBS 1987–90), and their efforts as pilot writers for Witt-Thomas productions brought them to the attention of Chris Carter. Carter gave Gordon 20 episodes to write in the first four seasons of *The X-Files*. He joined *Buffy* briefly, but would return later with new collaborator Tim Minear to re-join Mutant Enemy on *Angel*. Along with the returning Greenwalt and industry veteran Gordon, an entirely new writer joined the ranks: Marti Noxon. Still, though, there were only six writers on the staff.

The obvious response was to use freelance writers, among whom were Fury and Hampton whose own project had not been entirely successful and who now decided that they would work as freelancers on the show they had previously been encouraged to spurn. Among the other freelancers were Ty King who had, under the name David Tyron King, been executive producer on *Parenthood* (NBC 1990) on which, of course, Whedon had been a writer, and Matt Kiene and Joe Reinkemeyer who had written for *Buffy* season 1. This provided Whedon with a solid basis from which to launch season 2 with only episode six ('Halloween') of the opening eight of the season being written by a relative newcomer, Carl Ellsworth who wrote no more for Buffy (despite this being a wonderful episode) but who went on to write for a number of fantasy shows including *Xena: Warrior Princess* (Syndication 1995–2001) and to pen some screenplays. Episode nine sees two debuts as Gordon and Noxon co-wrote 'What's my line part 1'. Noxon's first venture into television writing was to be followed up in rapid succession by five more episodes including the last ever Monday night Buffy, 'Innocence', the first part of the two-parter leading to the re-launch of the show and the creation of The WB's Tuesday night line-up. This episode boasted the new highest ever drama audience rating for a The WB show of 5.2.

Whedon was significantly aided in developing his writing team by signing a four-year overall deal with Fox in the autumn of 1997. Worth US$16 million, the deal also gave Whedon US$1 million to develop Mutant Enemy and to executive produce its television offerings, as well as to write, direct and produce Mutant Enemy films (Pascale, 2014: 121–2). The security and the cash, as well as the growing critical and commercial success of *Buffy*, meant that there was a lot of confidence in him, as well as a realisation that his was a show you would want to be part of.

A combination of some writers not being re-hired and others choosing to move on meant that once again there were only three staff writers before the start of the third season of *Buffy*. Despite this, Mutant Enemy was going from strength to strength and Whedon's creative power was being given full support by Fox in the development of *Angel*. The company became incorporated and appointed a senior vice president of production and a director of development, and set about trying to appoint new writers. Jane Espenson, Doug Petrie and Dan Vebber were all brought on board, with Fury again preferring a less permanent relationship and working on an ad hoc basis. The six permanent staff writers and Fury's occasional scripts accounted for all the episodes this season and this group (minus Vebber) is still one that many would regard as the core Mutant Enemy team: Whedon, Greenwalt, Noxon, Espenson, Petrie and Fury.

By the season's end, a core team of writers under Whedon's leadership had created not just a show but a franchise, a phenomenon, and Fox and The WB were clearly keen that *Angel* would be able to deliver something similar. Much would depend on which of the core team could be kept on, who would take responsibility for running *Angel* on a day-to-day basis and how well the writing team could be strengthened in order to keep reliance on freelancers to a minimum.

One way of maintaining the staff you want is, of course, to recognise their contribution and this was duly done with Greenwalt being promoted to executive producer, Noxon being promoted to co-producer and Petrie to executive story editor. However, Greenwalt was to leave the *Buffy* stable to executively produce *Angel* with Whedon, though Greenwalt was to be show runner, thereby assuming day-to-day control of that show while Whedon, as best he could, kept day-to-day control of *Buffy*.

An obvious point to make at this juncture, but one well worth making, is the following: if, during a season of *Buffy*, Whedon was writing a script for the show or directing an episode, he was doing this while simultaneously fulfilling his role as show runner. If, however, he was writing an episode or directing an episode of *Angel* he could not be fulfilling his role as show runner of *Buffy* in the same way. And with Greenwalt in charge of *Angel* as show runner, there was no suggestion that he would have the same level of control on that show.

The first season of *Angel* offered significant challenges to Whedon. Despite an excellent team of writers in Mutant Enemy, as mentioned above, Greenwalt relied mainly on writers officially contracted to write for *Buffy*. With Greenwalt now exclusively on *Angel*, and Whedon not able to always be there on *Buffy*, Noxon was promoted to supervising producer, assuming operational control for those periods when Whedon was absent. David Fury finally agreed to join Mutant Enemy, primarily on the *Buffy* side, as a producer. Even though the opening episodes of season one of *Angel* carry some very strong names (Fury, Petrie, Espenson) they are effectively freelance and had a prior and important responsibility to the writers' room of *Buffy*. The writers' room of *Angel* was a collection of names largely unfamiliar to Whedon fans including Tim Minear, Tracey Stern, Howard Gordon and Jeannine Renshaw. These four were responsible for writing twelve of the remaining seventeen episodes (some in co-writer capacity). Gordon had already been part of the *Buffy* team of season 2 but had left to launch a show called *Strange World* (ABC 1999). He came back to *Angel* at Greenwalt's invitation and suggested that Tim Minear also be invited. As well as working with Gordon on *Strange World* and having worked on *The X-Files*, Minear had a host of experience writing for a number of shows including *The New Adventures of Superman* (ABC 1993–97). This experience would come in very useful for Minear as his responsibilities grew rapidly. It is interesting that he is the first of the 'new' writers to be entrusted with an aired episode of *Angel*, 'Sense and Sensitivity' (A S1E6). Along with Minear came Mere Smith who had been his personal assistant on *Strange World* and who was appointed script co-ordinator for season 1. Her promotion to writer in season 2 is a tale sure to warm the heart of any aspiring fan. As well as being Minear's PA, Smith had also been a long-time fan of *Buffy* and, as Nikki Stafford (2004: 160) describes, 'she posted often on the Bronze posting board and was a well-known admirer of Joss Whedon. Eventually she sent him a script, and he hired her as one of the writers on Angel.' Tracey Stern came from the exceptionally brilliant *Sports Night* (1998–2000), but despite the Aaron Sorkin heritage she only wrote two episodes and did not come back for the next season. Renshaw has three co-writer and one sole writer credit for the season and had a range of curious and tangential links with the Whedon world before her arrival. Most notably, she had been one of the creative influences behind *VR 5* (Fox 1995) (a show that Anthony Steward Head had appeared in) and which also had as one of its creators Thania St John whose idea for an episode was yoked together with a pitch from Jane Espenson to create 'Gingerbread' (B S3E11). As Espenson recalls:

> Also, this story has a shared credit. Thania is a writer who had pitched a witch-burning episode as a freelancer the year before I joined the staff. They never did the story. Then I suggested that we do a book-burning

> episode and the two stories were combined. Since we used ideas she had brought in, she was given the shared credit. I didn't actually meet Thania until 2007, when we briefly shared a writers' room at *Eureka.* (Personal correspondence, 23 January 2008)

Despite these seeming presentiments of success, Renshaw did not come back for the second season. While Renshaw lasted to the end of the first season, the departure of Stern after her only episode ''The Bachelor Party' (A S1E7) and of Gordon who left after 'The Ring' (A S1E16) to pitch a new series that was not picked up, meant that there was real strain on the writing team. The surprisingly speedy promotion of Tim Minear to supervising producer by the time of 'I've Got You Under My Skin' (A S1E14) suggests that his contribution to uncredited rewrites and credited episodes was such that he had become indispensable to the show. And the fact that only he and Greenwalt were left as full-time writers certainly constituted a crisis. Jim Kouf was bought in to replace Gordon, and a mixture of his history with Greenwalt, and his significant industry experience and connections helped to offer both a pair of hands and some stability. Despite Minear's efforts, Greenwalt's energies, the reappearance of Whedon for a co-writing credit and the final script from Renshaw, it was still necessary to seek freelance help in the shape of Garry Cambpell, from *Mad TV*. But the crisis was managed and on 23 May 2000 *Angel* aired its final episode of its first season. Mutant Enemy had provided two hours of quality television most Tuesday nights from 5 October 1999 to 23 May 2000 between 8.00 and 10.00 p.m. on The WB. Forty-four hours of television – twenty-two hours from *Buffy* using six writers; *Angel* used twelve (five 'borrowed' from *Buffy*). At least season 2 would not be so stressful.

The staffing situation on *Buffy* remained relatively stable with Forbes leaving and, in her stead, Rebecca Rand Kirshna arriving. Meanwhile, not content with running two shows, Whedon was developing an idea for an animated *Buffy*. Drafting in Jeff Loeb who had been a supervising producer on PBS for an animated series to work as executive producer, Whedon's pitch was greeted by Fox with a certain enthusiasm and a run of thirteen episodes was given the green light, to be shown on Fox Kids. Unfortunately, for Whedon and Loeb, re-structuring at Fox meant that they were less committed to their children's network. This network, barely a decade before, had (as so often with Fox) rewritten the television rule book by setting itself up as a co-owned enterprise between Fox, who would own part of the network, and the affiliated individual stations with the stations gaining a share of the profits. The greater the viewing figures, the greater the direct profit not just advertising revenue.

The first US$20 million profit for a sixty-five-episode kids' programme running five times a week for thirteen weeks (plus re-runs) would go to the producers. Fox would take 15 per cent of the remaining profit as a distribution fee, and the remainder would be split among affiliates based on audience share. Affiliate stations, therefore, had an incentive to promote Fox's children's output at the expense of all competitors and the commercial success of this placed Fox Kids high in the Saturday morning figures (Kimmel, 2004: 83–84). However, ten years on, the model had run out of steam: competitors had created more innovative programming and Fox Kids closed leaving Whedon and Loeb with the task of trying to find a network willing to buy their show. None wanted it. Whedon expressed his surprise about this a couple of years later, 'we just couldn't find a home for (it). We had a great animation director, great visuals, six or seven hilarious scripts from our own staff – and nobody wanted it. I was completely baffled' (Whedon, 2003: 27). It is tempting to speculate on why Whedon did not follow the lead of other animated franchises and choose to broadcast directly on the web as Vincent Terrance (2016) documents in *Internet Children's Television Series: 1997–2015*. Still, one positive to come from the experience was that Stephen S. DeKnight, who had been called in to work on the animated series, was offered two episodes on the live-action version and proved himself not only hard working but exceptionally talented (his first script 'Blood Ties' [B S5E13] requiring an enormous amount of sensitivity to the complicated plot lines of the season) paving the way for his eventual promotions on *Angel*.

In addition to developing the unsuccessful animated series, Whedon was also having to contend with the realisation that The WB were not going renew their option on *Buffy*. With this real dilemma occupying him, and with his continuing role as show runner on *Buffy*, as well as the three writer-director credits for the season, it is perhaps not altogether surprising that Whedon's credited contribution to *Angel*'s second season are his directing of Mere Smith's first script, and his co-credits for the story (though not the teleplay) for two further episodes. With Noxon still present as consulting producer but not providing any scripts of her own, and Whedon otherwise engaged, the full-time staff was effectively Greenwalt and Minear. Kouf was still present but as a freelancer. As mentioned above, Minear's PA from his previous show was promoted from script co-ordinator to staff writer, and Shawn Ryan was also hired and worked on five episodes before moving on to become executive producer on *The Shield* on FX (2002–8). The remaining slots were taken, again on a freelance basis, by Espenson, Fury and Petrie.

Season 3 of *Angel* was the first time it had not had *Buffy* as its lead-in because *Buffy* had moved to UPN. During this year, Whedon's energies included not just *Buffy* and *Angel*, the *Fray* comics, the mooted animated *Buffy* and others but also the production of a show whose genesis began in the summer of 1999 on holiday in England. Having read *The Killer Angels* about the American Civil War by Michael Shaara, and then a book about Jewish partisan fighters in the Warsaw ghetto (Whedon, 2005: 8), Whedon developed the idea of a space western focused on a group of outsiders, led by a man on the losing side of a war. *Firefly* would expand Whedon's imaginative real worlds considerably. In relation to the history of Mutant Enemy, one of the most telling contributions it made was the creation of Tim Minear as show runner. Having promised David Greenwalt that Minear would not be used on the new show because Whedon understood the extraordinary difficulty of running *Angel* and Greenwalt's need for Minear to enable that, Whedon appointed Minear anyway. The field was small and included Greenwalt himself, Marti Noxon who had assumed much of the running of *Buffy* and Minear. Without a 'second-in-command' on *Firefly*, Whedon was warned by a friend that he would never see *Buffy* or *Angel* again as he would be so busy. Greenwalt 'did not take that lightly' and for a variety of reasons left *Angel* (Whedon, 2006: 8). Noxon left *Buffy* to have her child and Whedon was without two show runners. Luckily, Minear 'was the guy ... and my god, from the first moment, he understood the show as well as any human being' (Whedon, 2006: 8). In addition, Whedon appointed Chris Buchanan, a long-time friend, to become president of Mutant Enemy and take over the running of the production company in 2002.

Sadly for Whedon, the Fox network was less understanding. He himself lamented his failure to 'understand' the network and their desires (Sullivan, 2004: n.p.) after the cancellation of *Firefly*. One of the network's needs, of course, is profit: a profit derived from advertising. Maximising advertising revenues at peak times is crucial to a network's financial viability, and Fox was seeking, after many years, to regain the capital income that had previously been achieved on their Friday night slot. Their trouble was that in desiring a show that would shine and flourish the network interfered and 'so second-guessed' it that the show could only 'fizzle' once it came to air (Kimmel, 2004: 269).

This desire for profit does not preclude high quality television, and there is no inevitable conflict between profit and aesthetic interest. Indeed, Peter S. Grant and Chris Wood (2004: 235) explain:

> Lavishly financed series like *West Wing, CSI* and *The Agency* have sharply raised the standard of production values by which audiences judge

> television drama. Broadcasters everywhere have reacted by scheduling fewer, albeit more expensive such shows, and filling the air with cheap but popular 'reality TV' fare.

Networks realise the marketing value of a high quality format and its associated franchise, but to afford this, less expensive forms of television are required to take up the slack. The decision as to what will and what will not be produced will be every bit as much driven by the market analysts as by any sort of aesthetic criteria. Indeed, the analysts' role is to determine the best match between aesthetics, markets, scheduling slots and franchise potential in order for them then to 'have a voice in determining the kinds of programmes made by identifying demographics in particular scheduling slots at which the company overall is aiming' (Nelson, 2007: 63).

Fox, in many ways, had been at the forefront of the growth of quality television and its 'reality' financer as well as the targeted notion of market segmentation. While the high-performing and relatively cheap-to-produce reality show *America's Most Wanted* (1988–2011) managed to be Fox's longest-running show in any format, the critically acclaimed Golden Globe-winning *Party of Five* (1994–2000) struggled to be renewed each year and rarely achieved high viewing figures. It could be argued that there is a mutual cross-subsidisation at play here: *America's Most Wanted* supports the financial cost of *Party of Five*, while the latter affords the network the cultural capital of award-winning drama. There is much to be said on this subject, but for the purposes of *Firefly*, the important questions relate to Fox's desire to reproduce *The X-Files* phenomenon, the slot into which the show was destined, and the nature of Fox's sports franchises.

Fox had seen enough of Whedon's work and his dedicated fan base to believe that Whedon was the man to recreate the Friday night 9.00 p.m. hit that had eluded them since *The X-Files*. *The X-Files* itself had suffered at the hands of Fox in its very early days. Peter Roth, who worked with Chris Carter to develop Carter's initial idea into a viable series, tells how: 'It almost didn't get greenlit as a pilot. It almost didn't get greenlit as a series. It was perceived to be too myopic and singular and not commercial' (quoted in Kimmel, 2004: 214). The eventual success of the show, and Fox's desire to recapture the audience that it had seen disappear with its demise, laid the foundation for a number of attempts to mine the same televisual gold. It was not only the ratings that Fox sought, but also the franchise. *The X-Files* had been its first franchise and the ancillary markets had provided huge revenue boosts. *Buffy* and *Angel* were successful franchises, and it was hoped that Whedon would produce another. Chris Carter himself had had two failed attempts: *Millennium* first aired in October 1996, in the midst of *The X-Files'* success. It achieved three seasons but never pulled in the ratings that *The X-Files* had. *Millennium* (1996–99) was replaced by another Carter program, *Harsh Realm* (1999–2000). Only nine episodes were filmed and not all of these were shown. The pattern had been set that would lead directly to *Firefly*'s demise.

Another effort to fill the vacated *The X-Files* slot was *Brimstone* (1998). An ex-cop sent to Hell for killing his wife's rapists is given a deal by Satan: if he tracks down and returns 113 evil souls who have escaped from Hell, he will be released. Beset by problems from the beginning, its executive producer Michael Chernuchin walked off the project before it had even aired. In addition to these internal difficulties, Fox now had to contend with ABC, NBC and CBS, as well as with the new The WB and UPN channels who had learned Fox's lessons well (The WB being set up and run by ex-Fox executives Jamie Kellner and Garth Ancier). *Brimstone* fared badly against a new The WB cult hit, J.J. Abrams' *Felicity* (1998–2002). Again, *Firefly* was destined to have a hard time.

The difficulty faced by *Firefly* was caused to a certain extent by a decision made nearly a decade earlier, in the same year that *The X-Files* came to the television screen. In that year (1993), Fox became a genuine player in the US networks by bidding US$1.6 billion for the rights to broadcast NFL football. Having ousted CBS from its position as the football network (and in the process demolishing CBS's Sunday prime-time strategy), Fox had shown it was capable of being a serious sports and outside broadcaster. Three years later it acquired rights to Major League Baseball, including the important postseason and its divisional playoffs and the World Series. The postseason takes place in September and October and brings in enormous numbers of new viewers. A difficulty, however, is that the regular schedule has to be moved around to accommodate the games. *Firefly* began its doomed brief season in the heart of postseason. Keith R. A. DeCandido (2004: 56) makes this point and observes that 'a big chunk of the advertising for the show was also shown during those games'. However, the demographic for baseball is not necessarily the same demographic that *Firefly* would be appealing to, and a quotation from an unnamed executive discussing the initial deal in 1996 is pertinent here: 'You can promote *The Simpsons* all day long, but if you're promoting it to a sixty-year-old male, he's not gonna watch' (quoted in Kimmel, 2004: 214).

Whedon's creation, then, was already in a difficult position. Fox had specific objectives for any show in that time slot and these included recreating the audience figures and the franchise potential of *The X-Files*.

Also, this mission had already been attempted by a number of programs that had faced various degrees of difficulty. In addition, the launch coincided with one of Fox's greatest assets, but an asset that played havoc with regular scheduling and something a new show could barely afford.

Despite this, Whedon had a crew he was very happy with, including a new director of photography David Boyd whose work Whedon described as 'cinematic, just beautiful' and who purposefully sought out old lenses 'that caught flares off of everything and really helped the look of the thing' (Whedon, 2006: 8). Old writers such as Espenson and Greenberg came from *Buffy* to join a new set, which included Edlund, Cheryl Cain, Brett Matthews and Jose Molina. As Whedon notes, 'The first year of staff is always difficult. But we actually started out very strong and that's rare' (Whedon, 2006: 9). The strength of the team was undoubted, Whedon's vision for the show strong and the move to Fox offered a new and expanded audience.

From the outset, though, Whedon's vision and Fox's were very different. The thirteen-episode order from Fox in December 2001, and the US$10 million given to Mutant Enemy to develop the pilot in January 2002 (Pascale, 2014: 203), was probably as warm as the relationship ever got, and the show lasted only eleven episodes before being cancelled. These episodes were shown out of sequence, and meant that three were left unaired. The importance of this for a reading of the show will be discussed in Chapter 7. But for Whedon it meant that his cast, crew and writing team had lasted less than half a season, and with *Buffy* coming to an end, the moment of three Whedon shows on television at the same time was brief indeed.

Angel would remain. At the end of *Buffy*'s fifth season, and its move to UPN, the questions raised over *Angel* with *Buffy*'s departure were significant. One obvious one was whether *Angel* would also be bought by UPN. The WB had no particular reason not to keep *Angel* as its licence was not being increased and, more pertinently, it is unlikely that they would have wanted to hand UPN a ready-made night of quality television, and have to fill two hours themselves. So, keeping *Angel* was a sensible plan, but it did raise the question of where to put it, and how well it would work without its lead-in progenitor.

In the 2001–2 season, The WB put *Angel* in *Buffy*'s old 1997 slot of Monday night at 9.00 p.m. with its lead-in show being The WB's top ranking *Seventh Heaven*. The change of day and lead-in show did not have any very strong impact on *Angel* in terms of audience. In the previous season, it had finished 125th in the TV rankings, and had an average audience share of 4.1. This season it rose one place to 124th, though its share fell a little to 4.04.

The end of *Angel*'s first season on its own at The WB saw it renewed so that in the autumn of 2002 Whedon had *Buffy* entering its final season on UPN, *Angel* beginning its fourth season on The WB, and Whedon's newest creation, *Firefly*, about to launch on Fox. Barely six months later and it was unclear whether there would be any Whedon shows in the next season.

Angel's season 4 was seen to be disenfranchising viewers and the network was seeking some reassurances about the following season if it was to be renewed. The season had been beset with difficulties before it even began shooting. David Greenwalt had left the production to work on developing his show *Miracles* (ABC 2003), which suffered a similar fate to *Firefly*, though it did manage to at least air all its fourteen episodes before being cancelled, despite being nominated for an Emmy. Whedon called Greenwalt's leaving a 'shock' (Topping, 2004: 345) but welcomed in the new show runner David Simkins with great enthusiasm. Indeed, Simkins' track record on (essentially post-*Buffy*) shows such as *Roswell*, *Charmed* and *Dark Angel* (Fox 2000–2) meant that he had both the genre-style experience and an uncanny network mirroring of Whedon too. He left the show after a matter of weeks. With Tim Minear, long-standing Whedon collaborator having left *Angel* to work with Whedon on the ill-fated *Firefly*, there was a distinct lack of direction at the helm, even though Minear maintained involvement in breaking the first few episodes of season 4 and returned to the show after *Firefly*'s cancellation.

The show was further hampered by The WB's decision to move its time slot yet again, after the Christmas break. It was to shift from Sunday to Wednesday nights where it would be in competition with *The Twilight Zone* (UPN 2002–3), Top-30 rated *The West Wing* (NBC 1999–2006) and top-20 rated *The Bachelor* (ABC 2002–present). It was not going to be easy to maintain audience figures, let alone build on them. Steven S. DeKnight comments that despite the time slot moves, *Angel*'s audience numbers remained largely stable, but of course the opportunity to gain new casual viewers was impeded (Abbot, 2005: 30). The fact that *Angel* was not among The WB's list of early renewal notices meant there was reason to be fearful that the show's fourth season might be its last.

It was picked up for renewal but on the twin conditions that James Marsters' character Spike be brought in as a regular and not just for 'odd appearances', and that the season be much more anthology-oriented. This drive towards the anthology-based season as opposed to the narrative-arc was not reserved for *Angel*. Abbott and Brown use *Angel* as an illuminating point of comparison with another show that shared a similar fate, *Alias*

(ABC 2001–6). Describing the network's unhappiness with two seasons of complex overarching narrative and its desire for a different emphasis in season five, they write, '*Angel* was likewise mandated to break from season-length arc narratives it had been exploring in the previous two seasons ... both shows were allowed to reach the 100-episode watermark required for syndication in the USA before the plug was pulled (Abbott and Brown, 2007: 3).

The 100th episode marked the return and final departure of Cordelia Chase (Charisma Carpenter). Laura Anne Gilman celebrates the character of Cordelia, and it is a truly unexpected development in *Angel* from the spoiled bitchy valley girl we are introduced to in *Buffy*. Gilman (2004: 185) writes of Cordelia, that 'in her humanity, we see the best points of the *Angel*verse: not the strong defending the weak, but the weak learning to be strong'. Many fans, and Carpenter herself, however, were unhappy with how the character was written out of the show towards the end of season 4 after a strong storyline. We see her become a Power that Is, return to Earth apparently (but hidden) harbouring the god Jasmine, have a sexual relationship with Connor, Angel's son who gets her pregnant (with Jasmine), and as the mother-to-be of Jasmine oversee the organisation of her birth and the destruction that comes with this. Jennifer Cruise (2004: 195) is far from a lone voice in asserting, 'we'd spent too much honest revulsion on the debasing of her character for us to go back to the Cordelia we once loved'. When the character ends up in a coma at the end of season 4, Cruise's feelings may have been assuaged had Cordelia returned in season 5. But she did not. Carpenter remembers the affair with some evident ire, 'my relationship with Joss became strained. We all go through our stuff ... I was going through my stuff and then I became pregnant ... I think Joss was honestly mad at me' (Pascale, 2014: 229).

Nikki Stafford (2004: 281) claims that not just on *Angel* but on *Buffy* too, 'season 4 was the weakest ... during season 4 of *Buffy* Joss was focused on starting up *Angel*, and during season 4 of *Angel* Joss was working on *Firefly*'. I disagree with this assessment and would be more in line with Stacey Abbott (2009: 25) who says the season 'serves as the culmination of the series' operatic arc narrative with its virtual abandonment of the episodic in favour of a sustained story line', but for the purposes of this discussion, it is not the story itself but rather the absence of both Whedon and David Greenwalt from much of the direct day-to-day running of *Angel* in season 4 that is of interest. Whedon, as noted by Stafford, was concentrating on *Firefly*, and Greenwalt had left to pursue other projects. It was Greenwalt who had suggested Cordelia's presence on *Angel*, and as Pascale speculates with his departure 'she no longer had a champion on the writing staff' (Pascale, 2014: 229). Her love interest, Connor (Vincent Kartheiser) did not feel much better written, feeling that he was doing the same scene 'over and over and over' (Pascale, 2014: 229).

Nevertheless, the writers wanted Cordelia back for the 100th episode. Despite her hurt and reservations, she agreed after Bell (promoted to co-executive producer after Tim Minear) left to helm *Wonderfalls* (Fox 2004) and David Fury also promoted to co-executive producer convinced her. They swayed her by assuring her the character would survive the episode. Bell and Fury had the difficulty of being new to the post that they shared, but with neither of them having been the show's creator. When Whedon did return 'it blew a lot of our stuff out the water ... as it should, it's his show' (Pascale, 2014: 239). On signing the contract she was told the truth (that she would die), and she 'felt totally betrayed' (Pascale, 2014: 239). Fury, however, outlined the idea for the episode, and Carpenter was won round, 'That's the story. It sucked that I died but I really felt it was a hell of a way to go' (Pascale, 2014: 240) (see Figure 3). Among other things, Cordelia's story arc and Carpenter's dismissal demonstrate how difficult the aesthetic desire for a progressive art can be when imbricated in an industrial system where power in the writers' room shifts, actors circumstances change, and show runners disagree with the one remaining creator: it implies a degree of tension.

Figure 3 Cordelia Chase, *Angel*, 'You're Welcome', season 5, episode 12, first broadcast 4 February 2004. The smiles of the character Cordelia Chase belie the significant tensions between Whedon and actor Charisma Carpenter over both the storytelling relating to her character, and the manner of informing her of his plans.

Back at the end of season 4, while Cordelia was being quietly written out, the set-up for the final season was being established in Minear's masterful last episode of season 4, 'Home' (A S4E22), and it afforded the opportunity for a very different *Angel* to be aired in season 5.

The nature of the renewal for season 5 was not all it seemed however. Whedon was not alone in assuming that the show had been picked up for a twenty-two-episode season, but only as the season was underway was the second half confirmed: the network called up and said 'We piggybacked you on the deal for another show,' I'm like 'Okay, so what you're saying to my writers is that they weren't picked up when they thought they were and now that they are it was because of something that has nothing to do with them. Okay. Great. Stop calling'. (Sullivan, 2004: n.p.)

They did not stop calling, and on 13 February 2004 issued a press release saying the show had been cancelled. Whedon's response was heartfelt:

> No, we had no idea this was coming. Yes, we will finish out the season. No, I don't think The WB is doing the right thing. Yes, I'm grateful they did it early enough for my people to find other jobs. Yes, my heart is breaking. (Whedon, 2004)

Eight months later on 26 October, a day after Whedon had hosted a fund-raiser for Senator John Kerry in his presidential race against George Bush Jr, Fox released a statement saying that at Whedon's request it was suspending his overall deal with the studio. Mutant Enemy closed its offices, and Whedon's future on television was uncertain.

The *Angel* years had been extraordinary. Changing networks with *Buffy*, the *Firefly* fiasco, the cancellation of *Angel*. Over 200 episodes of top quality television across three networks. New writers had been found, nurtured and developed. Producers had come and gone, as had show runners and the legacy of those years on later US quality television is immense. Mutant Enemy alumni have, since the cancellation of *Angel*, worked on a range of the most critically acclaimed and successful American television shows in the early twenty-first century

Whedon's reputation as a television maker is rightly high, but his contribution to the more broadly defined world of US television cannot be under-estimated. Whether it be as nurturer of talent or network scourge, the *Angel* years made Whedon a formidable presence in the US TV arena. And then he went away for nearly seven years.

'There are so many things I'd like to be': Multimedia polymath and mainstream cult 3

Between 10 March 1997 and 19 May 2004, there were over 260 episodes of Whedon-produced television broadcast for the first time on networks in the USA. Between 20 May 2004 and 13 February 2009 there were none. Between that date (the airing of the pilot of *Dollhouse*) and the end of the fourth season of *Agents of S.H.I.E.L.D.* in May 2017 there were a further 112 episodes. In the seven years from *Buffy*'s beginning to *Angel*'s cancellation Whedon had over 150 more episodes produced than in the following thirteen years. However, this decade has seen Whedon emerge as one of the most significant figures in the US cultural landscape both in terms of his contributions to a range of media, and in his direct interventions in political debates.

The main areas of his involvement with mass mediated art have been these: first, was the continuation through other means of the imaginative television universes created for *Buffy*, *Angel* and *Firefly*. These have been in the form of comic books, internet webisodes and films, as well as proposed new television series; second, has been Whedon's enthusiastic involvement with other franchises, initially in comic book form but latterly in film and television; third, has been his involvement in a range of new media enterprises ranging from viral marketing for his films, online comics, political intervention, acting and producing his own web series; fourth, has been his creation of new imagined worlds both online and on television and in film. A discussion of these areas will form the basis of the current chapter. Some of these areas intersect, of course, and it is, in some senses, the interstitial moments and the contradictions that they can present that are important for the analysis of this chapter. The different contradictions revolve around the major one: how is one to assert Whedon's role as cult hero, victim of the corporation, when he himself is now one of the most powerful media figures in the world in terms of box office takings and cultural capital? Allied to this, but different from it, is Whedon's involvement in the creation of so many intermedial and trans-medial productions. Indeed, as Valerie Frankel (2015: 1) asserts, Whedon is 'a trans-media event all by himself, as he transforms best-selling comics into shows, and also best-selling shows into comics'.

The twin poles of economic and cultural value has been at the heart of this book and in Whedon's output is probably best exemplified by the fact that he was directing the second *Avengers* movie at the same time as *In Your Eyes* came out. The budget for *Avengers: Age of Ultron* was estimated at US$250 million and its predecessor cost an 'estimated US$220 million' (Breznican, 2011) and together they grossed over US$3 billion worldwide (they are two of the top ten grossing movies of all time as of May 2017). It was produced by Marvel Studios and distributed by Walt Disney. The Walt Disney company reported overall long-term assets at 10 January 2016 at over US$92 billion (Nasdaq.com, 2017). Marvel Studios is a wholly owned subsidiary of Walt Disney. Isaac Perlmutter took control of the bankrupt franchise in 1998, side-lining Carl Icahn and Ron Perleman in the process. According to Forbes, in 'August 2009 Perlmutter sold Marvel Entertainment along with the rights to use its more than 9,000 characters to Disney for US$4 billion in cash and stock, with Perlmutter staying on as CEO' (Forbes.com, 2017).

Whedon's movies are part of one of the most powerful corporations on the planet, with all the attendant benefits and responsibilities that go with that. It will have worldwide theatrical releases with huge advertising and promotional campaigns. By contrast, *In Your Eyes* is a Bellwether Pictures production. Founded by Whedon and his wife Kai Cole and named after a script co-authored by his mother, Bellwether is a determined move by Whedon to both produce small, independent movies and to maintain his position as a non-mainstream, cult figure. The desire to 'do things on a smaller scale' after *The Avengers*, to 'do things that were not beholden to anything but our own indie imagination' (Whedon, 2013: 17) speaks to the tensions between blockbuster-Whedon and outsider-Whedon. The press release that accompanied Bellwether's first film said Bellwether is:

> a micro-studio created by Joss Whedon and Kai Cole for the production of small, independent narratives for all media, embracing a DIY ethos and newer technologies for, in this particular case, a somewhat older story. (Whedonesque.com, 2011)

The budget for *In Your Eyes* was an estimated US$1 million, and its release was at the Tribeca Film Festival at which an announcement made by Whedon (recorded on the set of *Avengers 2*, just to highlight the disparity in his respective roles) stated that it would be simultaneously released to Vimeo on demand.

The combination of Marvel, comics, new media, independent filming, public announcements, industry innovation, science fiction, major media companies and unabated public enthusiasm for his works (whether mainstream or indie; new franchises or established ones) characterises this period of Whedon's career: a period that begins with Whedon joining the Marvel team to write *The Astonishing X-Men*.

Whedon had been involved on the *X-Men* film project in 1994, although very little of his input can be seen in the final movie, and then in 2004 he was given the opportunity to take over the comic book series. The first two limited seasons had run in the 1990s, and Whedon with illustrator John Cassaday took the helm between 2004 and 2008. A review of one of the titles Whedon wrote, *Astonishing X-Men*, draws attention to the intermingling of tones, the centrality of teamwork over individual genius and the grasp of the franchise's allure for fans. George (2006: n.p.) writes, 'He knows how to write a team book with humor, action and drama. He knows how to handle team dynamics while allowing each character to have a unique personality' and goes on, 'Whedon absolutely nails the interpersonal dynamics. The team is small – Shadowcat, White Queen, Cyclops, Wolverine and Beast – but this lets the spotlight shine on everyone. No character dominates the page'. Cassaday's artwork is also highly commended and one can see here the trademark Whedon television aesthetic translated and adapted for comic books. Not only the aesthetic (great writing supporting an excellent story and great visuals bringing that into graphic existence) but also a politics associated with it: the democratising nature of the team over the fascist nature of the individual enforcer. The ability to work with a pre-existing franchise (and a franchise beloved by its fans) and to do so while retaining his own sense of aesthetic and political motivation would be rewarded later on with the opportunity to write and direct one of the biggest films ever made. And while industry recognition for his television work was hard to come by, Whedon and Cassaday won an Eisner Award in 2006 for best continuing series for their work, as well as two further nominations (comicbookdb.com).

His work on *X-Men* coincided with comic-book versions of all of his television series. While his work on *Fray* is the first example of a comic book spin off from a Whedon franchise, its extreme futurity means that, though canonical and important to the overall mythos of the *Buffy*verse, its relation to the world experienced by the audience is somewhat attenuated. *Serenity: Those Left Behind* is a limited series of three issues that bridges the gap between the cancelled *Firefly* and the fan-inspired movie, *Serenity*. Written by Brett Matthews with drawings by Will Conrad and colours by Laura Martin, the Whedon-created story is a canonical part of the *Firefly* world. Plot points of note include Inara's leaving, Book's decision to leave and the introduction of Fanty and Mingo and, more importantly, The Operative, who will play such a vital role in the film that Whedon wrote and directed after the well documented fan response to *Firefly*'s cancellation and subsequent efforts to raise money for the movie.

The production of *Serenity* highlights how important fan involvement can be (see Abbott, 2008: 227–38; Cochrane, 2008, 239–50; Milson, 2012: 270–84). But it also demonstrates the need for personal relationships with powerful people within the industry. In some ways, Whedon was still very much beholden to champions, as he had been back in the early 1990s when he was still at the start of his career. During that period he was friends with Jorge Saralegui, a junior executive at Fox who had recommended they buy the *Buffy* movie, as part of which Whedon was offered a development deal. He wrote a script for a comedy about a young boy who is trying to come to terms with the death of his mother (this was before Whedon's own mother's death) and who is also trying to stop the move of his girlfriend's family, which he tries through an ever-ambitious series of ridiculous schemes. This script, *Nobody Move* never got made but it did lead to a conversation with Saralegui, where Saralegui pitched an idea for a movie about a dog. Whedon, aware that his CV was very heavily oriented towards comedy and teen audiences countered by suggesting '*Die Hard* on a bridge' which was a joke about the many attempts to recapture the success of the *Die Hard* (John McTiernan, 1988) franchise, but also a plea that he be offered more exciting projects. Saralegui took the idea seriously and told Whedon to write the script, which Whedon duly did. It was called *Suspension* and was bought for US$1 million by Largo Entertainment, run by the producer of *Die Hard* and *48 Hours* (Walter Hill, 1982), Lawrence Gordon. Despite being replaced as the writer and the eventual decision not to make the movie after costs became impossible, the script marked Whedon out as a writer of considerable talent. The same year, 1993, Saraleugi was also the man who suggested Whedon to producer Walter F. Parkes, the man who had been brought in to try and rescue the script for *Speed* (see Chapter 1). Although the WGA arbitration did not in the end allow him to be credited as the film's writer, he was known within the industry. This perception was further enhanced the following year when his script for *Afterlife*, a science fiction drama, sold for US$1.5 million to Sony. The pathos, humour, sci-fi, action, comedy writer was widely sought after. Two scripts (*Buffy* and *Speed*) that grossed collectively almost US$140 million and two others taken into development – and all because of Saralegui's championing of Whedon's considerable talent.

Nearly ten years later, and Whedon was in need of a champion again. With all three television shows off air, but with DVD sales of *Firefly* proving that there was considerable commercial possibility in that world, he was eager to make a film based on the show. The head of Universal Pictures, Mary Parent, had been keen to work with Whedon for a while and had approached him a little while before, but as Mutant Enemy President at the time, Chris Buchanan, recalls, 'Joss would tell her that he had three shows on the air and didn't have time to do anything' (Pascale, 2014: 237). Once this was no longer true, Parent asked what he would like to do, and he told her of the *Firefly* movie plan. She agreed to the idea as long as Whedon worked within a US$40 million budget, a fifty-day shooting schedule and – most importantly – secured the rights to the show from Fox. In the event, Fox kept the rights to the name but sold the rights to the franchise, so on 3 March 2004 Universal announced *Serenity*. Not only this, but Parent agreed to a seven-figure deal that would see Whedon develop the film the script for *Goners*.

Goners, however, would have to wait while he worked on a script for *Wonder Woman*. Already five years in development, and having gone through a number of different writers, the project was always going to be difficult and the producer Joel Silver needed to work hard to convince him to take the DC franchise on. A previous excursion into DC territory had not gone well, when his script for a *Batman* origin movie was rejected by Warner Bros. in 2002, but Whedon accepted the job on *Wonder Woman*. In the event, over 18 months of writing and rewriting led nowhere, and the studio and he parted company in early 2007, with Whedon posting on whedonesque.com:

> Let me stress first that everybody at the studio and Silver Pictures were cool and professional. We just saw different movies, and at the price range this kind of movie hangs in, that's never gonna work. Non-sympatico. It happens all the time. I don't think any of us expected it to this time, but it did. Everybody knows how long I was taking, what a struggle that script was, and though I felt good about what I was coming up with, it was never gonna be a simple slam-dunk. I like to think it rolled around the rim a little bit, but others may have differing views. (Whedon, 2007a)

Later, he expressed much more frustration at the 'waste of time' that his involvement had been, saying he felt 'so ground down. Second guessing *everything*, unable to focus' (Pascale, 2014: 277, emphasis in original). In the same announcement, he insists that *Goners* is still in development and hints at more interesting projects to come.

Unfortunately for Whedon, his champion at Universal, Parent, left in order to take over at MGM's Worldwide Motion Picture group and 'the new people just completely shit-canned it ... And I wasn't ready for that' (Utichi, 2012: n.p.). But while *Goners* was no more, Parent's first job at her new role was to give the green light on *The Cabin in the Woods*. He had a champion, and the year was looking better.

Little could he or anyone have predicted that before the year's end the Writers Guild of America would call a strike that would have a definitive impact on Whedon's career, the future of his production staff, the face of new media production, Whedon's position as overt political commentator and also (and less dramatically, of course) this book.

The strike was called for many reasons, but the primary focus was to redistribute the profits that the major production companies were making more equitably (as the WGA saw it) to the writers. The dispute was called between the WGA and Alliance of Motion Picture and Television Producers (AMTP), a trade organisation including (but far from being limited to, but these organisations are important in terms of Whedon's industry trajectory) Walt Disney Company, Fox/Newscorp, NBC, Lionsgate and Warner Bros. In renegotiating the 2004 Minimum Basic Agreement (MBA), which forms the contractual basis for writers and is renewed every three years, no agreement could be found on the specific question of residuals for DVD and new media distribution. This MBA is a huge document (over 600 pages) that details everything from agreed definitions of such terms as 'writer' and 'format' to agreed minimum compensation for specific involvements in specific aspects of writing for film and television. For example in article 13, sub-section B.7.d. the document says:

> d. Network Prime Time (For all network prime time episodic series, one-time shows, unit series shows, once-per-week network prime time serials, and anthology programs. This subparagraph d. is not applicable to programs covered by Appendix A and other non-dramatic programs (for example, Wild Kingdom and travelogues). The rates set forth in this subparagraph d. are not to be utilized for the purposes of Article 15.B. of this Agreement.)

There then follows, in further sub-section 1, a chart that details compensation for a range of possible involvements. Someone credited with writing the story for an episode under sixty minutes but over forty-five minutes would receive a fee of US$11,763 between the period 11 January 2004 and 31 October 2005, which would rise to US$12,299 between 11 January 2006 and 31 October 2007. The writer of the teleplay for the same length programme during the same periods would have seen the fee rise from US$19,396 to US$20,278; while the writer of both the story and the teleplay would have seen the fee go up from US$29,482 to US$30,823) (Minimum Basic Agreement, 2004: 90–1).

While negotiations for these fees were developing relatively well, it was the so-called 'residual' fees that were causing significant disagreement. As Bennet and Brown explain (2008: 1): When DVDs ... were launched in 1997 in the US and the UK ... the potential impact on the economies of film and television production was unclear, leading to the WGA to agree to a deal whereby writers are paid 4 cents on each $15 DVD as a residual 'sell-through' of the artist's work. Yet by 2005, DVD players were in approximately 84 million homes in the US.' In other words, the DVD residual market was more lucrative than the ostensible primary markets and the WGA wanted this reflected in the new MBA. What is clear, though, is that the DVD issue was also an index for future concerns. The corporations' claims in the 1980s relating to video cassettes, which had set residual fees from the sale of these at 0.3 per cent and had then persisted into the DVD era, was that it was too soon to see what the future might hold. Now that future showed that DVD sales outstripped primary market sakes, the WGA felt it reasonable to forestall a similar claim. It is a claim made by Barry Diller, who was not involved in the negotiations but as a major player in the television and media world was unsurprisingly sympathetic to the corporations' view:

> What this strike is about is not revenues from first usage. It's about revenues from what happens in this digital age, of which right now there are none ... What they want to do is strike so they're protected for the future. The problem with that is right now it's a future that no one can figure out ... What they should have done is say, we're going to take the next five year period–we want to know where all of these revenues are coming from. We want to freeze this area until we can understand the revenues, which aren't going to develop for another few years ... There are no profits for the work that writers do that is then digitized and distributed through the Internet. (Finke, 2007: n.p.)

So, the WGA's action was 'as much concerned with the Hollywood studios attempts to extend the current residual payments structure to the new delivery methods offered by other digital platforms' (Bennett and Brown, 2008: 1). Whedon, in common with a number of other show runners, and a huge number of the people associated with Mutant Enemy, supported the strike.

However, Whedon was not content simply to strike. In part, one can assume, because of the restless creative energy that animates him, but also as a direct intervention into the practices being debated, Whedon chose to produce a web-based series.

Dr. Horrible's Sing-Along Blog marks an almost impossible to repeat form of political praxis. Writing and producing the series entirely outside of the control of the networks and production companies; developing a funding, distribution and compensation model that was similarly independent; while also staging the continuation of many of the questions that have interested him in the construction of previous televisual fantasy worlds (power, gender, consequentialist ethics), *Dr. Horrible* is, in some respects, one of Whedon's most significant works; while also being one of his least important.

One of the most significant changes to Whedon's career that *Dr. Horrible* introduces is the addition to his writing staff of his half-brothers Zak and Jed, and Maurissa Tancharoen. They had produced a YouTube video in support of the writers' strike that Whedon had loved. He promoted it on the website Whedonesque.com and when he began to formulate his ideas for the web show, their video encouraged him to ask them to join him.

Dr. Horrible is a transitional text in Whedon's career, and it marks a moment that can be read as sort of crisis. This book is not a biography, and I do not claim to have any sense of Whedon's emotional state, but in purely textual terms, *Dr. Horrible* and its associated media texts, present an aesthetic, political and industry-related challenge. Its coming into being is an overtly political response to the strike, and an effort by Whedon to exert creative control outwith the existing available structures. Given the fact that he had not had a new episode of television on air for years (and planned projects, such as the animated *Buffy* series, and the spin-off *Ripper*, were not any nearer agreement), and, despite *Serenity*, his film work was complicated and unfinished, the opportunity to work as an independent producer and, crucially, distributor must have been very appealing.

The show was streamed for free on the web over three days (15, 17, 19 July 2008), and then was released via iTunes and finally on DVD, as well as being available at different points on Amazon video on demand and Netflix. Whedon has stated that the time taken between initially pitching the idea to the writers to it being streamed was five months. The importance of this is that Whedon had total control, and this experience encouraged him later to develop Bellwether. Indeed, it is in response to a question about Bellwether that Whedon makes the remark:

> It's a reaction to all of my scary, eerily long years in the business. I've been doing this a long time, and I've had so many agonizing frustrations. Everything I've done, every movie's been delayed, every TV show's been put off till midseason or delayed or shut down. I've never had a process that went smoothly, with the exception of 'Dr. Horrible,' which was five

> months from the time I pitched it to the writers to the time we streamed it, because we were in charge. (Bercovici, 2012: n.p.)

Being in charge and having creative control is clearly desirable for any audio-visual narrative producer, but Whedon's enthusiasm both for Bellwether and for the *Dr. Horrible* project is more encompassing than that. The structure is a direct response to and attack upon the systems against which the WGA were striking. Whedon feels that the Union agreed to a lot less than they should have, 'in addition I created a structure wherein all the writers and leads were all profit participants, partially in reaction to how little we'd gotten out of the strike. I wanted to show a model where I'm the studio, here's how I work with the people and I still do the best' (Bercovici, 2012: n.p.).

And his best is considerable. *Dr. Horrible* remains the most successful Whedon project thus far in terms of income as a percentage of initial outlay:

> The initial investment was about $200,000. The budget with everybody actually being paid was about $450,000. With the movie and the soundtrack and everything we've been able to do with it, we made over $3 million with it. Now, $3 million doesn't get [CBS CEO] Les Moonves out of bed in the morning. But if you look at it in terms of percentages, that's a very healthy profit. And, more importantly, it continues to make money years after. It's on a limited basis, but the model is extraordinary. And we're all getting a piece of it, which is very exciting. And I'm getting the most, because I'm the studio. And that's very exciting *tooooo*! (Bercovici, 2012: n.p.)

So *Dr. Horrible* was a show that illustrated a different way of making mass mediated art that took full advantage of the opportunities afforded by new media, as well as creating new distribution and compensation models. It was also a huge critical success winning a range of awards from the Streamys to the Hugo, to the Peoples Choice to the Emmys.

Its critical and commercial success, its construction of new models of production, its use of new media and its sheer exuberance all contribute to a sense of the enjoyment of the show. However, the story we watch is potentially troubling in the light of Whedon's previous feminist-inspired narratives, and the musical *Commentary!* that supports it is, I contend, a kind of angry critique of the industry. This critique, of a piece with Whedon's liberal agenda, is complicated by the aesthetic decisions made and the purposeful collapsing of actors into their characters.

The story sees the shy and sympathetic Dr. Horrible seeking to join the Evil League of Evil. His nemesis is the superhero Captain Hammer, a vain, self-important hero caught up in his own mythology and lacking the 'nerdy alter-ego': 'there's no Clark Kent' (Whedon *et al.*, 2011: 13). Dr. Horrible is in love with Penny, a young woman who does work for homeless people. Inadvertently, Dr. Horrible places Penny in a dangerous situation that Captain Hammer recues her from. The two men compete over the girl and eventually an accident caused by Dr. Horrible kills Penny, allowing him to enter the Evil League of Evil, and sending Hammer into therapy. It is fast-paced, touching, funny, excellently produced and has great songs. And in its reversal of expected sympathies for the male characters, and the terrible accession of Dr. Horrible to the League, the series has Whedon's trademark combination of ethical considerations, and questions of political responsibility and power. However, it also has a very traditional and problematic representation of Penny. Maurissa Tancharoen, discussing the genesis of the story, remembers that 'we were talking about Penny: she needs to be something more than just a girl. She should have a cause, some interest', and while 'she's delightful and Felicia brings a lot to it ... she's the girl in the movie' (Whedon *et al.*, 2011: 12–13). It would be over-stating the case to say that Penny is the girl that Buffy was designed to repudiate in storytelling terms, she nevertheless is simply a device that allows the real story (and a very interesting and well told story it is too) to be told.

Alyson Buckman has written an excellent defence of the episode where Penny's death is located alongside Whedon's response to the recording and 'commemoration' of the stoning to death of Dua Khalil Aswad, a teenage girl mistakenly accused of converting from Yazidi to Sunni Islam. Buckman reminds us of Whedon's outrage at the filming and distribution of the images, and also of his linking the stoning to death to misogyny at play in general culture. Her (2010: n.p.) essay asserts Penny's death as resistive:

> Penny's death is not eroticised. She is not tortured in front of cameras in order to provide 'entertainment.' The penetration of Penny's body by parts of the death ray occurs off camera and does not serve to titillate. Nor is it treated – by characters, bystanders, or director – as being her fault. Horrible's discovery of the wounded Penny is also a linguistically silent moment: there is no dialogue or singing at this moment, marking it as one of the few quiet moments of the series. Her death, too, is uncinematic: she doesn't die beautifully.

While the essay is persuasive in its reading of Penny contra Aswad, the text of the series, shorn of the particular co-text is still problematic. As Buckman's essay notes, Whedon's willingness to comment on politics, his long-avowed feminism and his cultural capital mean that he will be held to a higher account than many other directors. It may be that reading Penny's death as an illustration of women-as-commodity, as passive object of male desire, and so on, rather than as promotion of these ideas, the text is resistive. However, the ease with which the text can easily be encoded within conservative gender constructions – an ease that then allows for Whedon to be castigated by left and right for his co-option into mainstream political discourses – is potentially damaging. Especially so, as the piece was produced by and from a position of a more typically Whedonesque radicalism.

The difficulties that *Dr. Horrible* throws up with regard to gender (difficulties in the senses both of the critique of alpha and beta males; and of Penny's representation) are made even more problematic in *Commentary!*. This text is one of the most remarkable things that Whedon has produced, and continues the expression of political, industry, aesthetic and personal anxiety that *Dr. Horrible* offered.

If a web super-villain musical was not enough of a new format, Whedon wrote *Commentary!*. Not, of course, a commentary in the accepted sense, this musical is a commentary on the possibilities and limitations of the commentary format. A product of DVD technologies, and an amazing resource for fans and scholars, commentaries have revolutionised the fans' ability to 'learn along' with the producers of television (Lavery, 2002a). The relationship between speaker and listener is predicated on a number of assumptions: first, the listener has to believe in the sincerity of the speaker; second, and related to the first, the listener has to believe that when an actor speaks it is as the actor and not as the character; third, the speaker has to assume that the listener will be interested in what is being said.

The commentary as a form, then, is one-directional, honest, sincere and interesting. It requires a naive but routine acceptance that the speaking 'I' is coterminous with the credited equivalent – if Whedon is speaking he speaks *as* Whedon and on behalf of himself as director/producer; if Amy Acker is speaking on a commentary of *Angel* she does so *as* Acker and not as Fred, and speaks on behalf of herself as actor and *about* her character. In *Commentary!* Whedon gleefully, maliciously exploits this naivety and in so doing provides an aesthetic-philosophic critique of the medium every bit as important as the political praxis of *Dr. Horrible*.

Like a normal commentary, *Commentary!* has to be seen as a subordinate text; possible only on the condition of the pre-existence of its primary text. Yet, *Commentary!* is also its own primary text, released for download on iTunes as well as available on the DVD. Unlike normal commentaries, this text does not reference its primary text especially often, certainly not in the sense of elucidating the production question of a particular shot, or the choices relating to the delivery of a line, for example. Most strikingly, it destroys the assumed relationship between listener and speaker. While the contributors to the ostensible commentary are all spoken to and respond as if they were themselves, they are all in fact scripted versions of themselves: they do not speak on behalf of themselves; they do not speak at all. They recite Whedon's lines. This obvious (indeed, axiomatic) fact is hugely important in considering the text's importance. (As an aside, the collapsing of the simulacrum into the real as happens in the case of Senator Perrin in *Dollhouse* might be thought of as an extension of this technique.)

Joss Whedon is responsible for eight of the fourteen songs with the remainder being penned by Jed Whedon, Zack Whedon and Maurissa Tancharoen. The songs often have dialogue after or before them, ostensibly spoken by the participants as *themselves*, or, at least, as fictional versions of themselves, rather than as the characters they played. In the case of Nathan Fillion and Neil Patrick Harris, the fictionalised versions of themselves also include (or seem to include) aspects of the characters they play insofar as the interpersonal relationship is presented with something of the animus that exists between Hammer and Horrible. In Fillion's song 'Better than Neil', Horrible's failure to seduce Penny is glossed as 'Look there Felicia goes / another deal you couldn't close, yeah.' Drawing attention to Buckman's assertion that Penny is illustrative of a commodity that can be 'dealt' by men, the lyric creates a complicated set of intersections where the male stars ventriloquise the attitudes of their characters and transpose the sexism of the fictional world (whether as critique or otherwise) into the ostensibly 'real' world of a commentary. The use of Filllion's song as a surrogate for actorly ego and the concomitant expose of sexist attitudes runs the risk, like the show, of having critique confused for iteration.

This is even more problematic in the solo given to Felicia Day, called 'The Art'. In part a simple and precise debunking of self-satisfied expressions of artistic integrity from actors on commentaries, it is also a problematic fictionalising of an actor whose role was itself problematic in terms of gender. As an engagement with the art of acting, the song is withering. Art is 'magic as a magic thing and lovely as love'; the much vaunted 'actor's process' is simply 'stand here and do what Joss says'; and finally art is, we are told 'really easy'. As an attack on pretentiousness, fakery and self-satisfied mediocrity it is a great song. But Day is not just an actor; she is a female actor and the song is uncomfortably close to sexist in its rendering of the fictional Day. Having already made her relationship with the whole notion of commentary very complex by repeating that she will not discuss her 'process', this debunking of the mystique is also presented as her inability to concentrate on her job because of her desire for Fillion. In a process of dizzying recursiveness the fictionalised Day says of the fictional Penny's stumbling and stammering (in other words of Day's acting of Penny's speech patterns) that practising them (acting) was itself 'just an act' because her implied desire for Fillion is 'all so real'. The philosophical questions and aesthetic questions here are very interesting – the limits of identity; simulacrum versus real; the relationship between the two texts. But these questions also give rise to the representation of gender. While Buckman's essay is very impressive in asserting the ways in which Penny's death-scene is resistive; the fictional Day presents a straightforward account of the scene as a lingering celebration of the dead female form, 'But my death-scene pumps are really dreamy / right when Billy dumps my corpse, it's steamy / to see me.' This is immediately followed by an apology from Day for having lost her train of thought and 'being such a bimbo'. In some ways, this can be argued as a knowing in-joke: Day is double major in maths and violin performance, a talented actor and the creator of web hit *The Guild*. The kind of fan who buys *Commentary!* is likely to know this and to read 'The Art' therefore as ironic, especially as the song has an extended reference to *The Guild* which 'she' also references in the preceding dialogue. The trouble with irony is that it is very much in the eye of the beholder. The song can be read (and probably should be) as a clever, recursive, ironic engagement with acting and with sexist assumptions about female actors. By playing the irony so straight, it runs the risk of being mistaken for what it ironises.

This is especially true because of the ways in which the first two songs set up the text overall. The opening song 'Commentary' sets up the aesthetic challenge; the second song, 'Strike' provides the political context. Both songs use irony and over- and under-statement to ensure that there can be no easy singular meaning attached. However, polyvalent does not mean inscrutable, and a broad sense of the piece can be established from these two opening songs. We are to be disabused of the notion that the 'making-ofs' tells us 'what it all means'; and we will discover that the 'insight' that we glean will be, most likely, the faux camaraderie and joyful reminiscence wonderfully captured in the following verse: 'And you'll be dazed by the haze of blazing praise / Arrays of ways to rephrase: "Those were the days".' The over-abundance of internal rhyme highlights the false and exaggerated nature of the supposed friendships and joys. Moreover, the song highlights the commercial value of the commentary as a component of fan-culture: 'moments like these sell DVDs' (with the panicked addendum 'we need to sell more / we've only sold four'). This song then, alerts the listener to the fact that this commentary (in addition to being 'uncommon' by virtue of being a musical) will undermine the modes of the commentary genre. I have already mentioned the display of rivalry between Fillion and Harris, and how Day refuses to discuss 'her process', and additionally we have interventions from the extras; ruminations on race in the television industry; a repudiation of the musical as a form capable of addressing serious issues (while also highlighting the nature of the broader Whedon family in developing the project in the first place) among others. This last, 'Zak's Rap' also highlights the commercial nature of the *Dr. Horrible* enterprise ('I was only in it for the horrible money'), a commercial context that essentially is the predicate of the show's existence, as addressed in 'Strike'.

'Strike' seemingly borrows the formal Manicheanism of the *Dr. Horrible* story with a clearly identified bad guy and the good guy. Here, however, the bad guy has no appealing vulnerabilities. The AMTP, here personified in the guise of Nicholas Counter, are introduced as drug dealers who will sell the ground up residue of the writers' guild cut with baby powder to underprivileged kids. The hyperbole is on par with the rest of *Commentary!*, but the anger is palpable. The AMTP are belligerent and confrontational, but also sly and manipulative. In a very telling phrase, the AMTP's public declarations that try to paint the writers as the villains are glossed as 'convincing as a cockney / Dick van Dyke'. A political stance is undercut by likening it to a bad performance in a musical (or at least the bad performance of a certain kind of accent and vocabulary) – politics is here a kind of performance (mendacious, illusory, false); just as performance is a kind of politics (engaged, questioning, progressive). The song describes 'splinter / Groups' who 'wonder what this Inter / Net is like'. While the detail is not filled in, this suggests Whedon and his team, who will use their 'dynamite plots ... to light the fuse or lose / the strike'. The song, then, is not just an artistic response to a political situation, it is itself a political gesture designed to enable the strikers to win. But they did not, and here Whedon is unsparing in his refusal either to claim a victory ('And lose we did / Impressively / Slunk back to our offices / Declaring victory') or to allow the writers to escape what he sees as their culpability in what he sees as their defeat: 'If you need your residual / Why did you all agree.' What is noteworthy here is the shift from 'we' to 'you'. For reasons discussed above, it is not possible to assert an uncomplicated relationship between the identity of the singer and the sincerity of the idea expressed. In this case, it is even more problematic as the singing shifts from Whedon singing about losing impressively to all the cast singing the 'Slunk ... agree' section. The lyrics are credited to Whedon but the safest claim would be to say that the song creates a tension between a seeming 'us' of the cast and production team who are also part of the 'we' that lost the strike; but that are positioned as separate from the 'you' who also went on strike but accepted terms and conditions that the 'us' of 'Strike' are exempt from. The 'good guy' is a precarious identity.

The new payment structure Whedon created for *Dr. Horrible* provides a clearer and fairer division of revenues between the participants, while locating Whedon as 'the studio' (see above). While the role of Whedon as studio (both for *Dr. Horrible* and for the Bellwether work) has provided for some innovative work, and for interesting modes of distribution and payment, it has not fundamentally changed the environment in which work is routinely commissioned and distributed. It has allowed him to maximise his capacity as a very powerful, influential and wealthy individual to produce work that might otherwise not have been released, and to to provide niche audiences with products they want to consume. However, in the ever-changing television market place, it is arguably providers such as Netflix and Amazon who are making most use of the opportunities for new content unmoored from the traditional television networks and advertising-related income generation.

By the time of the strike, Whedon had become a cult media figure. The decade since *Buffy*'s first appearance had seen him change from a highly respected but little-known film and television writer into one of the most significant figures in US network television. This was in no small way due to his willingness to engage in conversations with fans via websites, chatrooms, at live events like Comic-Con and via DVD commentaries. As discussed at many points throughout this book, Whedon's appeal is not just because of the television, film comic books and web shows that he has made (although that is obviously hugely important) but because of the sense of personal pride and responsibility he takes in these products, and because of his willingness to talk about all aspects of them. Indeed, it seems obvious that the skill and passion he demonstrates on the DVD commentaries is a further evidence of his desire to communicate, to express, to connect. It is for these reasons that the song 'Heart, Broken' is so surprising and powerful on the *Commentary!*.

'Heart, Broken' is the eleventh song of *Commentary!* and comes after Maurissa Tancharoen has sung 'Nobody's Asian in the Movies'. This song was the subject of a very interesting and to-date unpublished paper by Hélène Frohard-Dourlent (2012) discussing institutional racism in the television industry, including in Whedon's productions, at a conference of Whedon's work in 2012. In the context of the musical, it forms part of an arc that sees Tancharoen's song draw attention both to the issue of race, but also to her family dynamics and by extension to her role as part of the Whedon brothers writing team. In the commentary, she is upset and decides to sit in the corner and play her violin and '... math'. Jed, her husband and Joss Whedon's brother, warns Whedon, 'Joss, don't start' and after a couple of lines, Whedon begins 'Heart, Broken'. The reason for contextualising it within the series of songs is that there is a dramatic family-tension reason why Whedon would be upset at this juncture that it is important to recognise. However, the song's lyrics seem to have a much wider resonance than the family dynamics of the *Commentary!*, and they strike at the centre of a perceived truth about Whedon, which is his embracing of critical investigation, and his love of fandom.

The song sets up the conceit of audiences purely engaged with an artwork (cave people enjoying a painting of a bison; readers enjoying *The Odyssey*). The caveman is spared the tedium of explaining his choice of colour or subject matter; Homer does not have to explain the meaning of his poem, offer up deleted parts, or explain narrative choice as a function of focus groups. Both opening verses offer up the notion of the 'story' as the essential aspect of the art. For the caveman, 'What came before [the story] he didn't show / We're not supposed to.' This dangling participle is expertly located. Sung as written, the final line acts as an injunction against artists revealing their inspiration or the back story: the 'we' are artists. However, heard as sung, the line feels like there is an ellipsis, as though the expected rhyme has been submerged or swallowed: 'What came before he didn't show / We're not supposed to [know].' In this implied iteration, the 'we' is the audience who are not meant to have access to this information. The non-appearance of the rhyme allows the singer to inhabit the position of both artist and audience in a gesture of inclusion, precisely at the point of the commentary where he appears to be most separated. Whedon performed the song live on the NPR radio show, *This American Life*. I will have reason to return to this performance below, but for now it is worth noting that the pained, wracked artist that Whedon performs himself as at the beginning of the song makes this elided, collapsed identity even more pronounced, as he holds the 'to' over a couple of bars.

In the second verse, the story is again the important thing and, emphatically, 'He' [Homer] is not it: 'He's just the door we open if / our hearts need lifting.' Here the rhyme operates in the opposite fashion than the previous verse. It arrives, but a beat or syllable too soon so that although we here the 'lift', its gerundive form diminishes the possibility of the enunciation. In some ways this seems a likely (if subtle) manoeuvre if we remember Whedon's claims about art. He rarely asserts art as affirming in the way implied here. More frequently, he celebrates art like this, from a quotation used earlier:

> A writer has a responsibility to tell stories that are dark and sexy and violent where characters that you love do stupid, wrong things and get away with it ... that's what makes stories resonate, that thing, that dark place that we all want to go to on some level or another. (Lavery and Burkhead, 2011: 29)

The very fact that he was interviewed, and made the above observation, makes the chorus of 'Heart, Broken' odd. His critical engagement with journalists, academics, fans has been part of Whedon's appeal, yet here he bemoans that 'we' (academics and audiences) 'pick pick / Pick pick pick it apart' the effect of which is to find the 'Tick tick tick of a heart / A heart, broken.' Here again, Whedon's felicity with rhyme is crucial as the 'pick / tick' pairing suggests a mechanical as opposed to biological heart – one that does not beat, but rather ticks like clockwork. The examination, the questioning, the picking not only break the heart of the story, they essentially dehumanise it in the act of asking the question.

The picking that breaks the heart is part of a range of activities, some of which appear to be done to the art object by the audience; others of which are produced as by-products of the art object both to feed and placate an audience and (implicitly) to accrue greater revenues. The effect of this is that 'The narrative dies'. It dies, though because of what 'The audience buys'. As discussed in Chapter 1 and elsewhere, television art is art and business (indeed all art is both art and business) so it is intriguing to see Whedon penning a song where the commercial aspect of art is so antagonistic to the aesthetic expression. It is worth remembering that this point that *Commentary!* exists because of *Dr. Horrible* and *Dr. Horrible* exists because of the competing claims over the commercial returns on television production.

After another chorus, new voices enter the song. In the published versions (as with the other songs) names are attached to particular parts. Jed (Whedon's brother) has a verse asking Whedon why he 'rails against the biz' continuing, 'You know that's just the way it is' and adding that Whedon is making them all miserable with his diatribe. Then Zack, another of his brothers, accuses Whedon of being 'out of date', with the 'philosophies' he is espousing being better suited to the 'dinner table' and reminding Whedon of the commercial imperative, 'please / We have to sell some dvds.' Then both brothers are joined by Maurissa Tancharoen who together advise him that 'Without these things you spit upon / You'd find your fame and fan base gone' with Tancharoen providing the greatest threat yet, 'You'd be ignored at Comic-Con.'

In the recorded version, Whedon seems to be jolted out of his position by this threat and begins to elaborate on the more usual aspects of a commentary, introducing a thought about cinematographer Ryan Green, but no sooner has the name been said than he returns to his gloom. Now, though, the gloom is made worse by the sense that he feels betrayed by his family, 'Oh this is no good / I thought J-mo would back my play / Now Zack and they all say' and we return to the chorus. Again, Whedon's song writing skill is important. The 'good / would' rhyme allows for the accented stress to fall on 'back', which sets up the internal rhyme with Zack but more importantly highlights the sporting metaphor deployed here in the use of 'play'. The tactical sense of 'play' rubs against other senses such as theatrical production and an amusement. Its rhyme with 'say' leads narratively to the chorus and the major theme of the death of narrative; but also indicates a way of engaging with the song and, consequently, the commentary as a whole.

As I have stressed, this book is not a biography and I am not imputing any knowledge of Whedon's state of mind or motives. However, this song, written by him, performed by him and members of his family who sing lines written by Whedon as part of a debate about the status of the art object and the responsibility and/or complicity of the producer of mass mediated art objects, like television shows or web series, seems to offer an insight into some of the ways Whedon was articulating his position as cultural interpreter. And this song, probably more than any other artistic product he has made, illustrates the real tensions, the very immediate sense of strain and difficulty that an artist will encounter when she or he is both a proponent of art as meaningful, politically urgent activity, as a site of something like resistance to dominant tropes and histories; and as a successful, rich, increasingly culturally central figure. The twin imperatives of artistic integrity and commercial success become increasingly prominent on the mainstream global scene for Whedon in the years subsequent to *Dr. Horrible*, and the remainder of this chapter will be the beginnings of a sketch of this development. Before that, however, I'd like to return to the performance of 'Heart, Broken' by Whedon on *This American Life*.

For the most part, Whedon as performer is not a concern of this book. He has appeared in his own shows as an uncredited news caster on *Buffy* (B S1E8); memorably as Numfar who performs a dance of joy in *Angel* (A S2E21); as a man at a funeral in *Firefly* (F S1E14), and latterly he has appeared on Jane Espenson's web series *Husbands* (S2E1; S2E2) as well as being in episodes of *Veronica Mars* (UPN/CW 2004–7), 'Rat Saw God' (S2E6), *Robot Chicken* (Cartoon Network 2005–present), 'Rabbits on a Roller Coaster' (S3E3), 'Help Me' (S4E1), 'Immortal' (S6E20) and

Written by a Kid (YouTube 2012), 'Scary Smash'. In a different context, I would be interested as Whedon as performer of himself in interviews, but for now it is this one performance that is especially intriguing.

Originally aired on 1 May 2009, this episode of *This American Life* was recorded in front of live theatre audience and also filmed. The segment that Whedon was in was all devoted to *Dr. Horrible,* with a brief audio recording from the show, followed by an introduction to Whedon (2010) that is worth quoting in detail:

> So the commentary itself also rhymes, it's set to music. It both comments on, and critiques, the conventions of a DVD commentary, while synchronously existing with the movie. So it included this song where Joss Whedon got to express, as a filmmaker, what it feels like, what it means to do a DVD commentary, and have to return to his own work and talk about that work as part of his job. And he's agreed to play that song for us here today.
>
> Before we booked him for this show, he actually never had played in front of an audience larger than nine people. He actually taught himself piano to write musicals like this a couple years ago. He never had performed on a stage. He'll be accompanied – he wanted an actual professional musician with him just for backup – so he'll be accompanied on guitar by Matt Clark …
>
> Please welcome in his very brave musical, theatrical debut, film-making legend, Mr. Joss Whedon.

The legendary film maker (no mention of his television work) and self-taught piano player will sing a song from the commentary to a web show on the radio. Whedon says nothing as he takes to the stage and as he sits down he does not look at the audience. He begins to play the tune and then starts to sing. He looks at the top of the piano, his face serious. In the line 'They didn't ask "why?"' he places great emphasis on the word 'why', with eyes tightly closed, and small shake of the head. He is performing a certain kind of intensity that one would imagine befits a man who is expressing 'as a filmmaker, what it feels like, what it means to do a DVD commentary, and have to return to his own work and talk about that work as part of his job'. The audience is cautious in its laughter: some seemingly fans of Whedon and already in on the 'play', others uncertain as to whether the song, as yet, is funny. Moving into verse 2, Whedon looks up at the audience, briefly, before returning his brooding face back to stare at the piano. As the jokes about deleted scenes and testing well with teens arrive the audience appear wrong-footed. There is general laughter at the first one, but Whedon does not flicker; he maintains the seriousness of the song through the intensity of his expression: this is a serious artist; not a comic singer.

The second joke gets a much curtailed laugh, from many fewer people and this is not, I suspect, because they do not find it funny but because it is not at all obvious that Whedon finds it funny.

He sings the chorus and the next verse followed by the chorus, which gets us to the part of the song in *Commentary!* where his family join in. Whedon revises the lyrics to accommodate the fact that he is a solo performer, and wonders if an audience will just sit back and enjoy the show. He answers his own question: 'No the crowd won't rest 'til he explains / Like zombies clawing for his brains / Or anything that infotains / And that maintains my fame.' Describing the audience as zombies (brain-dead automatons who herd together to destroy life) is a challenging decision, especially as a few years later he will use the same motif to disparage Mitt Romney's presidential campaign in a video mentioned elsewhere in this book. Equally, the role of the commentary as a genuine aide to furthering knowledge, and as a helpful communicative tool between producer and audience is dismissed as 'infotainment'. What is apparent to him (or the version of him performing this song) is that this is the necessary condition for him to retain his fame, his 'precious quasi-fame' as he continues.

At this point the performance shifts. His head jerks upright on 'fame', and he turns it to the audience on 'quasi'. Here, at last, the audience can be assured the song is, if not a joke, at least a satire than can be laughed at, and laugh they do – as much from a kind of relief as from the humour of the piece. I am reminded of Becket's (1953/2009: 40) discussion of laughter in *Watt*:

> The bitter laugh laughs at that which is not good, it is the ethical laugh. The hollow laugh laughs at that which is not true, it is the intellectual laugh. Not good! Not true! Well well. But the mirthless laugh is the dianoetic laugh, down the snout – Haw! – so. It is the laugh of laughs, the risus purus, the laugh laughing at the laugh, the beholding, the saluting of the highest joke, in a word the laugh that laughs – silence please – at that which is unhappy.

Whedon acts as though he has been jolted into a kind of self-consciousness. The melody is replaced by a repeated phrase on the piano as he sing-asks, 'What am I doing / There's people watching' and he offers a half smile to the audience: a kind of embarrassed gesture of recognition and apology. He gathers himself, the melody re-emerges strongly and he sings, 'I sang some things I didn't mean', which gets a huge laugh. He asserts the quality of the commentary, and suggests 'Let's return now to the scene.' 'Return now' is spoken, as though a directorial instruction – Whedon the perfectionist, legendary film maker, in charge of his craft and his

Figure 4 Joss Whedon jauntily concludes 'Heart Broken' on *This American Life*, first broadcast 1 May 2009. Whedon performs a version of the song that draws fraught attention to the contradictions between the artist and the man, the creative and the commercial producer.

place in the industry: it is a brief but telling moment of performance. He discusses the process of writing the song itself and returns to the chorus. Musically it is the same and lyrically also, but performatively it is wildly different: Whedon sings it like a cabaret performer, all smiles and jaunty shoulder movements (see Figure 4), the chorus now a sing-a-long number that ends with the heart broken but, crucially, 'on sale, now'.

The song from the recording has been re-worked as a performance piece and as a performance piece it is a brilliant musical and visual expression of the impossible contradictions that Whedon has to try and negotiate. Even as he was singing the song, the transition that *Dr. Horrible* illustrates was well underway – Whedon was transforming from a multimedia polymath into the purveyor of (emblem of) mainstream cult.

If the period around *Dr. Horrible* and following is one of transition, the question has to be: transition from and to what? From the start of Whedon's career to the launch of *Dr. Horrible*, Whedon had worked in television as a writer, director and producer; he had been a script doctor, a script writer, a film director and film producer; he had written for comic books, both from his own franchises and others', and he had now produced a successful web series. Largely because of his television work between 1997 and 2004, he had accrued a huge following of fans who regarded him as a brave voice standing up for art/politics/culture/the little guy against the depredations of studios and networks. To locate Whedon as 'the little guy' or outsider was always something of a fan fiction; although his position as multimedia polymath is absolutely real, and his contribution to progressing the creation of high quality television is undoubted.

However, between 2004 and 2008, Whedon had produced relatively little to supplement this initial vast and important body of work. He directed two episodes (S3E17; S4E10) of the US version of UK comedy hit *The Office* (NBC 2005–13); had written and directed the award winning *Serenity* (the filmic spin-off from the short lived television show *Firefly*) and, now, produced *Dr. Horrible*. The writers' strike clearly impacted on his ability to produce work for television, but even so, the reduction in television output is very noticeable (see Appendix 2). His discontent with networks, discussed elsewhere in this book, would also seem to be an influencing factor. And while his audio-visual output was fairly modest in relation to the previous years, his writing contribution to comics was plentiful. Between the continuing *Buffy* and *Angel* comic book seasons (including the 'bold and striking' *Tales of the Slayer* [Dark Horse 2002] that had the 'distinction of being written by ... five *Buffy* TV scribes plus Amber Benson' [Miles *et al.*, 2003: 309]); his writing for the *Astonishing X-Men* series; as well as the *X-Men* (2001 #55) and *The Giant-Size X-Men* series (2005 #3); the *Serenity* comics; *The Essential X-Men* (2006 #143); *Runaways* (2005 #28, 30); and *Giant-Size Astonishing X-Men* (2008 #1), the canonical worlds of *Buffy* and *Angel* have continued since 2007 in comic book form: *Buffy* Season 8 (2007–11 #1–40, Dark Horse); *Angel: After the Fall* (2007–10 #1–40 IDW); *Buffy* Season 9 (2011–13 #1–25 Dark Horse); *Angel and Faith* (2011–13 #1–25 Dark Horse); *Buffy* Season 10 (2014–16 #1–30 Dark Horse); *Buffy* Season 11 (2016–17 #1–12 Dark Horse); and *Angel* Season 11 2017 #1–12 Dark Horse). Whedon's executive producer role in these displays every bit as much oversight, influence, care and control as was true for his television shows. Georges Jeanty, the artist on the Whedon-scripted *Buffy* Season 8 #1–4 said, 'the guy is such a mastermind, I'm sure. He's got the whole ... eighth season planned out in his head. And he knows where it's going to send' (Stafford, 2007: 371). Equally, Nick Lowe, the *Runaways* series editor describes how Whedon sent him a brief outline of what a story might be after he had approached him to see if he would be interested in writing some issues. He says, 'A week later he shot me what the story would be over to me and I was over the moon. He nailed it right away, and he had me tearing up to an outline. *The bastard*' (Pascale, 2014: 284, original emphasis). Whedon's polymathic skills were being well utilised. His comic book work contributed to the sense of him as a cult figure, and also ensured that when Marvel's plan to produce an on-going series of major movies was announced, Whedon's name would be in the pool of possible writers and directors. His perceived position as cult outsider would be what would help propel him to the centre of Hollywood and place him at the forefront of mainstream cult.

In 2008, the first two films in 'Marvel Studio's project to build a franchise around a series of self-financed, interconnected films and television releases' (Brincker, 2017: 207) were launched, *Iron Man* and *The Incredible Hulk* (Louis Lettier). A further fourteen have been released as of May 2017, including Whedon's two *Avengers* movies (2012 and 2015). In addition, there has been the Whedon executively produced *Agents of S.H.I.E.L.D.* and *Agent Carter* both on ABC; *Daredevil*, *Jessica Jones* and *Luke Cage* on Netflix to mention nothing of the many comic book tie-ins. The venture is one of the most comprehensively developed trans-media franchises in history, and Whedon's involvement across all three media is unique. The fact that Mutant Enemy alumnus Steven S. DeKnight is the executive producer and show runner of *Daredevil* points once again to Whedon's considerable contribution to the broader vitality of mass mediated popular art in the age of media convergence. In some ways, it is interesting that Whedon has not been more involved in some of the different opportunities provided by the wealth of new platforms. When asked, in the extraordinary publicity marking *Buffy*'s twentieth anniversary, what he thought of the new modes of all-at-once 'dumping' on platforms like Netflix, he said:

> I would not want to do it. I would want people to come back every week and have the experience of watching something at the same time. We released *Doctor Horrible* in three acts. We did that, in part, because I grew up watching miniseries like *Lonesome Dove*. I loved event television. And as it was falling by the wayside, I thought, 'Let's do it on the internet!' Over the course of that week, the conversation about the show changed and changed. That was exciting to watch. Obviously Netflix is turning out a ton of extraordinary stuff. And if they came to me and said, 'Here's all the money! Do the thing you love!' I'd say, 'You could release it however you want. Bye.' But my preference is more old-school. Anything we can grab on to that makes something specific, a specific episode, it's useful for the audience. And it's useful for the writers, too. 'This is what we're talking about this week!' For you to have six, 10, 13 hours and not have a moment for people to breath and take away what we've done ... to just go, 'Oh, this is just part seven of 10,' it makes it amorphous emotionally. And I worry about that in our culture – the all-access all the time. Having said that, if that's how people want it, I'd still work just as hard. I'll adapt. (O'Connell, 2017: n.p.)

The different televisual and trans-medial possibilities that the new platforms and models of production and distribution offer is discussed with great verve by Neil Landau (2016) in *TV Outside the Box: Trailblazing in the Digital Television Revolution*, with an interesting section on Marvel's/Netflix's *Daredevil*.

Before the enormous success of his involvement with the Marvel film franchise, Whedon returned to one of the other global powerhouses of world media, Fox Television where he was to be executive producer of his first television show in five years, *Dollhouse*.

After his fraught relationship with Fox in the *Firefly* period, his return to that network could have appeared odd, but Whedon was clear from the outset that a new set of people in charge meant that the show had significant network support. Fans became especially concerned about what appeared to be a repeat of the miscommunication between Whedon and the network that had so bedeviled *Firefly*, and was most apparent in the network's insistence that Whedon re-shoot the pilot. When news emerged that the pilot for *Dollhouse* had also been re-shot, Whedon sought to assuage fan concern and claim responsibility for the re-shoot for himself. In an interview with Maureen Ryan in July 2008, Whedon said:

> I'm glad you care. And also, you can be worried. The show could have all the support in the world from Fox and still not [be successful]. There's no guarantees in this business. The fact is, their support hasn't wavered, but they did sort of view what I'd done as a little bit different from what I'd sold. (Ryan, 2008: n.p.)

Whedon is clear on two things. First, even with network support, there is no guarantee that a show will be successful; and second, that the thing he produced was not exactly what the network felt he had pitched. He elaborates on this and says:

> I looked at [the first pilot] with a very cold eye, an executive's eye, and said, 'OK, I know what they want that they don't have,'' Whedon said. 'I asked them, 'Do you want [a new pilot]?' earlier, and they said, 'No, no, no, we just want to figure out how to make this work.' I said, 'Here's how you're going to make this work. I'm going to write you a new one.' They were very grateful. (Ryan, 2008: n.p.)

As with his comment about his being the studio with *Dr. Horrible*, Whedon understands the executive's position (a shift from his comments about not understanding what networks want immediately post *Firefly*), and in this instance was prepared to accept that it was his episode and not the network that was at fault. After the cancellation of *Dollhouse* at the end of its second season, he was less sanguine about this relationship, and offered a different version, wherein (as with *Firefly*), he contends that the network bought into a particular world, but then backed away. In another interview with the *Chicago Tribune*'s Maureen Ryan he says:

> Basically, the show didn't really get off the ground because the network pretty much wanted to back away from the concept five minutes after

> they bought it. And then ultimately, the show itself is also kind of odd and difficult to market. I actually think they did a good job, but it's just not a slam-dunk concept. (Ryan, 2009: n.p.).

Of particular difficulty for the network was the aspect of sexuality, the exploration of the client's fantasy worlds that, according to Whedon, had been a large feature of the original concept. Without that, and with the addition of the espionage component (that did add a degree of coherence to what could otherwise have been very disparate storylines), the show lacked the spark that had been part of its genesis. Once again, Whedon iterates one of his abiding beliefs as a writer of stories, as an artist and, therefore, as a purveyor of politics in its broadest sense:

> When you're dealing with fantasies, particularly sexual ones, you're going off the reservation,' Whedon said. 'You're not going to be doing things that are perfectly correct. It's supposed to be about the sides of us that we don't want people to see ... The idea of sexuality was a big part of the show when it started and when that fell out, when the show turned into a thriller every week, it took something out of it that was kind of basic to what we were trying to do. (Ryan, 2009: n.p.)

A more developed discussion of the themes of *Dollhouse* will be undertaken in the Chapter 8, but for now what is of interest is the extent to which the aspect of the show that garnered most criticism, especially because of the avowed feminism of Whedon, is, in some areas, he feels was the least well developed in the series. The idea that the show was a vehicle for some sort of glamorous valorisation of people trafficking, especially in the guise of sex work, was to mistake the depiction of an event with the event itself.

Whedon's attempts to interrogate both the limits and construction of identity through the conceit of the tabula rasa dolls, and his further intent to allow the malleability of the dolls to be a vehicle through which to look at desire, fantasy, sex trafficking and the abuse and manipulation of power never quite found its stride. However, even to phrase it in these terms, 'Whedon's attempts ...' is to repeat an error that this book has been seeking to address. Although the 'television auteur' handle is an enticing one, and despite the fact that Whedon asserts such strong creative control over his work, it is still apparent that part of this control is now devolved to trusted Mutant Enemy colleagues. *Dollhouse* sees the revival of the full-blown production team, its re-engagement with its history but also, and crucially, the creation of the next generation.

Although executive producer, Whedon passed responsibility for the day-to-day running of the show to the writing duo of Fain and Craft who had joined *Angel* in season 4 and became executive story editors on that show. Their experience on *Angel* and knowledge of Whedon's methods were certainly useful, but so too was the fact of their being women in charge of a show that was expected to have such a complicated relationship with gender, sexuality and power (Lavery, 2014b: 203). Alongside them were Mutant Enemy alumni such as Stephen S. DeKnight, Tim Minear and Jane Espenson on the writing side; and David Solomon and Michael Straiton on the directing. Along with these came actors such as the show's producer Eliza Dushku, Amy Acker, Alan Tudyk and Alexis Denisof. The much celebrated nature of the supportive and creatively productive Mutant Enemy team was here alive and well.

David Solomon's return is exciting because he had been part of Whedon's producing journey from the beginning, having been brought in to edit the *Buffy* pilot. Initially, the pair were at odds, but by the end of the process, Whedon asked Solomon if he would come on board if the show got the green light. The centrality of the editing process to the pilot's success highlights something of a gap in the analysis of Whedon's work, and television studies more broadly speaking. Rarely discussed in analyses of Whedon's work are the different editors with whom he has worked. What follows is far from a comprehensive engagement, rather an initial sketch into ways of considering the function of this role alongside that of the executive producer/show runner. While the writers and the actors of Mutant Enemy have received a considerable amount of deliberation, and directors have been discussed to an extent, editors are largely absent. In part, this is a truth about television studies in general – while textbooks on making television may include discussions of the role of the editors and highlight significant differences between the role in the USA and the UK (BBC editors are more akin to a producer, for example), discussion of shows do not frequently include the role of the editor.

As with my discussion of other staff members in Chapter 2, it might be instructive in the first instance to provide a presentation of some of the editors who have worked either on different Whedon shows, or on shows that have interesting links with Whedon shows, for example the David Boreanaz vehicle, *Bones* (Fox 2005–17); Jane Espenson's project, *Caprica* or Eliza Dushku's *Tru Calling*. The extent to which an individual is responsible for the whole editing of a single episode, or is part of the editorial team of a show in the editorial departments as, for example, assistant editor, is a complication in presenting clear and definitive figures. However, for the purposes of this (which is purely illustrative and is not intended to prove any statistical claim), the credit as editor is what will count, and if there is good reason to highlight additional editorial team involvement, I will make that clear. Table 2 is for Whedon's television and web work.

Table 2 Different editors who have worked with Whedon and their different credited contribution to the post-production process

	Buffy	Angel	Firefly	Dr. Horrible	Dollhouse	Agents of S.H.I.E.L.D.	Plus
Basinski, Peter	26				9		Tru Calling
Charson, Joshua	8					16	Tru Calling
Hodge, Sunny			5		7		
Kemble, Regis	32	1					Tru Calling
Lassek, Lisa	5		5	3			Serenity, Cabin in the Woods, Avengers Assemble, Avengers: Age of Ultron
Mazanini, Elena					4		
Miller III, Harry B					4		Caprica, Bones
Pilkinton, George		15			1		
Schoolnik, Skip	1	102 (as producer)					
Stern, Michael	1	21					Tru Calling, Battlestar Galactica
Trejo, Paul					8	16	

I offer little commentary on the overall picture other than to note that the pattern, if there is one, is not like that with writers and directors. Charson, for example, receives eight credits for *Buffy* and then has no involvement with Whedon shows until *Agents of S.H.I.E.L.D.* comes along, and then edits a very high percentage of the episodes. Trejo, by contrast, had no involvement with Whedon shows until *Dollhouse* (of which he edits a high proportion) and then has a high percentage of *S.H.I.E.L.D.* Regis Kemble is very prominent in *Buffy* (as it happens in the first five seasons, he edits no episodes in the UPN years), but then disappears from Whedon shows except for one episode of *Angel*. This implies a much looser, less engaged relationship between producer and editor than may be expected.

There is one very clear difference to this patter and that is Lisa Lassek. She joined Whedon's team on the only season of *Firefly* and the final season of *Buffy* in 2002. She was responsible for editing the eventually unscreened pilot 'Serenity', as well as the quickly re-shot eventual pilot, 'The Train Job'. To be trusted with both of these, especially given the importance of the pilot (see Chapter 7, and Pateman, 2014), gives some sense of the trust Whedon had in her ability. This is compounded by the fact that she edited the Tim Miner episode 'Out of Gas' (directed by David Solomon), widely regarded as one of the most impressive and difficult episodes of the season, and a tour de force of both narrative and editing accomplishments. She also edited the Whedon scripted and directed 'Objects in Space' another excellent episode and one that became the de facto finale after the show was cancelled. The trust shown in her in *Firefly* is matched in *Buffy*, with Lassek editing 'Flooded' (B S6E4) before she was given the responsibility of the musical episode 'Once More with Feeling' (B S6E7) (see Figure 5), the only credited Whedon episode in the season, and one that, as with 'Out of Gas', he also directed.

It is reasonable to speculate that the experience of working with her so closely on episodes that he both wrote and directed meant that Whedon developed a trust in her style, method and eye that suited his very well. Not that she is the only person who has worked closely with Whedon on episodes he wrote and directed. Of the sixteen that fall into this category on *Buffy*, Regis Kimble edited eleven, with a further co-edit credit. Indeed, in the first four seasons, the only Whedon directed and written episodes Kimble did not edit were 'Becoming 1' (B S2E21) and 'Becoming 2' (B S2E22) (Skip MacDonald and Kimberly Ray, respectively). In seasons 5 and 7, the Whedon episode editing went to Peter Bassinski, and in *Angel* the three Whedon episodes were edited by Mark Westmore ('Waiting in the Wings' [A S3E13]) who edited an additional thirty-four

Figure 5 Anya and Sweet, *Buffy the Vampire Slayer*, 'Once More with Feeling', season 6, episode 7, first broadcast 6 November 2001. This split-screen offers an overt example of Lisa Lassek's much under-analysed work as one of Whedon's primary editors.

through the series' run; and George Pilkinton ('Spin the Bottle' [A S4E6] and 'Conviction' [A S5E1]).

However, it seems to be the case that Lassek's work on the *Firefly* pilots, and on the *Buffy* musical (among others) encouraged him to call on her services when *Serenity* was brought into production. Since then, she has edited or been on the editing team of all but two Whedon film ventures. She edited *Dr. Horrible, Cabin in the Woods, Avengers Assemble* and *Avengers: Age of Ultron*. In other words, if one assumes that the triumvirate of writer/director/editor is among the most significant set of relationships determining the outcome of a film (or web series), then Lassek's contribution to Whedon's non-television career and the vision for his products in that time must be considered very high. Because of her involvement in *Cabin* and *Avengers* she was not available for *Dollhouse* or, so far, *S.H.I.E.L.D.* Amy Pascale (2014: 371), one of the few writers on Whedon to mention her, suggests that 'her rise was no doubt an inspiration to Joss's current assistant Daniel Kaminsky, who edited *Much Ado* on his laptop in Joss's office while the blockbuster was being shaped'.

While Lassek was notably absent from *Dollhouse*, a number of new faces appeared both on and off camera. In terms of the development of Whedon's television production work, the most significant names to appear on *Dollhouse* were two names who most Whedon fans and industry insiders would have been unaware of at the start of the writers' strike, but whose contribution to *Dr. Horrible* ensured that Mutant Enemy would no longer be *like* family, it would be family. Jed Whedon and Maurissa Tancharoen had co-written *Dr. Horrible* with Joss Whedon. Up until this point, Tancharoen had had two writing credits. One for an episode of Fox series *Oliver Beene* (2003–4) and one as the writer of video segments for the HBO music documentary *Britney Spears Live from Miami* (2004) which was co-directed by Hamish Hamilton, a specialist music video and music documentary film maker, and Tancharoen's brother, Kevin. Kevin Tancharoen, whose first film had been the Spears documentary, developed a reputation for dance-related shows and shorts, and directed the 2009 remake of the 1980 classic film, *Fame*. Released in 2009, it gets a mention in *Commentary!* on the cynical 'Ten Dollar Solo' wherein the conceit is that a wannabe actress called Stacey who plays groupie number two in *Dr. Horrible* gets to sing a solo in the commentary because she has bribed Whedon, who calls her Tracey and says her inclusion is 'good for the whole team, for the family. This is about *family*' (Whedon *et al.*, 2011: 83, original emphasis). Maurissa Tancharoen's husband, Jed Whedon (I will break with convention of surname usage here to differentiate Joss Whedon who I will refer to as 'Whedon' from Jed Whedon, who I will refer to as 'Jed') had had a credit on a DVD movie game called *Shout About Movies* (2004).

The pair began writing as a team early in their careers, with Maurissa struggling to write a pilot for a Fox show. She explained to Christina Radish (2013: n.p.) of *Collider*:

> I was losing my mind. We were dating, at the time, and I said, 'Help me!' We worked on it together, and it turned out really well. We said, 'Hey, let's write a feature spec. Why not?' So, we did, but then the strike happened. But, it went out wide and it got a great response. And then, *Dr. Horrible* happened, and right after that was *Dollhouse*.

This attenuated biography is helpful in seeing how rapid their move to the heart of Whedon's writing team was. The above interview is with both Tancharoen and Jed, and is discussing, among other things, their involvement as Show Runners on *S.H.I.E.L.D.* Tancharoen makes the important point that on by season 2 of *Dollhouse* they were 'on set constantly' due to the amount of writing they were doing on the show, so they have a good sense of the day-to-day running of a show. Equally, on the production staff of *S.H.I.E.L.D.* are Jeff Bell and Jeph Loeb. Bell's experience as executive producer of *Angel* would clearly be of benefit both in terms of the generality of running a show, but also of running a Whedon show. Loeb's experience is astounding. Executive producer of the yet-to-air *Buffy: The Animated Series* from 2004, Loeb's involvement with the television aspect of Marvel franchises makes his knowledge invaluable. Executive producer on the animated series, *The Astonishing X-Men* (2009); *Iron Man* (2010); *Wolverine* (2011); *X-Men* (2011); *The Avengers: Earth's Mightiest Heroes* (2010–12); *Marvel's: Avengers Assemble* (2013–14), his encyclopaedic knowledge of Marvel on television is beyond compare. Alongside these two great producers, Tancharoen and Jed also mention Whedon. Unlike shows where it is clearly the case that Whedon is in charge, here he is 'involved', although it is also clear that the idea for the show initially was his, but that the brief development meeting means that the idea as pitched is a collective effort of Whedon, Tancharoen and Jed:

> When Joss came to us and said, 'Let's make a S.H.I.E.L.D. TV show,' we were excited about the idea alone. And then, once we started diving into the world and inventing these new characters that would be a nice group around Coulson, it became a show that we want to watch, so hopefully other people share our feelings ... We talked about the show for about 20 minutes. By the time we were done, we had a rough sketch of who all those people were. Their names are a little different, but we had a pretty good idea, right off the bat, of who we wanted to surround Coulson with. (Radish, 2013: n.p.)

From joining with Whedon on an web musical and associated commentary, to being the most credited writers on *Dollhouse* (as well as, in Tancharoen's case, appearing in both shows), to show running the television spin-off of one of the most globally successful film franchises in history, Jed and Tancharoen have become, essentially, the televisual successors of Whedon. As his work has become more and more about film directing, producing and writing; and political activism, it is they who have taken the reins of the television shows that carry his name as executive producer. That said, while the show was still in its early days, Whedon did insist on a reasonable amount of involvement in the process of creating episodes:

> 'I'm reading every script, every story, and giving notes and re-writes,' Whedon says. 'I just can't be in the room every day. The group I have [including showrunners Jed Whedon and Maurissa Tancharoen] shares this hard-to-convey idea of how I want the show to feel.' (Hibberd, 2013: n.p.)

However, in the period during which *Dollhouse* and *S.H.I.E.L.D.* have been on television, Jed and Tancharoen have written as a team, and co-written with others twenty-four episodes across the two series. In other words, they have been jointly or partially responsible for writing almost one-quarter of all the Whedon executively produced material on television since 2009. By contrast, Whedon has written or co-written five episodes across the two shows. Jed and Tancharoren have written three times as many episodes as the next most prolific writers on the shows who are: Jeffrey Bell (eight episodes); Brent Fletcher (seven); Monica Owusu-Breen (eight); Paul Zbyszewski (nine) and Drew Z. Greenberg (eight). Jed has followed in his brother's footsteps by directing his first episode of television on a show he executively produces; and Tancharoen's brother, Kevin, has directed eight episodes across the four seasons of *S.H.I.E.L.D.* (more than anyone else except Vincent Misiano and Billy Gierhart who directed eleven each – making almost one-third of all episodes directed by one of the three: an exceptionally stable production unit). Whedon has written only one *S.H.I.E.L.D.* episode (which was co-written with Jed and Tancharoen) out of the eighty-eight that have been aired to date. In the same period, he has written, directed or produced five feature films and contributed significant ideas to at least three others. The six he has credited contributions to are: *The Cabin in the Woods* (2012: producer, co-writer); *The Avengers* (2012: co-writer, director); *Much Ado About Nothing* (2012: writer, producer, director [as well as contributing to the score and co-editing – this being the one movie Lassesk had no involvement in]); *In Your Eyes* (2014: writer, executive producer); *Avengers: Age of Ultron* (2015: writer, director).

This chapter began with these films and will close with them. The two *Avengers* movies have grossed over US$3 billion from theatrical release alone, to say nothing of the DVD, Blu-ray and associated sales. With operating budgets of almost US$0.5 billion, Whedon has worked at the pinnacle of global capital – Disney, Marvel and the cinema chains and distribution links that allow them to be. The 'quasi-fame' of the live performance of 'Heart Broken' has transitioned. As Eric Brown (2014) of the *International Business Times* comments, he has 'transitioned from a nerd icon into one of Hollywood's biggest (and most profitable) names' – one of Hollywood's biggest names: not one of directing's or acting's but the whole industry. At the same time, smaller projects such as *Much Ado* and *In Your Eyes* have provided Whedon with the capacity to have different outlets, on a much less global scale. These films (whether a conscious effort to retain the iconic outsider perception, or simply an expression of artistic desire) seem to offer new ways of thinking through production and distribution.

The decision by Whedon to circumvent the usual distribution channels with *In Your Eyes*, and go straight to Vimeo for a fee of US$5 was welcomed by some as a challenge to the established practices. For example, respected film blogger, Andrew Knighton (2014: n.p.), wrote, 'this is an incredibly bold step for someone in Whedon's position. He's risking a pet project on a new distribution method. He's standing up and being counted for change. He's leading the charge into a new era with the potential to democratise and reinvigorate the film industry.'

Other critics were less convinced that this model was anything more than a vanity project with little or no impact on the industry standard. Eric Brown (2014: n.p.) says:

> Digital distribution might sound like an egalitarian utopia for artists, but the reality is that without the right marketing or a big name attached to the project, it's easy to flounder and get buried. The upshot of traditional film distribution is the stability – and more important, the promotion – that comes with aligning with a large studio.

Brown offers a brief account of other major artists who had sought to use the Vimeo method. He draws particular attention to the stand-up comic Louis C.K. who was the first major artist to try. The obvious point is that the artist assumes all the risk of distribution and promotion costs. By virtue of being so famous, Louis C.K. was able to advertise his show, and because it was a recording of his stand up, the production costs were considerably lower than the (for a film) incredibly low *In Your Eyes*. Even so, it cost C.K. about US$200,000 to produce and distribute the film. He did make a profit of nearly US$1 million. As successful as this was, Brown highlights other stand-ups who also tried the Vimeo model and lost money, and points out that C.K. himself has chosen to go with HBO for his next project. Others have foregone Vimeo in favour of companies such as Netflix – a different model than the established, but much more similar than Vimeo. Brown concludes, 'in the end, Whedon's experimental release structure for "In Your Eyes" is exciting, but it's largely a vanity project, something cool for Whedon to do for himself and his fans but not really possible for creators who don't have his kind of money or clout' (Brown, 2014: n.p.).

Whedon's power and wealth enable him to produce interesting, exciting, possibly challenging, art alongside the much more blockbuster movies. These products will, doubtless, continue to encourage the 'pick pick pick' of fans and scholars who continue to find his artistic and filmic vision compelling and profound. But as he becomes more and more powerful, more and more central to the US and global film industry, it becomes harder to maintain the sense of outsider that once seemed to identify him. The feminism inevitably becomes more difficult to engage with (even though his films maintain the sense of interesting and strong female characters), and the tensions between artistic and political desires become more awkward to propose – the insistence of a democratic team ethos, built in *Buffy* and continued elsewhere, strains when placed within the much more individualistic world of superheroes.

If the tensions of Whedon's success for his status as a film maker are problematic, they demand a similar set of queries for his status in relation to television, and they pose, I suggest, a challenge to scholars in the field of so-called 'Whedon Studies'. It is true that *S.H.I.E.L.D.* is a Whedon show, but it is surely as much (or even more) a Jed Whedon and Maurissa Tancharoen show; or a Marvel show.

In the script book for *Much Ado About Nothing*, Whedon is emphatic about the joy he felt on that project: 'it was a perfect storm of things I love, and all of it came out' (Whedon, 2013: 32). The intimate nature of the production, working with a whole range of friends and colleagues in his own house, away from the colossus that was Marvel, he could express his love of Shakespeare, his delight in working with actors, his directorial acumen. Once more, he could develop and learn ('if we're not learning then why are we working? [Whedon, 2013: 18]) while doing the job he loves. The second part of this book will discuss the television shows he has given us and seek to explore the work and learning they engendered and the love they inspired.

Readings of Whedon's works: Narratives, formats, characters

Part II

'Someone else around who can explain these matters': The exposition scene in *Buffy* 4

Joss Whedon has commented before that the title *of Buffy the Vampire Slayer* carries within it a clear suggestion of generic hybridity. The three main terms indicate comedy, horror and action, respectively, and taken together what the title offers is an artistic mission statement. This case study will look at one of the standard features of *Buffy*'s format – the exposition scene – and discuss the ways in which Whedon establishes this, and then seeks to play with the format through generic commingling. To do it, I will first look very briefly at the setting up of the exposition scene in the pilot episode, then will investigate the way it is manipulated in an episode that, although important in many ways, is not usually considered one of the series' stand-out episodes, 'Pangs' (B S4E8). 'Pangs' I will argue, is an exemplary *Buffy* episode, and I will use it to discuss some of the more general ways that the series uses generic hybridity. I will then consider 'Hush' (B S4E10) in some of its generic splendour, and will finish by seeing how the exposition scene can act as a barometer of an episode's willingness to work outside not only genre but also expected format requirements.

An obvious point about a pilot episode is that it is intended not only to introduce characters, location and themes that will be central to the show, but also it needs to do this by asserting the generic and format-specifics of the show. The *Buffy* two-hour pilot (subsequently referred to as two individual episodes 'Welcome to the Hellmouth' [B S1E1] and 'The Harvest' [B S1E2]) did an excellent job of establishing character, theme, generic hybridisation and format. As part of the format construction, the audience learns about Rupert Giles, the new school librarian and, it transpires, watcher of Buffy. We and (to a much lesser extent) Buffy rely on him to provide the explanation for what is happening in the realm of the supernatural, to provide the mythic information to make sense of the episode (for the viewer) and the events (for Buffy and her friends). His first exposition scene is effectively shared with Buffy and the scene's function is twofold. First, it tells the audience who both characters are in terms of title (Buffy is a vampire slayer and Giles is a watcher) and it explains what these terms mean. Both characters already know what a slayer and a watcher are (in simple terms anyway, the series will add layers and layers of subtlety and complexity to both roles but especially to Buffy's) so the exposition is largely for the audience's benefit. However, the scene also shows that the format will never be satisfied with simple expository description. The exposition scene also has to, as far as possible, tell us about character and has to do so by bending generic forms to allow maximum versatility to the storytelling. So, in the first exchange between the two we learn an enormous amount about Buffy's character, about the conflict that exists between the young girl and the superhero, the emotional trauma of being a teenager in a new school and having this destiny-heavy function to fulfil. We learn about Giles's knowledge and, although we are offered a man seemingly buttoned up and very British, we also see the individual behind the authority figure – the man who will not only send away for the *Time Life* series of the supernatural but will also break off from his exposition to offer a slightly sheepish admission of this in response to his slayer's question.

A similar interaction between slayer and watcher occurs at the local nightclub, the Bronze, thereby establishing both the school library and the nightclub as central features of the group's existence, and providing us with detail about the characters as personalities as well as furnishing us with knowledge of the supernatural. Most tellingly, it sets up one of the on-going debates of the show, which is between authority and personal freedom, especially here in the ways that Giles expects a certain kind of discipline and rigour to inform Buffy's arcane and esoteric abilities while she utilises everyday culture to distinguish evil from good: she spots a vampire at the club because of his very outdated clothes; Giles wanted her to 'reach out with your mind' (B S1E1). The two approaches to slaying typify the initial antipathy but growing trust and respect between this student and teacher, surrogate father and daughter. So this exposition scene provides for the audience knowledge of the characters' functions to be transmitted, but only in a situation where the characters learn at least as much about each other as people in the imagined worlds they inhabit as we do about that imagined world. It is one of the central strengths of the format that a scene will offer as much emotional as factual satisfaction to an audience.

In the second half of the pilot, we have the first exposition scene proper, one in which the remaining members of the gang, Willow and Xander, are present and the three young people find out from Giles, after contributing their own questions and thoughts, what is going on.

After Buffy has saved Willow and Xander, but not Xander's friend Jesse, from an attack by minions of the season's main adversary, the Master, the three of them go back to the library. We see a shot of a globe, full screen, filmed from below: it is spinning. Giles enters from the left, behind the globe and it and he fill the frame. Both in terms of his position as the person controlling the globe and, metaphorically, the knowledge of it, and from the fact that he is positioned above us in terms of where we 'see' him from, Giles is afforded a significant presence of authority. He remains above us as the camera follows him along the corridor of the library, to the stairs and down to where the Xander and Willow (and effectively, we) are. He continues the lecture he has been giving, which introduces the series' major myth system. Willow and Xander express their upset, incredulity and confusion, and Giles tries to provide an explanation, especially to Xander's question, 'So vampires are demons?'

As Giles begins his answer, he is framed to the left of Xander and the camera begins a slow move towards him, very gradually knocking Xander out of frame and making Giles the centre of our attention. There is a sharp cut to Buffy and Willow, and Giles's voice continues off screen. While this is a very ordinary technique, it serves to reinforce the notion of Giles's authority by having his explanation have the power of a documentary-style voice over: he is effectively the narrator for a brief period. We cut back to Giles as he continues, and he is now in medium close up, centre screen, centre of our attention and unambiguously the man we should trust. His affinity with the lore he is discussing is enforced when he finishes his explanation with the chilling warning that the vampires are waiting for the 'old ones to return', at which point we have a slow dissolve from Giles to a vampire lair providing both narrative continuity and thematic emblamatisation of Giles's knowledge. Everything has been done to ensure the audience's belief in Giles, and these framing, editing and audio decisions have established Giles's expositions as a foundation of the show.

The vampire lair is extremely darkly lit. There is a small patch of very cold blue light to the rear right of the screen but beyond that we have some meagre gold lighting coming from the top right of the screen. The special effect faces, black clothing, gloomy lighting all provide clear horror genre aspects, and as well as this the similarities between the two groups (older wiser man holding court over a group of younger acolytes) allows for the implication of the dissolve from Giles to play out (horror and normality are intimately connected). Luke, the Master's most devoted follower, begins to suggest that the girl from the crypt 'may be ...' and the Master concludes, 'The Slayer?' and we cut back to the library. Xander continues the dialogue begun in the lair, thus establishing another format feature, which will be discussed in more detail in the analysis of 'Pangs' below. Xander asks, 'And that would be a what?' So, the edits imply both an intimate relation between the supposedly normal and the horrific, the monstrous and the mundane, while also asserting their difference. The relation is made clear through the formal echoing of composition, and the completion of sentences from one scene by a person in the adjacent scene; however, the ethical and emotional distance between the groups is also clear. Giles's exposition is not just telling us a brute fact, it is being orchestrated to offer texture, depth, aesthetic and ethical overview, as well as to provide us with a sense of characterisation.

After Xander's question, 'That would be a what?', presumably in response to Giles describing Buffy as the slayer, but in narrative terms, presented as being in response to the Master's expression of such, we, the audience, expect a return to Giles and his authoritative explanations. We do indeed return to him, and he begins to explain a slayer to Willow and Xander. However, he remains seated, there is no tracking into close up and he is interrupted by Buffy who cheekily interjects, 'He loves this part.' He might be knowledgeable, but he is not infallible and he is not above mocking. Within minutes, the exposition scene has been set-up and redefined. Giles's knowledge is essential, and he is worthy of respect and admiration, but he also has to continually earn it, and neither he nor we can assume that we will just sit back and take his word for it. The serious, even essential task of transmitting information – dramatic exposition – is every bit as prone to comedic subversion as any other part of the show. The format undermines its own premise to expand its possibilities. Giles continues his exposition in a much-curtailed form. 'Alright, the Slayer hunts vampires. Buffy is a Slayer. Don't tell anyone.' Even here, though, the comic recasting still allows for the important assertion of the significance of what Giles says. After 'vampires' there is a cut to Buffy and Willow as Giles continues off screen. The narrative voice-over authority persists, even if curtailed and mocked. The exposition scene has been established, and Whedon and his team have demonstrated how a necessary, functional, even predictable aspect of a show can be manipulated, inter-penetrated by different genres and be seen as a measure of the rest of the show's abilities.

Whedon's creative vision and control (as discussed in Part I) is most heavily exerted in the episodes where he is writer and director. The next section of this chapter is going to offer analyses of parts of two of Whedon's most famous writer-director episodes, 'The Body' (B S5E16) and 'Hush' (B S4E10). The emphasis of these analyses will be to see how

Whedon manipulates generic convention to suit his narrative, character and the thematic needs, as well, again, as to constantly refresh the show's format by recasting some its most central features.

'Hush' is one of the most innovative episodes in *Buffy*'s history. Indeed, critics such as Nikki Stafford (2007: 227) are not beyond making claims such as the following: 'This mind-blowing episode is one of the best hours of television ever.' Most famous for the fact that about twenty-seven minutes at the heart of the episode have no dialogue, it is often mis-identified as being 'silent' – and this mistake extends even as far as official *Buffy* merchandising, such as the *Watcher's Guide Volume 2*, which has a sidebar about the show calling it 'almost completely silent' (Holder *et al.*, 2000: 220). 'Hush' is emphatically not silent: not a silent movie; not a silent television episode. Indeed, one of the aspects that make it such a memorable and successful episode is Danny Elfman's score. This to say nothing of the parts of the episode that do have dialogue, and the very many sound effects. Jowett and Abbott offer an illustration of just how central sound is to the horror of the episode. In describing the cutting of the heart out of the mute student, unable to scream, immobilsed by the terrifyingly serene Gentleman, they (2013: 135) say:

> 'Hush' does not show the cutting of the heart in graphic detail, but makes the actions explicit through other means ... in TV horror a substitute often takes the place of the gore that cannot be shown in detail ... In this case the squleching sound [of flesh being cut off screen] serves this purpose ... .

To stress this point about the presence of sound and dialogue-by-other-means is important because the formal requirements of the show (its characters' inability to speak with each other leading to lack of dialogue for a large section of the episode) are driven by the thematic concerns that propel the writing. In this case, as is famously known, Whedon wanted to focus on the problem of communication, a problem that is introduced at the opening of the episode via the device of Professor Walsh's psychology class being based on that subject, and continued through Buffy's dream in which she both engages in sexual and loving communication with Riley Finn, as well as hearing an eerie nursery rhyme thereby being part of communicative process dating back centuries and operating both as a mechanism of infantile education and adult fear. While Whedon has also made it clear that he thought that it would be interesting as a challenge to himself to write an episode minus an aspect that was routinely applauded by critics (the witty dialogue), he is equally adamant that is not just an exercise in whimsy. He has said of 'Hush' that he came to it because 'I felt I was becoming lazy as a director. I thought that I needed to push myself visually. That evolved into the question, "What if I had no choice"' (Ruditis, 2002: 62). This is expanded upon elsewhere, where Whedon goes so far as to claim that he was 'degenerating' as a director and that at points he was falling into the trap of viewing television as 'radio with faces' (Whedon, 2002b: n.p.). This emphasis on visuality, which I have addressed elsewhere, is one of Whedon's great contributions to television drama. It is quite difficult to see an episode pre-'Hush' that would confirm Whedon's directorial degeneracy, but be that as it may, he states that he wanted television to be 'visceral, visual, and cinematic' (Whedon, 2002b: n.p.). Choosing to work without dialogue in order to push the visual part of his directing allowed for him to write a story in which the theme developed that 'when people stop talking they start communicating' (Whedon, 2002b: n.p.). So, 'Hush' is a self-imposed challenge to expand the visual possibility of television drama. The skill that Whedon brings to this is to do so while retaining the format that had made *Buffy* such a successful show.

Indeed, it is not that the episode is a 'silent' movie that makes it interesting in terms of genre but rather it is the way that the show's usual mixing and subversion of genres operate when faced with this, quite emphatic verbal restriction and visual augmentation. Added to this, there is the question of how the format is able to accommodate such a challenge to its expected structure.

From the very first episode, Giles has been the person who is able to explain to both the audience and the Scoobies what is going on in terms of particular demons, general trends, mythos and so on. Whedon's ability to keep this central component of the format always new and fresh is one of the reasons for the show's success. As early as 'The Puppet Show' (B S1E9), the writers were drawing attention to the convention of Giles's exposition in the quotation in the title of this chapter. The centrality of this as an organising principle is absolute. Indeed, it can be argued that the loss of Giles as a character for much of season 6, and his role as anchor in terms of organisation of narrative exposition, is one of the reasons why that season is felt by many to lack the coherence and integrity of other seasons. Be that as it may, Giles tells us and the Scoobies how things are.

There is an obvious and very profound difficulty for a character in the exposition role when the main tool at his disposal, speech, is taken away. Whedon devises a quite superb scene in which Giles is able to perform the role of expositor, and does so in a fashion that is both formally extraordinary, generically consistent with the show's ambition of genre-busting, thematically integral to the episode and also manages to link a number of character lines in the season as a whole.

The point of the exposition scene is to explain to Buffy and the gang who has been causing the voice-loss and the violent deaths, and how to stop them. We have already seen the who, prefigured in Buffy's opening dream, as well as in their gruesome murder of a young student. The Gentlemen, who are the creatures under discussion, are among the scariest ever seen on television. Whedon is clear that he wanted them to be iconic, to live long in the minds of children who saw the show. He designed them himself, based in part on a figure who came to him in a nightmare when he was young, and in part on a range of other figures. In the shooting script, one of them is described like this in the stage direction, 'he's old, bone white, bald – Nosferatu meets Hellraiser by way of the Joker. Actually, he looks kind of like Mr. Burns, except that he can't stop his rictus-grin, and his teeth are gleaming metal' (Whedon, 2002d: n.p.).

The range of references extends to Whedon's own nightmares, late twentieth-century horror movies, comic book, cartoons, silent-era expressionist cinema. Whedon's huge reservoir of filmic and televisual knowledge can here be seen to be utilised in the creation of a creature of genuine fear – a nightmare, fairy-tale bogeyman, who also manages to offer cultural and historical critique. In describing the process of developing the Gentlemen, Whedon draws attention to the metal teeth, and equates this precisely with late Victorian considerations of science's ability to supersede both supernatural explanations of curious phenomena, as well as being an aspect of improving nature. To this extent, Whedon is not only mining an archive of representations for their formal qualities, but is making an explicit effort to afford those aesthetic attributes a cultural value and investment. By insisting, as he does, that the Gentlemen's Footmen, the straitjacketed, crouched, feral expressions of instinctual violence, are a revisiting of the inmates in the asylum in *Dracula* (Whedon, 2002b: n.p.), he also places the fusion of fear, the supernatural and science in the context of Jonathan Harker's considerations in the same novel.

All of these elements come together in the exposition scene. The scene is set up by Olivia, Giles's brief girlfriend, drawing a picture of the Gentleman who she saw in a moment of truly terrifying television when he appears a matter of inches from her, serene and gruesomely smiling on the other side of Giles's window. The drawing prompts a thought in Giles's mind and he goes to a book on his shelf called simply

Fairy Tales. At that we cut to a new scene. In the shooting script it is described thus by Whedon (2002d):

> NT. LECTURE HALL– CONTINUING (DAY)
>
> The lights are low – it's dim but not dark. Xander is closing the last of the blinds. He heads down from the back to the front where the other are gathered. Buffy, Willow and Anya are in front row seats, Willow all ready to take notes. Giles is pulling the screen down. He has an overhead projector and a series of transparencies set up on the desk. Xander stands to one side, waits with the rest.

This is materialised on screen under Whedon's direction in a quite marvellous fashion. What is not mentioned in the script is the post-production over lay of the sound of the footfalls. These are very prominent, as are the sounds of the overhead projector (OHP) screen being pulled down and secured by Giles. There is, at this time, no music. Giles is lit mainly by the light from the OHP, which shines brightly on the screen in front of him, and he then moves to the front of the desk so that we have two environments collapsed into each other. The first is the lecture theatre, a place of learning, transmitting knowledge, offering exposition; the other is a cinema, a dark place where the only light is a screen on which a series of frames are shown in rapid succession. The set-up manages to exactly mimic the episode's cultural antecedents (a silent movie theatre) as well as to offer the opportunity for fabulous parallel between Giles in his role as transmitter of arcane knowledge and cultural authority, and Maggie Walsh who opens the episode in Buffy's dream in exactly the same spot as Giles now is. Two forms of knowledge, two kinds of authority figure, two mentors. Giles's antipathy to Maggie will find a wonderful moment of expression two episodes later in the Espenson-penned 'A New Man' (B S4E12). Discussing Buffy, Giles calls her a 'girl' prompting Professor Walsh to correct him and call her a 'woman'. Giles's response, 'Woman, of course, how wrong of me to choose my own words' exemplifies Giles's pride in his linguistic acumen ('Giles is proud of how he speaks, and is a bit defensive when called on an infelicity of wording', Espenson, personal correspondence, 9 January 2008), an acumen of course, sorely lacking in the exposition scene under discussion.

What we have then, is a lecture scene that has within it a fairy-tale film, though the frame speed is exceedingly slow. The lecture provides information for us and the gang, as well as allowing some excellent moments of comedy stemming, in part, from what Whedon calls 'fun miscommunications' (Whedon, 2002b: n.p.). The fairy tale offers us a tense mini-narrative with suspense, horror and gore.

Providing the music for both lecture and fairy tale is Saint-Saëns's *Danse Macabre*. The choice of music was, according to Whedon, difficult and a number of pieces were used, each being played over the top of the sequence before this piece was chosen. In retrospect, this 1872 composition seems inevitable as the musical choice with its peculiar, eerie orchestration, strange rhythm and, importantly, final pianissimo heralding the dawn and the return of the skeletons. What is interesting here is the generic requirement for the music. Giles's expositions do not need music as an accompaniment and often do not have them. The fairy tale, by contrast, needs the aural stimulus to reinforce the pictures. What is also noticeable in terms of the show's format is its willingness to use intradiegetic music. This is most noticeable, of course, in the musical episode. It is also very explicit in Giles's other great season 4 exposition scene in 'Restless' (B S4E22) where he sings his findings to an ecstatic cigarette lighter waving crowd at the Bronze (see Pateman, 2006). But it is also a more general aspect of the show where bands playing at the Bonze provide the musical backdrop to the scene, and which can then become extradiegetic as the scene might move but the song remains. Other instances often involve Giles either singing music or listening to it (Pateman, 2006). Most emotionally intense, perhaps, is its use in 'Passion' (B S2E17) written by Ty King.

The similarly impressive horror of 'Hush' is given some kind of explanation by Giles as he prepares to offer his exposition. Giles cracks his knuckles to introduce the lecture, and continues the DIY feel of the scene and his lecture (to be contrasted with the hi-tech efforts of Maggie Walsh and the Initiative) by placing his first transparency back to front on the OHP. The response of the gang to the lecture is an excellent example of the cast's acting abilities. Whedon describes how they each had to learn a new way of acting, especially insofar as taking time over scenes was concerned. Deprived of their voices, the actors had to find other ways to express their characters. As Katy Stevens (2010: 85) observes, 'the voice represents something of the "essence" of a subject, and its materiality brings to life an enigmatic element of the individual'. Shorn of this enigmatic materiality of voice for their character, and without the architecture of dialogue to provide clear makers and beats, the cast needed to find new ways to express emotion, story, response, to 'separate moments without standard dialogue' (Whedon, 2002b: n.p.). After rehearsing the first scene, each actor had made the adjustments, and, as Nikki Stafford points out, the response, especially in this scene, is excellent. She (2007: 227) calls this scene 'the highlight of the season' and expands, 'Giles goes on and on and on (complete with illustrations and music); Xander's mind is in the gutter; Willow offers helpful suggestions; Buffy simply assumes they can go off and kill the creatures with a stake ... and Anya couldn't care less.' That these, and more character traits, are expressed in a relatively short period of time and without the aid of dialogue is a testament to the actors, but also to Whedon's ability to write and direct. As the transparencies tell their story and ask their questions we have the creation of a mini-narrative replete with its own tension and horror. This is undercut as we cut away from this narrative to the object of its transmission who seek to engage with it. Willow answers the question, 'What do they want[?]' by putting up her hand and then, when reluctantly pointed to by Giles, pointing to her chest. Xander mouths 'boobies?', Buffy, Willow and Giles look aghast, and Giles puts on the next sheet, the next frame, the next part of the narrative (which needed no interjection from the floor) and we see three hearts drawn and the word 'hearts'. As the music builds and Giles projects more frames we see a picture of a single Gentleman and next to it, in capital letters, the word 'THEN'. Just as we have had the briefest of time in which to read the pictorial and linguistic message of the frame, we cut to a medium close up of Giles. Lit only from behind by the OHP and from some dim practical lighting, he raises a finger sharply, emphasising the 'Then' and creating an unambiguous moment of dramatic and horror-related tension that cuts across both the fairy tale and the lecture. The moment is augmented by the music having reached a point in the score where it is silent for a couple of bars. Short scenes, emphatic gestures, clear and brief pictorial and linguistic markers of narrative suspense, dim lighting giving 'maximum creepiness' and a crescendo leading to silence in the score – all the formal requirements of a scene of action-horror suspense created during a lecture of low-fi proportions with no dialogue. The suspense and tension is maintained by the drawings (childlike and inexpert as they are) now having splashes of bright red pen as we see macabre visions of bodies having their hearts cut from them (see Figure 6). Buffy and Willow share a look implying a recognition of the real horror they face despite the curious context of the exposition.

Xander asks the important question, 'How do we kill them?!' and Buffy offers a straightforward mime of staking them. Unfortunately, the gesture, without stake, looks much more like vigorous masturbation. The capacity to mis-interpret is gleefully utilised by Whedon to make a deliciously lewd joke. A similarly rude gesture (though this time determinedly meant) occurs later in the episode as Anya signals to Xander that she would like to have sex with him. This gesture, at the conclusion of a brilliantly contrived situation for comedic misapprehension, is hilarious and even though the executives at the network were, like Giles, Olivia

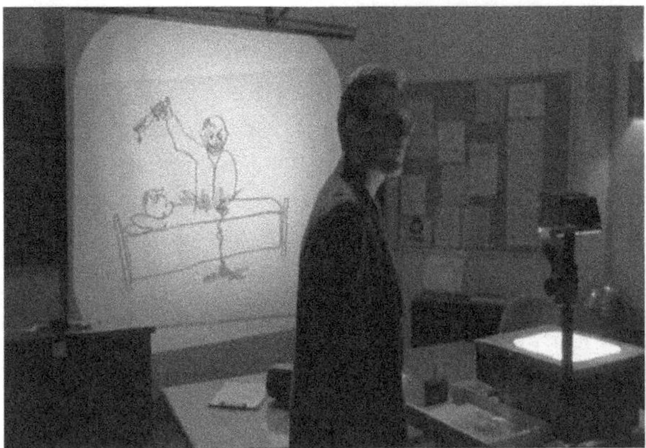

Figure 6 Giles, *Buffy the Vampire Slayer*, 'Hush', season 4, episode 10, first broadcast 14 December 1999. One of the central conventions of a *Buffy* episode – Giles's exposition – is beautifully re-crafted when he is denied access to spoken language.

and Spike, 'a little grossed out' by the gesture they allowed it to stay in because it was 'too damned funny' (Whedon, 2002b: n.p.). Comedy is central to much of *Buffy* and in these examples, the sheer brilliance of Whedon as a director and writer of comedy is clear.

Further points for comedic moments in different genres continue, not least Willow's mime, which tries to suggest that a CD might kill the Gentlemen. As the scene begins to come to an end, Giles places a frame on the OHP that has a rudimentary picture of a girl and a caption saying that Buffy will patrol. The music here shifts into the final pianissimo, and the comedy also subtly alters. The previous points of humour had come as a consequence of misapprehension or miscommunication all directly related to trying to defeat the Gentlemen. Here, Buffy's dismay that the picture implies that she has fat thighs is a lovely twist back to her as a young woman. The pianissimo alerts the viewer to a shift in tenor and tone and the movement to the woman rather than the slayer allows yet another of the show's central themes to be engaged with. While it is in no way as extreme as the lighting effects mentioned in Chapter 1, it does once again show how Whedon only ever uses the formal devices at his disposal to further the core features of the story or the characters and never just as an exercise in self-congratulatory excellence. Here, the mixtures of genre and their relationship to the episode's main theme and the show's core principles is magnificently undertaken.

The final episode discussed in this section is different again. 'The Body' (B S5E16) is the least normal *Buffy* episode insofar as it sits outside of almost all the expected format rules. It also deploys a visual syntax that is generally very far removed from any easily categorisable genre. Much has been written, quite rightly, on this episode, so I will make only a couple of preparatory observations before moving into the analysis of two scenes, one of which is a heavily modified exposition scene.

This episode offers us the characters' response in the immediate aftermath of the death of Joyce, Buffy's mother. In order to allow for the maximum focus, each character or group of characters is given a whole act before they come together in the final act. So, Act 1 focuses almost exclusively on Buffy's response to the discovery of the body. This Act is itself introduced atypically by there having been no 'previously on' section, and the teaser is incredibly short and is effectively the last few seconds of the previous episode, 'I was Made to Love You' (B S5E15) written by Jane Espenson, except this very last scene. Espenson notes about her drafts, 'Notice that it lacks the final scene, which was never included to try to keep it from leaking out. I know I wrote a version of it at some point, but mine was not used, obviously, in favor of Joss's' (Espenson, private correspondence).

The use of Whedon's scene at the end of this episode makes perfect sense when it is going to be the exact introduction to 'The Body'. The short teaser leads into the credits and we then have a short sequence where a Christmas meal is coming to an end. Buffy, Xander, Willow, Tara, Anya and Dawn are all there, as is Joyce, the host, and Giles. Whedon has commented that he made a mistake with this section insofar as a lot of the action focuses on the guests, with Joyce, Giles and Buffy in the kitchen arranging things (Whedon, 2002c: n.p.). As Wilcox (2005: 183) notes, however, it offers a version of one of Buffy's greatest desires, 'the whole communal scene in a happy family ritual of the sort regular viewers know Buffy longed for (cf. 'Pangs 4.8)'. However, when we do move into the kitchen, the closeness, the domesticity, the love between Buffy and Joyce, and the conviviality with Giles, all present a picture of gladness. As Buffy knocks a dish off the sideboard and it crashes to the floor, we have a sharp cut back to the silence of the living room, in the present with Buffy looking at her mother's body. For the remainder of the scene, Buffy is the centre of our attention: we have an off screen 911 operator, the paramedics who arrive and the brief appearance of Giles. There is also one other scene, which I shall discuss below.

Act 2 takes place at Dawn's school, though, like every act, it opens with a scene of Joyce's body, which in this instance is being zipped up in a body bag in Buffy's living room. This act plays out Dawn's upset over a taunt made about her by another girl at school, sees her in an art class and then Buffy arrives to tell her the devastating news. Dawn's collapse as Buffy tells her of her mother's death is seen silently through the widow of the art class she has been in, and is utterly compelling as a piece of drama. Much of the construction of the scene and its dialogue is changed from the shooting script and Whedon can be argued to be reprising his ideas from 'Hush', but here it is not fear that we see amplified without dialogue, but grief – and the effects are staggering.

Act 3 focuses on Willow, Tara, Anya and Xander. Again, a shift occurs between shooting script and produced version. In the shooting script all the action takes place in Willow's dorm room, but in the episode we see Anya and Xander's arrival in their car. This allows for the Willow and Tara scenes to have a much more specific focus, and for Willow's distress at her choice of top to be uninterrupted, as well as for the first kiss between Tara and Willow to have its full force open to it. Not only this, though, but having Xander and Anya arriving from outside allows Whedon the chance to play with the interior and exterior in a fashion that hints at, even if it does not replicate, Buffy's perusal of the outside 'real' world during her confusion and disorientation in Act 1. The final shot of Act 3 is a beautifully crafted pan from across the dorm, to the window, through it and down to see Xander's car being given a ticket for illegal parking. The quotidian irritations continue, even amid extreme personal tragedy.

The final act brings everybody together in the hospital and shows the boredom of waiting for information, character responses, provides the exposition scene, which I shall discuss soon, and even has a vampire to slay. Whedon insists that this was essential in the show, and points to the fact that this was unlike any other vampire fight – the choreographed, almost balletic athleticism of most sequences of fighting is replaced with close-up, close quarters, messy, brutal, aurally disturbing images of real exertion, genuine physical effort (Whedon, 2002c).

So, the episode uses the act structure uniquely for the *Buffy* format. There is no sub-plot. Action remains largely in one location with no cuts to different locations (except the shots of Joyce's body) and, among other formal innovations, there is no soundtrack. And there is little to identify it as a genre show, not even a polyglot genre show. It stands in large measure outside of generic classification, except to say that it is an exceptional piece of television. One clear genre piece is the opening of Act 2, which, as Whedon says, is a 'teen high school story' but one into which the unclassifiable excess of her mother's death will intrude. Notwithstanding that, the episode still has an exposition scene, but it is one in which the episode's formal desire to alienate the audience in order that they share, at least vicariously, the 'in-the-moment-of-it' of the death means that it is distorted and reshaped. The emotional disorientation that the formal strangeness of the episode encourages is further enhanced by the way that voices are recorded (either with an extremely close boom or attached lapel microphones) to achieve an uncomfortably close relationship between speaking voice on screen and listening ear of the audience:

> The acoustic close up of 'The Body' obliterates distance between performing body, apparatus and spectator body. The proximity of the voice opens up intimate access to its textures, intonations, and delivery that reveal a 'liveness' not otherwise accessible ... for an audience subjected to such intimate access, the 'presence' of the naked and vulnerable voice draws one into the emotional space of the text. (Stevens, 2010: 87–8)

The exposition occurs in the final scene, which makes it already structurally unusual. What makes it narratively unusual is that what is being explained is not a supernatural phenomenon that requires magic and arcane lore, but a medical phenomenon that requires medicine and science. To this extent, Giles is in no position to provide the necessary explanation. He has, in fact, been notably absent from the episode. He arrives at Buffy's after she has called him but he is confused, believing that he is there because of something to do with the season's Big Bad, Glory. It becomes clear that the expected (or at least plausible) format has been disrupted. He sees Joyce lying there, rushes to her but is impotent in the face of her death, and has to do nothing as Buffy shouts that they are not supposed to move the body.

At the hospital, Giles offers some kind of consolation to the Scoobies simply by being there, though he as ineffectual, for the most part, as the rest of them. He does become useful as the exposition scene draws to an end, but until that point Whedon has divested him of his usual knowledge-derived authority. The person who does have the authority is the doctor. We first see his hands as they conclude his examination of Joyce's corpse. He turns from her body, goes to a desk and fills out some paperwork, walks through the doors and along the corridor. The walk along the corridor occurs in real time, and we watch the entire journey from morgue to hospital waiting room. The effects of this are various. It helps to insist on the reality of the space, and Whedon has commended Carey Myer's ability to build sets that connected in such a fashion that the viewer was never let out of the scene, so that they know Joyce's body is, genuinely, just along the corridor (Whedon, 2002c). No cuts, no edits, just the continuing journey of a man in real time. Allied to this point, and made more powerful a little later as Dawn undertakes the journey in reverse, is that the morgue, the corridor, the hospital are all very ordinary for the doctor: they are part of his daily experience. Dawn's fearful, much gloomier walk to the morgue in order to see her mother's body is the exact opposite of her normal life; she is experiencing something exceptional. The doctor's walk to the waiting room may be an expression of normalcy for him, but it is one further example of the formally alienating efforts of the episode. By offering us an uninterrupted, mundane walk without simply cutting from morgue to waiting room with the doctor appearing, we are given a scene that is 'real' to the extent that the reality of the walk is not edited or tampered with any way, but whose very realness serves to distance the viewer from the action because it is not realism.

There is no such thing as realism, of course, simply a set of techniques that proffer a fictional world that can be believed. Among these techniques would be plot content and in *Buffy*, the decision to have monsters and the supernatural means that the show is a long way from a sense of realism predicated on a factual congruence between the fictional world and the world of the viewer. However, other factors also contribute to the believability and almost none of these is based on replicating real world actualities, but rather on creating format-specific approximations or versions of these actualities. A normal choice for the realism of *Buffy* would be to see a person leave a room or building and then cut to them either mid-journey (perhaps a shot in a car), or else arriving at their destination. The contraction of time to allow for the traversal of space via cutting between moments in the journey rather than witnessing the whole journey is such an ordinary technique that it is easy to barely notice it. By choosing not to use this familiar technique, Whedon defamiliarises the viewer, draws attention to the formal technique and by so doing enforces the episode's sense of formal strangeness. The paradoxical effect of this is that the emotional intensity of the experience, the reality of the affective experience is amplified. Non-realist form contributes to extreme realist sensation. This moment then is in many ways synechdochic of the show as a whole – its unrealism in terms of plotting and in terms of production technique (lighting design, soundscapes, score and so on) all contribute to allow for Whedon's desire that the show should be *felt* as real.

As the doctor arrives at the waiting room, Buffy, Dawn and Giles move towards him to hear the results of his examination – to have the exposition. The doctor explains what happened, making it clear that even had Buffy arrived at the instant of the stroke, it is unlikely she could have prevented the death. This prompts a brief and intense fantasy scene in which Buffy does arrive and her mother is saved, and then we are back in the hospital with the doctor continuing his explanation.

This fantasy scene parallels one that Buffy had in the first scene, during the paramedics' attempts to save Joyce. In this sequence, the formal estrangement of the episode allows Whedon to play with generic stereotype in a way that highlights genre typicality at the same time as deploying it to make it strange and further intensify Buffy's emotional bewilderment. The medics are trying to resuscitate Joyce and suddenly she gasps, and awakes. One of the medics comments that 'we've never brought one back this late before' and we then cut to a shot of the swirling lights of an ambulance with its sirens wailing, then to the interior of the ambulance with smiling Buffy holding Joyce's hand and the doctor declaring it as a 'miracle, a beautiful miracle', and then to a scene in a hospital room where a recovering Joyce is bathed in warm, golden light and her happy daughters are at her side as the doctor tells them that Joyce is 'good as new'. On a first viewing, these scenes do two things simultaneously. They provide us, like Buffy, with a fantasy of Joyce's recovery: we see her come back to life, be declared fit and healthy. However, while each scene operates on a stock medical drama cliché (impossible recovery, ambulance lights, ambulance interior, recovery room), they take place too quickly. The cuts happen with extraordinary rapidity. Even as we wish for Joyce's salvation through stereotype, we feel the unfamiliar form and the last violent cut back to the still, quiet desperation of the reality of the scene is unwanted but not unexpected.

Whedon has manipulated form, format and genre to make an episode of astounding emotional intensity and honesty. Indeed, much of the reason for its intensity is its manipulation of form, format and genre. This, episode along with 'Hush' and also episodes like 'Once More With Feeling' (B S6E7), 'Superstar' (B S4E17), 'Normal Again' (B S6E17) and 'Storyteller' (B S7E16) are the extreme versions of *Buffy*'s general aesthetic – an aesthetic that seeks out emotional reality through stories, structures, forms and hybrid versions of these that purposefully estrange the viewer from a recognisable 'real world' or stable genre or format.

The refusal to assume that an audience would recoil from the narrative and generic tricks being played, and that instead, they would respond with power and profundity that moves the drama beyond a 'like to see' and into 'must see TV' is one of Whedon's great contributions to television. As executive producer, he showed networks that there is a smart audience willing to watch on a weekly basis smart shows. For the networks of course this is cultural and financial benefit: '"must see" television is designed to appeal to affluent, highly educated consumers who value the literary qualities of these programmes, and they are used by the networks to hook this valuable cohort of viewers into their schedules' (Jancovich and Lyons, 2003: 3). The next chapter will assess how Whedon extends the opportunities presented to storytelling by having two separate 'must see' shows sharing the same televisual universe.

'I love a story with scope': *Angel* – cross-overs, complexity and conclusions

5

Angel ran for five seasons in the USA, first airing on 5 October 1999 and having its finale on 19 May 2004. It remained on The WB network for all five seasons, initially being aired directly following an episode of *Buffy*. This was not possible, of course, after *Buffy* moved to the UPN for its final two seasons. This means that for seasons 1 and 2 of *Angel* there was the opportunity for there to be episodes that not only directly followed on from *Buffy* but that also crossed over, with characters from the one show appearing in the other. For seasons 3 and 4 of *Angel*, after Buffy's move to UPN, there was still the opportunity for there to be limited cross-reference and even more limited cross-over; while the final season of *Angel* aired after *Buffy* had concluded.

To locate *Angel* so squarely in a relationship with *Buffy* is purposeful. While it is clearly its own show and 'is a shining example of television drama at its best – supernatural or otherwise' (Middleton, 2012: 116), and while it develops characters in directions that would have been difficult to predict and impossible to actualise on *Buffy*, it is nevertheless the case that it is, at core, an extension of the *Buffy*verse. It is this aspect – the tele-mythopoeic – that is so fascinating, and that provides such challenge and opportunity to the show. I discussed in detail the issues relating to the production, writing and show running of the show in Chapter 2: here I want to offer a discussion, or exegesis, of the stories presented in what Helen Wheatley (2006: 159) calls, in relation to *Buffy* and *Angel* together, 'perhaps the most successful example of parodic, hybrid, Gothic television'.

The *Buffy*verse is one of the most successful tele-mythopoeic worlds invented. Situated in the high fantasy, rather than sci-fi tradition, the *Buffy*verse produces a deep, textured mythologically dense, self-referential world that is open to expansion and revision. This occurs within *Buffy* but also across *Buffy* and *Angel*. The worlds expand far beyond the televisual, of course, into comic books and other outputs, and this trans-medial universe can be understood as the super-diegetic world of the *Buffy*verse. This chapter is concerned with the tele-mythopoeic aspect of this super-diegetic *Buffy*verse. Possibly the most important addition to the *Buffy*verse that *Angel* offers (and it is one that does not find its way back into *Buffy*) is introduced in the very first episode and is the law firm of Wolfram and Hart. Initially, more of a satire on the nature of evil, and the depredations of a certain version of corporate America (Harrison, 2005: 117–31; Sutherland and Swan, 2005: 132–46), it develops over the seasons in to one expression of the pan-dimensional body called (or made up from) the wolf, the ram and the hart. Implicit in this comment, but central to much of the architecture of the storytelling apparatus of the last four seasons of *Angel* is the notion of multi-dimensionality. These two concepts together (wolf, ram, hart and the presence of many dimensions) help to extend the *Buffy*verse in ways that *Buffy* alone could not have done. Glory (the mad god in season 5 of *Buffy*) is from another dimension, and the final episode of that season is a battle to stop the dimensions collapsing in on each other, but *Angel*'s expansion of the concept into almost a predicate of the mythos is an important aspect of its storytelling potential.

As with *Buffy*, the basic unit of storytelling in *Angel* is the episode. These are, in the opening seasons, usually self-contained stories relating to the solving of some kind of supernatural mystery. The self-containment of the specific story is supplemented by continuing threads of character development and, as the seasons develop, broader narrative context. I will look at the relationship between the episodes and seasons arcs presently, but for now, I want to look at the ways in which character development is an integral aspect of the storytelling.

In her excellent introduction to the show in *Joss Whedon: the Complete Companion*, Stacey Abbott (2012: 162) identifies *Angel*'s 'association' with *Buffy* and equally asserts that it 'transforms' the character of Angel from teenage love interest into a 'noir detective, losing himself in L.A. to escape the pain of the past'. The extension of the tele-mythopoeia occurs not just at the level of dimensions and law firms, but through the generic and aesthetic differences built into *Angel* the show, and Angel the character. This fundamental shift in Angel from *Buffy* (damaged noir detective) is part of the effort to make the show about 'the big, bad grown-up world and the people first entering it' (Whedon in Lavery and Burkhead, 2011: 15). This decision to locate the show in LA in the dark, in the noir/adult world and away from the sunshine, bright colours and high school/college juvenile world of *Buffy* further allows the expansion of the world created, but also allows for characters who had a certain trajectory in *Buffy* to be taken in very different directions in *Angel*. And these differences are perhaps most explicit and offer some of the most texture and depth in the episodes that allow characters to cross over from one show to the other.

The crossing over between the shows takes a variety of forms and offers the writers an array of ways of expanding the storytelling capacity of both worlds. I shall briefly list the episodes where cross-overs occur. In each case, I shall provide a description of the kind of cross-over and what this contributes to the overall mythology. In what follows, I am describing the narrative and affective potential of the shows as they were first aired in the USA. Having the shows run consecutively on the same day meant that the writers could assume immediate memory and context in *Angel* for an event from the previous episode of *Buffy*, and reasonably good recall for *Buffy* from the previous week's *Angel*. I discuss the notion of temporality and televisual narrative more fully in Chapter 7.

The first cross-over episode is *Buffy*, 'The Freshman' (B S4E1). Having left high school, Buffy and Willow are both starting university in Sunnydale. Angel has left Sunnydale to move to Los Angeles. In this episode, we see Buffy answer the phone in her mother's kitchen. No-one speaks, and Buffy hangs up. This small and insignificant detail is made sense of in *Angel*, 'City of' (A S1E1). This opening episode of the new show sees ex-*Buffy* love-interest Angel trying to help the helpless with the help of his non-cross-over helper Doyle. Angel attends a party to protect a young would-be actress, and here he meets ex-*Buffy* alumnus Cordelia Chase. We also see him call someone, hear the phone get picked up and see him hanging up without speaking. So, in addition to the appearance of characters in *Angel* who are familiar from *Buffy*, we also have a very economical reminder of the amazing love story between Angel and Buffy, and their mutual inability to either let it go or address it directly.

Buffy 'The Harsh Light of Day' (B S4E3) and *Angel* 'In the Dark' (A S1E3) sees Oz promise to take a gem to Angel in LA because his band has a gig there. The gem allows a vampire to move in daylight without burning up. Spike also goes to LA in search of the gem. We are provided with an expansion of our experience of Oz seeing him in LA where he is entirely at home and retains his unforced cool, responding directly to Doyle's query to Cordelia as to whether Angel and Oz are 'always like this' as they exchange brief, undeveloped sentences with 'No, we're usually laconic.' The contrast between the city of LA and the suburban setting of Sunnydale is vital to the theme and tone of the two shows, and while Oz traverses the twin locales with ease, Aaron C. Burnell (2011: 55) is clear that 'the leading characters in Buffy are (sub)urbanites in a suburban setting'. We also see the re-emergence of Spike's dislike of, but fascination with, Angel (and have been re-acquainted with his cruelty in his treatment of Harmony in the *Buffy* episode). Characters traverse the two worlds in the development of plots (Spike wants the gem, Oz is seeking to protect it and Angel) while we build our trust in the trio of Angel, Cordelia and Doyle and the mission they are developing. This mission is helped by Doyle receiving visions from the Powers That Be. These give clues to the identity of the victim Angel has to protect. At the end of *Angel* 'The Bachelor Party' (A S1E7), Doyle has a vision of Buffy in trouble as the show ends. The next *Buffy* ('Pangs' [S44E8)] sees the pattern of cross-over shifted as Angel returns to *Buffy* in order to protect her. His presence is known to all of the gang except Buffy herself, until Xander blurts out that Angel was there fighting with them as they have Thanksgiving dinner. For fans of *Buffy* who have not watched *Angel*, his return is a pleasing reminder of former character who still looms so large in Buffy's consciousness; for viewers of the new show who are also watching *Buffy*, Angel's return offers the contrast between the two Angels identified by Abbott (the love interest and the noir detective). In the *Angel* episode that follows ('I Will Remember You' [A S1E8]), Buffy comes to *Angel* to confront him over his secret trip to Sunnydale. This is, jointly, the sixteenth episode that both shows have been running and the seventy-second of the tele-mythopoeic world. In it, Angel is infused with the blood of a demon that turns him human. He and Buffy have the chance to be together, to live and die together. The show gives the characters and fans of this televisual relationship the very thing that they both desire. But Angel is not just mortal now, he is weak and his capacity to help the helpless, let alone Buffy, is significantly diminished. He implores the Powers That Be to let him re-live the day, to kill the demon before he is infused so that he can continue to serve good by being a vampire. He will be the only person in the whole *Buffy*verse to remember the day as it occurred. He chooses service, and sacrifices his love for (and possible future with) Buffy. She leaves, knowing only that their love is over. The episode has been an emotionally intense and moving affirmation of the separation of Buffy from Angel and *Buffy* from *Angel*. Although *Angel* continued to benefit from *Buffy* departees, as the stuffy and largely inept supercilious watcher, Wesley Wyndham-Price ('the most fascinating character on the show' (Berner, 2004: 146) turns up in LA as a rogue demon hunter in *Angel*, 'Parting Gifts' (A S1E10), where Angel and Cordelia are mourning the death of Doyle, a death that leaves open the chance for Wesley to join forces now that Cordelia hosts the visions.

These twin separations of the title characters and their shows are made even more manifest towards the end of *Angel*'s first season. Having been put in a coma at the end of *Buffy* season 3, Faith, the wayward and dangerous vampire slayer, wakes up in *Buffy* season 4 and wreaks havoc on Buffy. She swaps bodies with Buffy, sleeps with Buffy's new boyfriend Riley and creates chaos. She leaves Sunnydale and goes to Los Angeles where she arrives in *Angel*, 'Five by Five' (A S1E18). Phil Colvin (2005) makes the important point that Faith's appearances in *Angel* are typically part of the US television cycle called the 'sweeps'. The global consumer data organisation, Nielsen, send S diaries to certain households and asks the occupants to fill out a log of what they have watched. The diaries are then collected in a very specific order beginning in the northeast USA and 'sweeping' across the nation in a particular order. This occurs three times a year and the results will often determine if a show will stay on air, by virtue of being able to measure how many new viewers have been added in which markets. It occurs in February, November and May, and audiences have become used to shows having star guests, astonishing stories or, as in the case with *Angel*, cross-over episodes.

As Colvin rightly summarises, and I have indicated above, the cross-over episodes follow a structurally similar pattern with a character from Sunnydale *Buffy* arriving in LA in *Angel* as an antagonist, wanting something from Angel. They leave unfulfilled and both Angel and *Angel* assert their independence from both Buffy and *Buffy* (Colvin, 2005: 20). With Faith, the pattern is different. The emotionally unstable and violent Faith comes to LA as an agent of Wolfram and Hart, with a brief to assassinate Angel. In the course of her efforts, she tortures Wesley and manages to separate Buffy and Angel, as Angel insists on the possibility of Faith's redemption in *Angel* 'Sanctuary' (A S1E19). Buffy's fight and her role as guardian in Sunnydale does not translate to LA where it is Angel's responsibility to determine the moral actions. Buffy's rage at Faith offers a sense of the always fluctuating morality of the *Buffy*verse, and its recognition of (and dramatic use of) contextual limitations. As Faith seeks to apologise to Buffy for the hurt and damage she has caused, Buffy's response is simply to silence her with a threat that if she continues she will 'beat her to death' (A S1E19). Faith's presence, then, allows for a dark cross-over that illustrates both the core mission of Angel's team – the insistence of the possibility of redemption – and a dramatic and painful dissolution of one of the romantic storylines that had been so central to the *Buffy*verse. That this was done in a 'sweep' period is not accidental, and illustrates that absolute centrality of industry contexts to both character stories and the narratives that include them.

The next week's *Buffy* episode ('The Yoko Factor' [B S4E20]) sees Angel back in Sunnydale to apologise for how he spoke to Buffy. In so doing, he meets her new boyfriend, Riley, and the two men admit to mutual dislike: the Buffy–Angel romance seems to be truly over and Angel and *Angel* are very much going their own way. *Angel's* first season ends with the reintroduction of a character who was the very first female character to appear on *Buffy* labelled simply 'Timid Girl' in the shooting script but who came to be known as Darla – the sire and 150-year lover of Angelus. Staked in *Buffy*, 'Angel' (B S1E8), the character has been seen in the flashback sequences that offered us Angel's history in *Buffy*, 'Becoming Part 1' (B S2E21) and in *Angel*, 'The Prodigal' (A S1E15). In *Angel*, 'To Shanshu in L.A.' (A S1E22), Darla is reincarnated by the law firm Wolfram and Hart, for reasons that unfold over the next seasons, but which are part of the process of shifting the emphasis of the show away from Angel solving crimes and rescuing people, and moving towards struggle for redemption. Darla's role in this is central, in part because she (despite her seeming cold and callous attitude to humans) is similar to Spike. Both of them are ruled at least as much by love and sexual desire as they are by the need to feed. Darla, even in reincarnated human form, loves Angelus with a ferocity that eclipses all of their shifts in state and status. While Spike's path allows him to transfer his affections for Drusilla to Buffy and even to have a final, validating, apostrophising of his love for Cecily while he was still William, Darla is killed by Angel in *Buffy*, resurrected as a frail human, impregnated by Angel, re-sired by Drusilla and finally kills herself giving birth to their impossible son, Connor. I shall mention the role of motherhood and heterosexual love in the section on *Dollhouse* (II.5), but for now it is worth mentioning Lorna Jowett's (2005: 74) observation that it is her passion for Angel that provides the necessary weakness for her character development in *Angel*, 'this is clear from the way she was a relatively minor character in *Buffy* but is key to revelations about Angel in his own series'.

Darla is part of the work of using cross-overs to tie the two worlds together in a single tele-mythopoeic *Buffy*verse, and to differentiate them from each other that continues in the second season. The presence of so many *Buffy* characters in *Angel* (Angel, Cordelia, Wesley, Darla) the inter-penetration of both shows is quite evident, but there are fewer appearances by cast members of one show appearing in the other show in the present tense. Angel goes to visit Faith in prison, where she has voluntarily allowed herself to be placed as part of her redemption storyline (*Angel*, 'Judgement' [A S2E1]) but as Faith is no longer a recurring character on *Buffy* this may be more thought of as allusion than cross-over.

The seventh episode of each show provides for an astonishing use of flashback and cross-over to question televisual objectivity and point of view. In *Buffy*, 'Fool for Love' (B S5E7), Buffy gets Spike to describe in detail how it was that he killed two previous slayers. The story is told with sequences of flashback, especially to the time of the first slayer he killed in China during the Boxer rebellion. In the flashback, we see Spike, Angel, Darla and Spike's sire, Drusilla, with whom he had terrorised Sunnydale in *Buffy* season 2. In the flashback, we see Spike kill the slayer. In the shooting script, Doug Petrie wrote:

> EXT. CHINA 1900 – NIGHT
>
> NOTE: THIS SCENE MATCHES EXACTLY THE SAME SCENE IN ANGEL EPISODE SEVEN.
>
> Spike and Dru walk out of the burning building and into the bloody chaos of rebellion all around them. Spike's long period-era coat flows out behind him as he walks. He's no longer the unsure, overcompensating vamp he was before. Now he radiates true confidence. (Petrie, 2000: n.p.)

Spike and Drusilla tell Angel and Darla of their feat. Angel appears moody and unimpressed, seemingly annoyed to have had Spike do something he has not yet. They talk about how the smell of fear is exhilarating, but Angel simply asserts that the rebellion is starting to bore him. In the companion episode, *Angel*, 'Darla' (A S2E7), this scene is provided with significantly different context. Angel has already been re-ensouled, and he is asking Darla to still be with him, as he is still a vampire. She insists they 'reap the whirlwind' but we see Angel try to hide a cowering family. Directly after this we have the repeated shot of Spike and Dru from the *Buffy* episode and now the audience reads Angel's response not as jealousy or moodiness, but as disgust and upset. The slow-motion camera work as the four leave the burning ravaged city, Spike jumping over a blazing box, shifts from a triumphant Spike and sulking Angelus to a triumphant Spike and a tortured Angel unable to be a vampire, but not ever a human. The two episodes have provided two origin stories (Spike's and Darla's), which, in turn, have deepened and broadened the tele-mythopoeic world, while also challenging the convention of the neutral and 'true' objective eye of the camera by showing us the same scene differently contextualised and once more affirming the general premise of Whedon's work, which is that storytelling has to be careful, subtle, multi-layered and challenging. This is never for its own sake – the two scenes in the two episodes are formally stunning, narratively clever and the cross-over is a *tour de force* of television writing: but it is the emotional pain of Angel and his need to live with and through that for another 100 years that is the point (along with Spike's glee, a glee that in the *Buffy* version will be short lived as Buffy humiliates him at the end of the episode).

Drusilla appears in the present of the show in episodes 'The Trial' (A S2E9), 'Reunion' (A S2E10) and 'Redefinition' (A S2E11). Brought in by Wolfram and Hart to re-sire Darla she fulfils her mission before returning to Sunnydale in *Buffy*, 'Crush' (B S5E14), to try to tempt Spike back. When he declares his love for Buffy, Drusilla leaves and never returns, although the character's form is taken by the First Evil in season 7, and appears in flashbacks on both *Buffy* and *Angel*. The passions, violence, histories and relationship tribulations that have beset Angel, Darla, Drusilla and Spike furnish the mythology with great storytelling depth and texture across both shows, multiple time frames and a formal ambition that produces the emotional power and realism so central to the *Buffy*verse.

The emotional intensity of the *Buffy*verse rarely, if ever, reached the astonishing mixture of grief, boredom, pathos, anger and confusion expressed in 'The Body' (B S5E16). I discussed this in Chapter 4, but I want to briefly address the episode that aired the following week, 'Forever' (B S5E17). In this episode, the grief of Buffy and her sister Dawn at the death of their mother is overpowering. Dawn decides to try and bring Joyce back and enlists Spike's help. The spell works, to an extent, but Buffy is furious at them both right up until the point when it seems as though Joyce (or Joyce's zombie-like body) appears at the door. At this point, Buffy plaintively calls for her mommy, while Dawn destroys the talisman that brought the body forth, thereby making it disappear. Buffy, the little girl, is saved and comforted by her little sister Dawn, whose act of emotional maturity and emotional courage marks an important (though not constant) shift away from her more usual selfish teenage needs.

Preceding all the high drama, near the beginning of the episode, there has been a very quiet, very moving conversation between Buffy and Angel. Having heard of the death, Angel came to Sunnydale, and he and Buffy have been sitting all night under a tree. Although he is comforting her, and she is expressing her need and her fear at not being able to cope, it is ultimately she who realises that he cannot stay and understands that she will have to find the strength to cope. The gentle care and the deep sense of love from each to the other offers, in the wake of more tempestuous encounters earlier in the season, a more adult, modulated and sustained friendship. Meanwhile, in the following *Angel* episode ('Disharmony' [A S2E17]), Cordelia's friendship with school friend Harmony is given some comic relief when it becomes clear that the person who has arrived to stay with her is now a vampire whose presence in Angel Investigations is both unwanted and ultimately betrayed.

The final episode of the season has one of the shortest cross-overs but one that is crucial to both the narrative shape and production histories of the shows. The episode, 'There's No Place like Plrtz Glrb' (A S2E22), is the final of the three-episode mini-series that ends the season. Set in another dimension (a kind of medieval fantasy dystopia from a human perspective) the story revolves around rescuing Cordelia and in the process also finding the student Winfred Burkle who was transported there some years earlier. By virtue of the dimension-hopping, and bringing back the new character Fred, the trio of episodes expand the mythos. The absence from the *Buffy* dimension is crucial because she is fighting the God Glory – also intent on opening multiple portals to other dimensions – and it is unlikely that anything other than inter-dimensional paralysis would have stopped Angel from going to help, so the writers needed a drastic solution. An audience watching both shows at the original time of airing will have just watched Buffy die in her quest to save the planet. The high fantasy and mildly silly story provide a jarring juxtaposition but the two worlds well and truly recombine as Angel, Cordelia, Gunn, Wesley, Lorne and Fred enter their workplace to see Willow sitting there, grief struck, silent. As she stands, eyes fixed on Angel, Angel understands. The episode, the season and the production capacity for follow-on cross-overs all end.

With *Buffy*'s move to UPN, and with *Angel*'s day of broadcast changed by The WB, the opportunity for these follow-on cross-overs disappeared, and with them a rich source of mythos-expanding and emotion-deepening storytelling. The two worlds still interpenetrate in terms of story, with off-screen phone calls and meetings (Willow calls to inform Angel that Buffy is alive; and Buffy and Angel meet between episodes). Nevertheless, there were still characters who traversed the networks. Faith is broken out of jail to fight Angelus and returns with Willow (who has come to LA to cast a spell to put Angel's soul back) to Sunnydale to help Buffy fight the First Evil. After *Buffy*'s conclusion, Spike and Harmony both end up on what would be *Angel*'s final season, where Angel now runs the LA branch of Wolfram and Hart. The character of Andrew, who has been introduced as a would-be villain in season 6 of *Buffy* but who finds redemption in season 7, appears in season 5 of *Angel* and provides information to Angel (and the viewers) regarding the characters from *Buffy*.

In some ways, what is more interesting during these years in terms of the cross-over is not so much the notion of narrative and character in one show being developed in the next episode of the other show, but the use of actors across the worlds created by Whedon. This has been discussed by Jeffrey Bussolini (2013), but for the purposes of this chapter it is worth noting actors who moved from *Buffy* to *Angel* but also actors who moved from *Firefly* to *Buffy* and *Angel* to provide what Bussolini calls the 'intertextuality of casting'.

I am not talking here (although Bussolini does) about actors who appear as minor or one-off characters in different shows; rather I am looking for actors who appear as the same character repeatedly in one show and then either as that same character on the other show, or as a new character in a different *Buffy*verse. Moving from *Buffy* to *Angel* there is David Boreanaz, Charisma Carpenter, Alexis Denisof, Eliza Dushku, Tom Lenk, James Marsters, Mercedes McNab, Julie Benz and Juliet Landau. From *Firefly* to *Angel* we had Gina Torres and Adam Baldwin, and from *Firefly* to *Buffy* there was Nathan Fillion. And if we expand this to include the remainder of the televisual worlds created by Whedon then the intertextuality of casting begins to become a vast and complex source of involutional complexity and delight.

Back in the world of *Angel*, though, I want to return briefly to the nature of the ensemble who perform it. Narrative is a function of storytelling, and televisual storytelling, as I hope has been made clear throughout this book so far, is as much a function of network requirements, industry contexts, advertising revenues, audience uplift and Nielsen ratings as it is of creativity. Or rather, the test of the creative capacity of a production team is to be able to produce stories that have the emotional and moral richness and texture that keeps an audience interested, while simultaneously meeting all the corporate targets.

Angel struggled to achieve all of these requirements, partly for the reason outlined in Chapter 2 and partly because it was a less clearly defined format. As Nikki Stafford (2004: 4) identifies, the first season was intended to be a much more conventional week-by-week anthology show like *Law & Order* (NBC 1990–2010) but 'because the writers were from *Buffy* and were accustomed to more serialized content, the format soon changed'. This ability to be agile, to shift format to satisfy competing demands is one of *Angel*'s strengths, but also means that from one season to the next, there were nearly always format shifts that both allowed significant shifts in characterisation, but also had the possible effect of either alienating existing viewers or putting off possible new viewers.

The shift from 'anthology' to series arc required a shift in focus around the character of Angel himself. Rather than him simply being the hero who helps the helpless by solving a supernatural mystery each week, the show focused on his redemption as a core feature. For Dale K. Koontz (2008: 130) redemption is central to Whedon's shows, but that the redemption must involve 'action on the part of the penitent, who cannot rely on empty ritual and hollow words to achieve renewal'. The series shift to redemption as the major theme required action from the writers as well as from the characters to re-orient the stories to perform this function. This required the shift of the previously important but rather abstract Wolfram and Hart into a genuine and personal threat. As a consequence, we see the emergence of two of the lawyers as particular adversaries who threaten and menace Angel. The previous set up of Angel Investigations solving crimes and running foul of a police force that did not believe in monsters (described by Stafford [2004: 5] as 'slightly clichéd') was sidelined and the importance of redemption, personal threat and the global nature of the fight highlighted. Wesley Wyndham-Price from *Buffy* was brought across (to begin the most complex character arc in the whole *Buffy*verse) meaning that all three main cast members were Sunnydale alumni. A new character, Charles Gunn, was introduced immediately following Faith's chance for redemption as offered by Angel. The shift in focus from Angel 'being guardian to becoming the protagonist in a mythology' (Colvin, 2005: 23) necessitated a broadening of the terms of that mythology, which, in turn, needed a larger ensemble capable of delivering that extension of the tele-mythopoeia. Gunn was introduced 'expressly to become a series regular and "build up the ensemble"' (Colvin, 2005: 26). This was expanded further in season 2 with the addition of Lorne, the demon from a different dimension and owner of a karaoke bar (the commingling of demons and humans, and the inter-dimensional aspect of Lorne's being are further developments of the tele-mythopoeia). As mentioned, the disappearance of Cordelia through a portal to the dimension that Lorne is from offers a three-episode sojourn in a wholly different fantasy world (a necessary disappearance given the cataclysmic battle taking place on *Buffy* – a battle Angel [and possibly *Angel*] would otherwise have taken part in). Coming back from this dimension, they bring Winifred Burkle (Fred), the brilliant scientist who had been transported there by her unscrupulous professor and who becomes the latest addition to the ensemble. This group of Angel, Cordelia, Wesley, Gunn, Lorne and Fred remains the core team until Cordelia falls into a coma in season 4. Angel's unlikely son, Connor, is present throughout season 4 as member and antagonist, and returns briefly in season 5, where Spike and Harmony are also introduced, and Fred is replaced by the ancient god Illyria. This mostly stable ensemble as well as a host of characters who are frequent inhabitants of the *Angel* world (the lawyers Lyndsey and Leila, Gareth Park, the time travelling vampire hunter, Holz, Darla, Drusilla) provide two contrasting but complementary methods of expanding and enriching the *Buffy*verse. The first is by creating new characters, new plotlines and environments, organisations and possibilities; the second is by taking familiar faces and stories from *Buffy* and cross-fertilising them with the new *Angel*-world. As I have tried to describe, this cross-fertilisation provides for some of the most rewarding and textured storytelling in the whole mythos.

Despite this, after five seasons its viewing figures led The WB to cancel the show. The press release on 13 February 2004 expressed its admiration for the show, pointed out that *Frasier* (NBC 1993–2004) and *Friends* (NBC 1994–2004) were also being axed, wished everyone well and was very polite. It provoked a storm, as up to that moment there was a sense that *Angel* was improving in the ratings and was safe after celebrating its 100th episode just days before. On the Bronze message board, Whedon wrote the following:

> Some of you may have heard the hilarious news. I thought this would be a good time to weigh in. To answer some obvious questions: No, we had no idea this was coming. Yes, we will finish out the season. No, I don't think The WB is doing the right thing. Yes, I'm grateful they did it early enough for my people to find other jobs.Yes, my heart is breaking.
>
> When *Buffy* ended, I was tapped out and ready to send it off. When *Firefly* got the axe, I went into a state of denial so huge it may very well cause a movie. But Angel ... we really were starting to feel like we were on top, hitting our stride – and then we strode right into the Pit of Snakes 'n' Lava. I'm so into these characters, these actors, the situations we're building ... you wanna know how I feel? Watch the first act of 'The Body.' (Whedon, 2004: n.p.)

Likening his response to Buffy's numb, bemused, shocked grief at her mother's death provides a very precise measure of Whedon's emotional state, though his trademark rueful humour is also evident a little later when he writes, 'Two roads diverged in a wood, and I took the road less traveled by and they CANCELLED MY FRIKKIN' SHOW. I totally shoulda took the road that had all those people on it. Damn' (Whedon, 2004: n.p.).

A few weeks after the announcement and almost exactly coterminous with the broadcast of the final episode of *Angel*, Whedon was interviewed by Jeff Jensen for *Entertainment Weekly*. His assessment of the networks (while clearly tempered by his experiences over the previous two years) is remarkable. His observation regarding the cancellation of

Angel demonstrates the ways in which networks find what they believe to be a winning formula and then fail to either develop it, or to see that the formula they see is different from what actually makes the show a success. Whedon says, 'I believe the reason *Angel* had trouble on The WB was that it was the only show on the network that wasn't trying to be *Buffy*. It was a show about grown-ups' (Jensen, 2004: n.p.). A specific network's inability to see beyond a passing fad is broadened into a scathing attack on a general failure of nerve and reliance on cheap, sensationalist programming. Whedon denounces each network in turn:

> The reality television thing. I've definitely been the guy in *Singin' in the Rain* who's like, 'Talking pictures – it's just a fad!' The face of the marketplace is changing; none of the networks are doing that well, and they're all scrambling. ABC is kind of falling apart, NBC and CBS are entrenched, my history with Fox [as a network] is ... not great. The WB basically said, We have to do more reality, we don't have room for Angel – this, when Angel had always done well, and was doing better ... I'm not sure what else I needed to do! (Jensen, 2004: n.p.)

Angel's ending was unexpected for Whedon and show runner, at the time, Jeffrey Bell. The cross-fertilising and deeply mutually implicated stories of *Buffy* and *Angel* meant that when the cancellation of *Angel* was announced, the writers had to provide a conclusion not just to a season, but to a whole series, and moreover a series that was itself a constitutive part of a broader fictional universe, the *Buffy*verse. The finale had a lot of work to do. Earlier in the year, at the discovery of the half-show pick-up, Whedon explained that he was ready for any eventuality and could end the season appropriately, whatever the context, 'With *Angel*, we do as we have always done on *Buffy* where the season ender will either have a lot of closure or a huge amount of open-sure' (Sullivan, 2004: n.p.). As Alexis Denisof points out, however, in his fascinating interview with Nikki Stafford, The WB's decision did produce a certain shift in some of the story and character directions. Wesley's character 'got a little compressed' (Stafford, 2004: 94), so much so in fact that he was killed in the final episode, a fact that provides the title to the interview as Denisof lays the blame for his death directly, if semi-ironically, at the door of the network: 'So, Thanks WB – you killed me' (Stafford, 2004: 96).

The work any finale may be expected to do is, with *Angel*, made more problematic by the unexpectedness of the cancellation, its need to offer some kind of thematic and character-oriented resolution, and its requirement (attenuated but real) to affirm the mythopoeic relationship with *Buffy*. As such, the plot aspect of the finale is very simple. As co-writer and director Bell asserts, 'we didn't need a whole lot of plot' (Bell, 2005: n.p.) because the focus was going to be on the characters and their response to a final battle that was likely to kill some or all of them. That said, as Roz Kaveney (2005: 70) points out, in addition to concluding the *Buffy*verse, the episode needed to 'lead logically to a sixth year should one be commissioned, and to further *Buffy*verse material should it be called for'. The sixth season on television, according to David Fury, was 'going to launch into a post-apocalyptic show ... It was going to be Angel in *The Road Warrior* which I thought would be awesome' (Pascale, 2014: 246). As the worlds of *Buffy* and *Angel* continued as comic books a couple of years after Kaveney's observation, the attenuated plot was still important.

Such as it is, the plot of the episode is that each of the characters has to kill one of the members of the Circle of the Black Thorn, a secret society that is the most powerful force of evil working in the world. Before the killings, they each have some time to themselves. This very simple plot structure, which is leading with determined narrative force to the final battle, allows for the thematic and mythopoeic elements to be addressed with great focus.

There is a simple but important mythopoeic link between the two shows in terms of character. The *Angel* finale has five characters who first appeared on *Buffy*: Angel, Wesley, Spike, Harmony and, the occasional character, Anne. The last is vitally important to the thematic element of the show... Gunn chooses to go and visit Anne during his time off before the battle. First seen as a vampire wannabe called Chanterelle in *Buffy* season 2 ('Lie to Me' [B S2E7]), then as a runaway in *Buffy* season 3 ('Anne' [B S3E1]), in *Angel* she has become a hard working member of a team who seek to protect and shelter vulnerable young people. When challenged by Gunn (who is aware of the higher powers, and seemingly hopeless fight to come) to say what she would do if she knew all her work was pointless, she simply asserts that she would move the stuff on the truck they are packing and carry on. This normal human young woman, who has travelled her own path of recovery/redemption, provides a simple, pragmatic response to the futility of struggle: it is one that echoes the over-arching theme of the episode, the show and the mythopoeic world constructed by Whedon and his team. In short, in the absence of a secure moral framework, one has to work and carry on working, pragmatically, locally, in response to immediate ethical need.

This case-by-case morality, unmoored from the security of a clear theology or political philosophy obviates the notion of the hero secure in his or her moral position, above or outside of moral quandary. However, it also places competing moral systems into conflict, with a seemingly universalisable notion of good and evil being juxtaposed with contingent ethical choices. The most distressing of these becomes clear towards the end of the finale as the character Lindsey, who has himself seemingly fought his own demons and decided to fight on Angel's team after five seasons of intermittent but very real evil, is shot by Lorne.

Lorne is a character who has been largely peaceful: a demon who loves to entertain, who reads people's futures when they sing, and who revels in song and conviviality for their own sake. Lorne's agreement to kill Lindsey marks his last involvement with Angel. The act of assassination may be justified in a larger scheme (Lorne has read Lindsey's future and, although the audience is not told, the implication is that his future will be evil again, despite his current fighting on the side of good) but it is both cold-blooded murder and a betrayal of trust. The greater good demands Lindsey's death but the manner of its achievement is brutal, disloyal, mendacious and cruel. Lorne has done bad to do good; a utilitarian choice, a pragmatic ethics. Angel has made him a murderer. Importantly, the point of Lorne's most complex and disheartening moral action is the point where he is most fully integrated into the visual fabric of the team. As Lorrie Palmer (2011: 88) asserts, *Angel*'s 'male characters ... are depicted as notably metropolitan in attitude and costuming and in their skilled navigation through Los Angeles'. Season 5's metropolitan look is dominated by browns, deep reds, ochres, fawns and beiges yet Lorne remains joyfully besuited in greens, blues, pinks. He begins this episode in blue, is seen in an orange-brown jacket as Angel gives each team member his job (though the audience does not know Lorne's) and as he murders Lindsey and walks away, he has a fawn leather trench coat and brown jacket: he is visually as murky as the rest of the team (see Figures 7 and 8). Lindsey dies in striped shirt and blue jeans – an outsider.

During a discussion between Angel and Lindsey earlier in the episode, where he pretends to welcome Lindsey as a group insider, Angel offers a brief observation to counter Lindsey's belief that the fight is unwinnable. Angel observes that 'once this world was theirs [the demons] and now it's not'. Jeffrey Bell tells us that for scheduling reasons, the scenes with Lindsey were shot about six weeks before the rest of the episode with Whedon writing all of them. It is important that Whedon writes a line for the final episode of the *Buffy*verse that is so closely reminiscent of a line from the first episode of the *Buffy*verse. In the second half of the *Buffy* premiere, Giles explains to Buffy and her friends that 'contrary to popular mythology, [Earth] did not begin as a paradise. For untold eons demons walked the Earth. They made it their home, their ... their Hell. But in time they lost their purchase on this reality. The way was

Figure 7 Lorne, *Angel*, 'Not Fade Away', season 5, episode 22, first broadcast 19 May 2004. Lorne, early in 'Not Fade Away' dressed in blue and sitting, is clearly visually removed from the colour palette and ethical murkiness of the rest of the team of Angel, Wesley, Gunn and Spike who are all in muted browns, ochres and black.

Figure 8 Lorne towards the end of *Angel*, 'Not Fade Away', season 5, episode 22, first broadcast 19 May 2004. Lorne, later in the same episode, now in brown and black (and leather jacket rather than cotton suit) after his murder of Lindsey – an act of significant moral ambiguity, leaving Lorne unable to return to the group at the point where he is most visually similar.

made for mortal animals, for, for man.' Angel's recapitulation of this central mythopoeic foundation at the end of the series is enormously important in asserting not just character consistency but mythological and thematic unity across and between the shows. It also allows Lindsey, soon to be betrayed and murdered, to mock Angel's 'speechy' –ness but also to commend his being a 'vampire with big brass testes' (A S5E22).

Angel's brutal pragmatism for the greater good, Lorne's visual and moral merging with the group and Anne's more positive pragmatism all provide both character-related and thematic points of assertion and summation. However, a more clearly invoked form of narrative closure occurs for Spike. Having been the main enemy in *Buffy* season 2, Spike's first appearance in *Angel* was in the third episode of season 1 where his sadism, selfishness, humour and charm are all evident. His re-appearance as a permanent fixture in Angel season 5 keeps all of the above qualities except the sadism: Spike has saved the world at the end of *Buffy* and his path to redemption seems secured. But there has always been another aspect to Spike, a part of his vampiric make up that has marked him out as different from the majority of vampires in the *Buffy*verse, and that is his emotional vulnerability. Whether with Drusilla or Buffy, or even at times with Harmony, Spike has needed to love and be loved. In *Buffy* season 5 we have seen the pre-vampire Spike as an ineffectual late nineteenth-century English gentleman called William. He is in love with, and writes poetry for, a woman called Cecily. The poetry is mercilessly mocked, and his advances are firmly, even cruelly, declined ('Fool for Love' [B S5E7]). In the *Angel* finale, as Gunn visits Anne and Lorne sings karaoke, Spike heads to a bar. Setting the audience up to believe he is simply going to get drunk and fight, what he actually does is get drunk and read his Cecily poem. It is rapturously received. The poet, the lover, the emotionally vulnerable Spike is affirmed, celebrated. Later he will revel in the violence of the fight; here he (and we) can revel in the depth and texture of a fictional universe that creates characters of such multi-faceted, contradictory and complex aspect. This is a narratively satisfying moment, and one that not only offers us a partial resolution of a wonderfully crafted character, but also a renewed declaration of an aesthetic ideal that the *Angel* and *Buffy* have lived up to: characters grow, develop, respond, remember. Spike remembers William and over 100 years of biography and history are concentrated in the moment.

Yet, Spike's is not the most moving finale moment, though it may be the funniest – another central feature of the show is its commitment to constantly shifting the generic ground within an episode: comedy one moment, drama the next, horror the next, and these moments may be merely seconds apart. And nor is Spike's the most astonishing journey a character takes.

Initially comic foil and object of ridicule on *Buffy*, Wesley's journey on *Angel* has been into despair and alienation. Following great mythic and literary models such as *The Aeneid* and *Heart of Darkness* (both of which are implicitly or explicitly evoked in the mythopoeic world of the *Buffyverse*), he is seen to be striving for recovery and reconciliation in season 5. One aspect of this is his eventual recognition that he and Winifred Burkle (Fred) are in love. At almost that exact moment she dies and her body is inhabited by an ancient god, Illyria. As an aside, it is worth noting that Fred's journey is not as interesting, but the actor who plays her, Amy Acker, gets to play two entirely different characters; in the finale within seconds of each other.

Wesley, having journeyed into darkness chooses, like Marlow in *Heart of Darkness*, a lie from his intended. While the others go off to their various pursuits, Wesley stays in the offices with Illyria. Confused as to his motives, Illyria has to have it explained to her by Wesley that he has no special place he would like to be or special person he would like to be with since Fred is dead. Illyria offers to assume her shape but Wesley adamantly refuses to accept the illusion of Fred over the fact of her absence saying 'I won't accept a lie'. Later, after being mortally wounded and nearing death (see Figure 9), Illyria finds Wesley and the following exchange occurs:

ILLYRIA
Would you like me to lie to you now?

WESLEY
Yes. Thank you. Yes.

Figure 9 Wesley and Illyria / Fred in *Angel*, 'Not Fade Away', season 5, episode 22, first broadcast 19 May 2004. Wesley dies in the arms of Illyria, having accepted her offer to lie to him and assume the form of Fred.

WESLEY
Hello there.

FRED
Oh, Wesley. My Wesley.

WESLEY
Fred. I've missed you.

FRED
It's gonna be OK. It won't hurt much longer, and then you'll be where I am. We'll be together.

WESLEY
I-I love you.

FRED
I love you. My love. Oh, my love.

Wesley dies.

Apart from being one of the most heart-wrenching moments in any television show, let alone simply *Buffy* and *Angel*, due in large part to the exceptionally understated and emotionally compelling acting performances, the choice of the emotionally sincere lie over the morally sincere truth locates the culmination of Wesley's journey into his heart of darkness structurally and emotionally adjacent to Marlow's. Like the moral pragmatism offered earlier, the show provides us with conflicted and conflicting versions of moral choice.

Illyria's willingness and ability to assume the shape of Fred and to cry at Wesley's passing provide both a visual lie (she is not Fred, but is pretending to be) and an emotional truth: Illyria (who like many characters in the show is trying to understand humanity) is crying at Wesley's departure – either because she feels the pain of his dying (sincere grief) or because she realises this is what Wesley needs to see (sincere empathy). She is learning humanity.

The character who not only wants to learn humanity but become human is Angel. The reward for his works, according to a plot mechanism called the Shanshu prophecy, is that the vampire with a soul will become human. Angel signs away in blood his chance to attain this reward in order to convince the Order of the Black Thorn of his commitment to their evil cause. However self-sacrificing this gesture may appear, it is not quite the selfless gesture it may at first seem. For a start, there is enough doubt in the prophecy's detail to imply Spike may be the ensouled vampire mentioned. Also, on a number of occasions, Angel has had the chance to act like, or be, human through a variety of mystical routes and he has always forgone them in order to continue the fight. As he says in this episode, if the fight cannot be won, the importance is that the fight continues. Signing away his chance to ever be human is the same thing as saying he will remain as he is forever: in other words, he will still be able to fight, with a soul, for good – even if his tactics are morally dubious. Reward is not the point; the fight is.

For this reason, the episode ends with Wesley dead, Gunn dying, Lindsey murdered (all the strictly human main characters are beaten); Lorne has left; and Spike, Angel and Illyria stand to face the legions of hell. Angel, in a rather more pressured context, echoes Anne's earlier pragmatism: against apparently insurmountable odds they will fight on: 'Let's go to work', he says as he wields his sword and the screen goes black. Mid-battle, in the heart of the fight, with no obvious chance of victory the show ends, the finale wraps up the televisual *Buffy*verse.

Characters have been given the chance to conclude their tales (Angel's son Connor makes a return and helps his dad in the fight; Harmony gets to say goodbye; Eve, the liaison to the Powers that Be, has a poignant and lonely shot; Doyle and Cordelia get a mention); production values of palette and narrative have been given creative and ethical weight and energy; moral and ethical complexity has been affirmed; and generic mutability and emotional multiplicity have been given their necessary freedom.

The repeat of a line from the pilot of Angel ('let's go to work') at its very end is another sign of the respect the writers pay the viewers, and is a structural analogue to Angel's recapitulation of Giles's line about demons from the *Buffy* aired pilot, as well as mirroring the structure of *Buffy* itself that has Giles repeat the line about the earth being 'doomed' in both pilot and finale of *Buffy*. This level of detail, of attention to story, character and theme is relatively common today in the world of quality TV. It was not always so. The *Buffy*verse deserves much credit for that fact. Not just a vampire, but a show, a whole mythscape, with a soul. And, as the shows that have come after it attest to, however obliquely, a long and growing legacy, not the least of which is a significant fan and scholar awareness of writers and producers. The next chapter will be a study of the interplay between producer and writer, as well as a discussion of one writer in particular: Jane Espenson.

'Come with me now gentle viewers': Popular culture and (non-Whedon) authorship 6

The purpose of this case study is to assess episodes that are not written by Whedon, or which are not credited to him as writer. In part, this is to show just how pervasive his control is, even when not directly credited; but it is also to demonstrate how he created in the Mutant Enemy production team a group of writers whose capacity to bring his vision to light is remarkable. It is interesting to note that even when discussing shows from years before Whedon's work was on television, it is to Whedon that scholars and critics look to make points of comparison. Hence, Alan McKee (2007: 239), in his fascinating discussion of *Dr Who*, when seeking to highlight the quality of the dialogue in an episode from 1977 says it, 'includes the same kind of verbal playfulness we now see in *Buffy the Vampire Slayer* ... where lines not only make narrative and character sense, but also delight in their own poetic play with language'. And it is this quality that is found in episodes not credited to Whedon that is the subject of this chapter.

I have chosen Jane Espenson for a number of reasons. First, as a casual viewer, before I began to study Whedon, I noted that it was her scripts that I tended to enjoy the most across the (at the time) three available shows. My delight in her work is obviously shared, and there is now the critical term 'the Espensode' to refer to her work (Kociemba, 2009: 23–41). Also, Espenson has been remarkably open in discussing her methods, process and ideas. This is in many interviews, her blog and, for the duration of the writer's strike in 2008, a series of email correspondences in which she very graciously answered as many questions as I could ask. These are collected as Appendix 1 at the end of this book.

The episodes I am focusing on, 'The Harsh Light of Day' (B S4E3) and 'Pangs' (B S4E8) from *Buffy*; more briefly, 'Shindig (F S1E4) from *Firefly*, have been chosen because of the ways in which they engage in different ways with aspects of popular culture. As will be discussed,

'Pangs' is a very direct confrontation with the popular cultural event of Thanksgiving, and the episode provides an excellent, if problematic, critical engagement with the histories – both personal and political – that contribute to the celebration of this 'ritual sacrifice with pie' (B S4E8). 'The Harsh Light of Day', which will be examined first, provides a brief, but nevertheless important, critique of that most pervasive of popular culture media – television. 'Shindig' will discuss the rewriting of the teaser section to discuss how its eventual location in a pool hall draws together the character issues the episode sets up, while also offering an excellent introduction to the themes of elite versus popular culture in the episode.

All the episodes will also allow for an illustration of the ways in which the initial story becomes a script, and the ways in which that script both allows the credited writer's lines to be heard, but also has the inevitable traces of Whedon. Whedon states in interview that 'if somebody does something right, I will not change a word' (Lavery and Burkhead, 2011: 32) but also reminds us that the disappointments he had with his film scripts ('I had such a specific vision, and nobody was seeing it') meant that relinquishing control is 'hard for me'. Espenson describes *Buffy* as a 'top-down show (as opposed to, say, *Battlestar*, which is more group-driven). Every *Buffy* episode came very much from Joss's brain' (Espenson, personal correspondence, 5 January 2008). Despite this, as Kociemba (2009) observes, Espenson is more than 'an adept craftswoman' and across the range of her work (*Buffy*, *Angel*, *Firefly*, *Tru Calling* [Fox 2003–5], *Gilmore Girls* [The WB/CW 2000–7], *Battlestar Galactica* [SciFi 2004–9] as well as her 2011–13 web series, *Husbands*, co-created with Brad Bell, and her work as writer and consulting producer on *Once Upon a Time* [ABC 2011–present] and co-creator of the spin-off, *Once Upon a Time in Wonderland* [ABC 2013]) there are identifiable aspects to her work that he cites as evidence of her being regarded as an artist in her own right. Whedon's skill, as Espenson observes, is to have a room of writers who write episodes in which 'the original voice of the show's creator is allowed to shine through with minimal interference' (Kociemba, 2009: 26) yet still allows the individuality of the staff writer to be heard.

The oscillations between writer's voices (and therefore characters' voices) can be seen in a brief section from the third episode of season 4. 'The Harsh Light of Day' is credited to Jane Espenson as writer and James A. Contner as director. From season 2, Contner was an ever-present on the *Buffy* director rota, even being charged with the season 6 finale, 'Grave' (B S6E22). In addition to this episode, Contner directed Espenson on two further occasions, both, coincidentally, the third episodes of their respective seasons: 'The Replacement' (B S5E3) and 'Same Time

Same Place' (B S7E3). About, 'The Replacement' Espenson (personal correspondence, 26 January 2008) wrote:

> Notice that although this appears to be a Xander story – Xander has the A-story, the Buffy story concludes the episode and is, in a way, deeper – Buffy is worrying that Riley prefers the non-Slayer parts of her, when in the end we learn that the problem between them actually comes from her not loving him. A powerful, deep little story. Joss always asked 'What's the Buffy of it?' when we were trying to break a story, and this is a great example of how even an apparently Xander-centric story has a strong 'Buffy of it'.

The 'Buffy of it' in The Harsh Light of Day' is her attempt to overcome her sense of loss and grief at Angel's departure at the end of season 3. The first two episodes of season 4 (written by Whedon and Marti Noxon, respectively) have introduced us to the main characters in their post-high school lives, and have shown Buffy to be ill at ease and out of her depth in the new environment. In the opening episode, 'The Freshman' (B S4E1) Buffy, apart from being unsure and out of place, is humiliated by a lecturer in a popular culture class.

Whedon's worlds are many things, but all of them are celebrations of popular culture in its many guises. Most notably, each of his major shows exists as a hybrid concoction of a range of popular genres (gothic, noir, sitcom and so on). In their very form, then, Whedon creates shows that are quintessentially located in popular culture. But while this may be true at a general level, it is also the case that, as Sue Turnbull (2004, 12) has argued, there is, 'the niggling possibility that the creators of this series [*Buffy*] can't help but construct fandom for popular culture as somehow inherently "funny"'.

Turnbull illustrates a number of occasions when characters in the show are ridiculed for their delight in popular culture. This is most striking in the case of season 6's supposed Big Bad, the trio of Andrew, Warren and Jonathan, but it is also true of a range of other examples including the main characters who are either marked as amusing for liking popular culture, or pass their own negative judgements on popular culture.

In considering the opening episode of season 4 of *Buffy*, Turnbull (2004) comments on the scene in which a course Buffy might study as a freshman at University, 'Images of Pop Culture', is held up for mockery, or at least incredulity: how could watching television be worth credits? The professor who runs the course is bullying, arrogant, offensive and repugnant, and humiliates Buffy before expelling her from the class. Turnbull (2004: 3) asks:

> Is Joss Whedon, who wrote this episode, really suggesting that the study of popular culture shouldn't be taken seriously? Or is he simply rehearsing

> the general prejudice in order to make fun of it? Or is Whedon (as usual) having it both ways, mischievously mocking the notion of an academy which would dare to take popular culture (and therefore his creation *Buffy*) seriously, while having a dig at those who don't?

I would like to continue Turnbull's examination, both of the 'general prejudice' and then of Whedon's relationship with popular culture and television. I will do the latter via an analysis of Espenson's drafts for 'The Harsh Light of Day'. In particular, I shall be focusing on a scene wherein Xander, Willow and Oz discover that Giles owns a television. This discovery compels Xander to exclaim that Giles is 'shallow like us', a phrase that I shall return to.

At the same time as Buffy is trying to overcome her heartbreak at Angel's departure, Spike has returned to Sunnydale after having left at the end of season 2, and returned once in season 3 ('Lover's Walk', B S3E8), and he is found to be the unlikely lover of Harmony who was turned into a vampire in 'Graduation Day II' (B S3E22). Spike is searching for the famed Gem of Amarra, which will enable him to exist normally in the light. With Buffy absently seeking clues and hoping for a potential new boyfriend, Parker, to return her telephone call at the University campus, Giles, Willow, Xander and Oz are trying to find information about the gem of Amarra at Giles's house.

When Xander moves some objects out of the way he discovers that Giles owns a television. His response is, 'Whoa. Giles has a TV. Everybody, look at this, Giles has a TV! He's shallow like us!' This prompts Oz to admit to being a 'little disappointed' and pushes Willow to speculate that it exists as some kind of 'art'. Giles defends his ownership by saying it is for PBS programming.

I want to look at this clip from two different but related positions. First, I want to address some of the ways in which the chat about Giles's television might be considered in relation to a broader conception of the debates concerning art, television and popular culture. Second, I want to look at how the chat we are watching came to be on the screen in terms of its development from idea to outline to various drafts to actual aired episode. The second of these positions has a direct relationship with the former as through the drafting process, among other things, we can see the debate being played out in the writers' minds and also see the extent to which Whedon's vision is central, even as Espenson's voice is resonant.

An instructive and useful starting point for discussion is Xander's outburst: 'Whoa. Giles has a TV. Everybody, look at this, Giles has a TV! He's shallow like us!' The brief expostulation comprises two phrases. In the first, Xander describes something about Giles in terms of ownership: 'Giles has a TV.' The second offers a proposition about Giles based on the object owned in the first: because he *has* a television, he *is* shallow. The simple correlation between object and character is unambiguous: the object itself, in its own right as an object and with absolutely no reference to the kinds of uses to which it could be put is sufficient to provide a judgement about an individual's cultural and possibly even intellectual abilities.

More than this, though, is that Giles's newly revealed shallowness operates to identify him as part of a group. He is 'like us'. For Xander, this 'us' presumably is supposed to mean the other people in the house at that time (Oz and Willow) and by extension the Scoobies from which Giles is seen as separate. This separateness is relatively easy to explain: he is notably older; he holds (or has held) positions of institutional authority; and he is English. Together these attributes can be seen to mark Giles out as not only culturally separate but also superior, at least in the mind of Xander. This superiority is fatally compromised by the discovery of the television.

Oz's 'disappointment' comes very quickly after he has been expressing his delight in Giles's record collection, especially his copy of the Velvet Underground's *Loaded*. Already then the scene is figuring popular culture as a category whose breadth and range is in excess of easy simplifications of it: popular culture includes music and television, shallowness and the avant garde (albeit, in the Warhol factory, an avant garde itself predicated on a kind of celebration of the shallow, ephemeral and reproducible).

Willow's comment offers a beautifully inverted response to Xander's. She tries to claim for the object a position of art itself. Much like Duchamp's toilet, Willow sees Giles's television as a mass produced object whose meaning could be re-inscribed as art if a sufficiently radical re-contextualisation has taken place. For Xander, the object demonstrates the 'shallowness' of television; for Oz it is the other side of popular culture (perhaps he could envisage a series of Phillips where the Heinz cans used to be); and for Willow the possibility that object can be divorced from its function is what makes it potentially art (as long as the medium is *not* the message, we are all ok).

The chat about the television has revealed a little bit more about each of the characters (not least Giles himself, of course) and in so doing has offered the audience the chance to extend the brief discussion about the role of television. That this should take place in a television show is in itself interesting, and may point to self-referential knowingness, may indicate a genuine desire for television to confront its critics head on, or may simply have been a convenient way of presenting essential plot information with a soupçon of character development.

The brief scene, unremarkable in many ways, is fascinating in relation to Turnbull's question about Whedon's shows presentation of popular culture. This however, unlike 'The Freshman', is not credited as a Whedon episode. What is interesting here is to look at the development of the script and to see how certain decisions regarding each character's position change. It is worth also remembering Whedon's very clear sense of his ownership of and responsibility to every episode:

> I'm responsible for all the shows. That means that I break the stories. I often come up with the ideas and I certainly break the stories with the writers so that we all know what's going to happen. Then once the writers are done, I rewrite every script ... Then I oversee production and edit every show, work with the composers and sound mixers. Inevitably every single show has my name on it somewhere and it is my responsibility to make it good ... Every week that show is on, I'm standing in the back row, biting my nails, hoping people like it, so I feel a great responsibility. The good thing is that I'm surrounded by people who are much smarter than I am. So gradually I have been able to let certain things take care of themselves, because my crew, my writers, my post-production crew, everybody is so competent, that I don't have to run around quite as much as I used to. (Lavery, 2002a: n.p.)

What is interesting is how other people within that process view their role and their contribution, especially a writer who, as Whedon states (much more forcefully than in the earlier quotation), will definitely have his or her work rewritten. Espenson (personal correspondence, 5 January 2008) has remarked how *Buffy* in general was a 'top-down' show, and she continues:

> 'Pangs' was not an exception to this. It was almost a case of watching Joss break the episode, in fact. He was, of course, very much involved in the *Angel* episode that accompanied 'Pangs', so he made sure to construct 'Pangs' specifically so they would work together. If both eps have, in essence, one writer, the co-ordination.

To call Whedon the 'writer' of the episode is, of course, to significantly undervalue her own centrality in the episode being the fabulous example of television that it is. However, the quotation does highlight just how clearly there is an overarching consciousness behind *Buffy*, and a consciousness that has repeatedly demonstrated the extent to which it has a vision that is both culturally vital and aesthetically stunning. Just to affirm both points (Whedon's control and his sheer ability),

Espenson also says that 'Joss was the ultimate authority' on the show 'often, the five most memorable lines in a script are the ones that Joss declared during the break'.

In the example being discussed here – the discovery of Giles's television in 'The Harsh Light of Day' – the jokes do not appear to be Whedon's, but some important changes are. Espenson's draft scripts, and her responses to some of my questions, will help to illustrate this.

Once an episode has been assigned to a writer, her first task is to create an outline script that describes each scene in each act. There is indicative dialogue and a sense of the 'beats' of emotional intensity. For 'Harsh Light', we get the following at scene 34.

> 34 GILES'S APARTMENT 34
> (Giles, Willow, Xander, Oz)
> Giles, Willow, Oz and Xander looking through books. Xander gets bored and turns on the TV ... a story about unauthorized tunnelling or something. That's Spike. Giles sends Xander to find Buffy and meet us there. They're off.

As we can see, this scene is a very straightforward plot scene. The gang is researching for clues, a bored Xander turns on an un-remarked television and a news story provides the impetus for action. The wonderful economy of Espenson's direction 'They're off' is worthy of note, but there is nothing here to suggest any of the characterisation and thematic probing to come.

This outline turned into the first draft, which I do not have but which Whedon was not entirely happy with. According to Espenson (personal correspondence, 23 January 2008), Whedon was concerned about the character of Parker in this draft, feeling his 'insincerity was too clear' and so suggested a rewrite. The rewrite has a very clear focus, which is to make Parker less insincere-seeming. While this does not impinge on the scene being looked at here, it is a clear example of Whedon's involvement, care and vision.

Written just two days after the first draft (21 June 1999), the second draft offers us a more fully developed scene than the outline, and we can also see that a further seven scenes have been added from the outline:

> 41 GILES'S APARTMENT 41
> Giles, Willow and Xander are still poring over books and maps. They look pretty burned. Oz is going through Giles' record collection.
>
> OZ
> Okay, I'm either borrowing all your albums or I'm moving in.

GILES
Oz, there are more important things than records right now.

OZ
More important than this one? Oz holds up a CLASSIC ALBUM (Pink Floyd's 'Animals'?).

GILES
Yes, well, I suppose an argument could be made ...
Xander is moving stacks of books ... and accidently reveals a TELEVISION SET.

XANDER
Whoa. Giles has a TV. Everybody, look at this, Giles has a TV! He's shallow like us!

OZ
Gotta admit, a little disappointed.

GILES
I'm not ... It's not ...

WILLOW
Maybe it doesn't work. It's like, a statement.

Xander turns on the set. It works fine.

GILES
I keep it– Public television– Look, everyone, we have vital work to do. If this gem falls into vampire hands, the Slayer is in terrible danger. Television isn't going to help us now.

41.

CONTINUED:

(CONTINUED)

WILLOW

(re TV news)

What's that?

INSERT: TV
A reporter narrates helicopter video of a muddy sinkhole with a roadway partially collapsed into it.

REPORTER (V.O.)
– around noon today near Brookside Park. Officials attributed the formation of the sinkhole to unexplained weakening of the topsoil support nearby. City work crews deny that any tunnelling has been done in that area ...

Over the continuing report:

XANDER
I love TV.

GILES
It's Spike. Come on. Xander, find Buffy and meet us there.

This is quite an extraordinary expansion. A fairly simple plot scene has become the site of a series of characters interacting and, in so doing, providing an attenuated debate about the status of television. Xander offers a blue collar average Joe response; Oz provides a kind of counter-cultural perspective that nevertheless echoes a high culture viewpoint; and Willow seeks to redeem the discovery in terms of high art, though here art itself is a 'statement' such that Giles's television, if it is to be redeemed at all, is to be redeemed through a self-referential, ironic didactic denunciation. Giles's defence is to claim that his viewing habits are highbrow – they reside in the sphere of public television. Given the emergence of so-called 'high-end' TV in the mid-1990s, of which *Buffy* was such an integral part, it is, perhaps, a shame that none of the characters is able to offer a positive reason for having a television and seem, rather, to share a perception of television as inevitably unworthy of serious study, or even serious pleasure.

An interesting shift from draft to screen is the album that Oz holds up as an example of truly important popular culture. Giles rebukes Oz's general enthusiasm by saying there are 'more important things than records', itself a generic dismissal of a depleted form, but the specific example, Pink Floyd's *Animals* allows for a revision of the general disavowal in favour of the specific approbation. This shift (*Animals* in the script, *Loaded* in the aired episode) allows two different types of analysis. On the one hand, one can speculate about what prompted the change. Given Giles's musical choices elsewhere in season 4, especially his listening to David Bowie's 'Memory of a Free festival' in 'The Freshman', a case could be argued for an attempt to provide Giles with the kind of art-house yet edgy musical tastes that fits more readily with Lou Reed, Nico and the rest than with post-Syd Barrett Pink Floyd. I offer this up as a point for minor debate. The more interesting invitation to analysis comes from Espenson's comments on this episode. She (personal correspondence, 2 May 2008) says, 'I recall him [Whedon] dictating that 'classic album' exchange ... even the choice of album was something that came directly from him'.

This level of detailed change is instructive. It is instructive not only because it provides a clear example of Whedon's intervention, but also because of what happens to this intervention. Whedon is not only suggesting a rewrite but is developing an idea or set of ideas that are, at this juncture, unstable, as we shall see. In the next draft the scene has changed again. It is important to remember that this scene, while providing vital information regarding Spike's whereabouts, is far from being central to the main thrust of the episode. It is an episode in which we see Buffy not having got over Angel, being duped, and betrayed; it is an episode where Spike's viciousness and cruelty are played out against the return of the sadly abused Harmony; it is an episode in which Anya's potential for hurt and confusion are writ large. These are the truly significant aspects and the reason, one supposes why, for Espenson (personal correspondence, 23 January 2008) says:

> This is one of my favorite scripts ever. I love this one ... My only regret with this one was that I think the central notion that Buffy was acting out in response to Angel's), absence got lost. Many fans felt that she had forgotten Angel too quickly, when in fact, this episode was intended to demonstrate how she had NOT moved on at all.

So the reason for the episode, its power, the purpose of it (which is to advance our feelings for these characters and especially for Buffy's continuing loss of Angel), is what drives the writing. Yet the third draft still has changes to a scene that has minimal impact on these parts of the story:

> 41 GILES'S APARTMENT 41
> Giles, Willow and Xander are still poring over books and
> maps. They look pretty burned. Oz is going through Giles'
> record collection.

41.

CONTINUED:

(CONTINUED)

OZ
Okay, I'm either borrowing all your
albums or I'm moving in.

GILES
Oz, there are more important things
than records right now.

OZ
More important than this one?

OZ HOLDS UP A CLASSIC ALBUM (PINK FLOYD'S 'ANIMALS'?).

GILES
Yes, well, I suppose an argument
could be made ...

Xander is moving stacks of books ... and accidently reveals a

small TELEVISION SET tucked into a corner.

XANDER
Whoa. Giles has a TV. Everybody,
look at this, Giles has a TV! He's
shallow like us!

OZ
Gotta admit, a little disappointed.

GILES
I'm not– It's not–

WILLOW
Maybe it doesn't work.
Xander turns on the set. It works fine.

GILES
I keep it– Public television–
Look, everyone, we have vital work
to do. If this gem falls into
vampire hands, the Slayer is in
terrible danger. Television isn't
going to help us now.

WILLOW

(re TV news)

What's that?

INSERT: TV

A reporter narrates helicopter video of a muddy sinkhole with

a roadway partially collapsed into it.

42.

CONTINUED: (2)

(CONTINUED)

REPORTER (V.O.)
– around noon today in Brookside Park. Officials attributed the formation of the sinkhole to unexplained weakening of the topsoil support nearby. City work crews deny that any tunnelling has been done in the area ... Over the continuing report:

OZ
Tunnelling.

GILES
It's Spike. Come on. Xander, find Buffy and meet us there.

In this draft, we still have Xander proclaiming Giles's shallowness, we still have Oz holding up *Animals* and being disappointed by Giles's television, but Willow has changed her tune considerably. No longer a statement, she now simply expresses a hope that the television does not work. The implication that a television deprived of any utilitarian value would reduce its negative cultural implications might tend towards an idea of its being a statement or an art object, but it is much less pronounced than in the previous draft, and significantly removed from the comment in the episode as aired (see Figure 10). The scene has moved from simple plot device to character-driven interaction with plot discovery and action-creation at its climax. It has also created a debate it is itself engaged in: how does one read Giles's television? And, as part of this debate, how should a character, who has in some ways the most in common with Giles (Willow is bookish, ethnically distanced and who has even quite literally taken the place of his lover, though in very different domain), respond to this unexpected and seemingly

Figure 10 Xander discovers Giles's television in *Buffy the Vampire Slayer*, 'The Harsh Light of Day', season 4, episode 3, first broadcast 19 October 1999. Xander discovers Giles's television behind a stack of books and boxes, prompting his comment, 'Giles has a TV! He's shallow like us!'

unpleasant discovery? From a 'statement' to a simple desire that it be 'broken' to a declaration that it could be 'art' Willow's differing responses demonstrate a hesitancy that is fascinating, but ultimately inconclusive. Who it was who took the decision to include the word 'art' in the aired episode is unlikely to be discovered. Espenson says:

> In order for the idea to be cut and then make its way into the produced episode, it would almost certainly have been either Joss, or me, changing my mind – not, on our show, the director. Gotta be Joss or me. I simply don't remember which, but I'd guess it was Joss.

It is clear from what has already been said, that whoever changed the word would have needed Whedon's ok anyway. So, it is possible to suppose that Whedon is proposing a claim that a television that does not work is potentially art, but a television that works produces consumers who are simply shallow.

Except that the television has the last laugh. Giles, for the second time in as many minutes, disavows a medium from his position of high cultural separateness, only to be proven wrong. Television at about its most utilitarian and parochial (local news) is what provides the necessary clue for the gang. A staple of US television through its network and post-network (or TVI and TVII) days, local news still offers an essential function in the digital-global context of post-1995 TVIII.

It can be seen then, in this small scene, just how attentive to detail Whedon is, and how much control he asserts in this show. However, it is also clear that Espenson uses her own considerable talents to provide the characters with great dialogue, and to unfold the brief debate, The combination of writers (Espenson and Whedon), the debate about a cultural form and the drafting process allow the twin strengths of Whedon's shows to be seen: his intense and firm vision *and* his hiring of extremely talented individuals to enable that vision to come to life.

I now want to turn to 'Pangs' for a slightly different examination of a non-Whedon credited episode. Like 'Harsh Light' it confronts a popular cultural phenomenon, but here the phenomenon is the celebration of Thanksgiving. What Thanksgiving represents is part of the episode's purpose to explore, especially in the first act. My desire here is to provide an analysis of the episode as it was aired (with some important references to the drafting process), and to see how the episode provides us with Whedon's vision not just in terms of what is written, but also in terms of the continuing evolution of the format, and its adherence to some fundamental *Buffy* attributes.

'Pangs' was directed by Michael Lange. In addition to having directed the Marti Noxon scripted 'Surprise' (B S2E13), which was the first of the crucial two-parter that saw *Buffy* move to its new Tuesday night lot on The WB, Lange had also directed 'Band Candy' (B S3E6) which was Espenson's first credited script on the show. Experienced both in Whedon's general vision, and in Espenson's particular script-writing strengths, Lange would be able to direct a perfect example of a very ordinary episode. The 'ordinary' *Buffy* episode is still usually a very impressive 42 minutes of television art but is one that uses the show's established format to tell excellent stories and to develop characters in certain ways. By this I mean that it does not have a plot or character development of such proportions that it becomes a stand-out episode in terms of emotional intensity or story direction. Also, it is not an episode that deploys clear formal invention at the level of plot such that format or thematic expectations are significantly shifted. Less narratively dramatic than, for example, 'Passion' (B S2E17) where Jenny Calendar is killed; less mythos expanding than 'Out of Sight, out of Mind)' (B S1E11) where there is evidence that government agencies far beyond Sunnydale know about the supernatural; less formally innovative than 'Hush' (B S4E10) where there is little spoken dialogue for much of the episode; 'Pangs' is nevertheless an important – yet ordinary – episode.

'Pangs' is important in terms of its treatment of the history of Native Americans (see Pateman, 2006; Wilcox, 2011), and it is also a cross-over episode as discussed in Chapter 5. But its key import here, is that it is exemplary in terms of how the show mixes genre as a matter of course 'Pangs' is a generic hybrid because that is how *Buffy* has been created, not because of any ancillary thematic or discursive reasons. In addition to this, its writer (Espenson) has had a season's worth of experience of the writers' room and the creative process, and the director has been involved with the show since the middle of season 2. In this way, we can be confident that the team involved in the creation of the episode is working very closely to a well-understood Whedon vision of which they are already aware.

The discussion of 'Pangs' will offer an almost scene-by-scene description of the earlier part of the episode, which will seek to indicate the ways in which the episode mirrors the show's desire to work with comedy, horror and action in the presentation of a drama that offers acute character definition and story development. In so doing, it also seeks to indicate some of the ways in which Whedon organises and controls his shows. It will also, address the exposition scene as discussed in Chapter 1.

Espenson (personal correspondence, 5 January 2008) is very clear about where the genesis of the story came from, and very firmly classes it as a Whedon episode:

> This was an episode in which he had an extremely clear vision and I was just there to carry it out. He determined every scene and every act break. He also extensively rewrote act three ... the yam recipe that Giles is working with is Joss's personal recipe, for example.

Not only the general story, then, is largely Whedon-created, but also its thematic drive and character response. However, the writer's job is to provide the episode with its particular shape, detail, resonance and Espenson certainly does that. As she (personal correspondence, 5 January 2008) points out:

> BUT ... I am very proud of the personal touches I managed to insert. I only had a few days to write the episode, and I started by doing some short-and-intensive Chumash Indian research. It was when I found the list of ways that the Chumash had suffered (cut-off ears, syphilis, etc.), that Joss realised those could help shape the story. Spike getting shot with arrows was not part of the original plan, either, but was something that came out of my first draft. And, of course, the dialogue was largely mine. 'What's a ricer?' 'You made a bear, undo it,' 'Sorry about that Chief,' 'A yam-sham.' (However, the iconic Spike speech about the plight of the Indians was pretty much all Joss – I never wrote a version that was quite harsh enough).

One of the instructive things here is that Espenson highlights some of the most memorable lines of the episode, and they are memorable because they are funny. Comedy is such a central plank of *Buffy* that it can be easy to overlook just how unusual it is to have a drama so heavily engaged in comic moments. Whedon seems almost brazen in his belief in his writers' capacity to be funny: 'All of my writers are extremely funny, so it's easy to make [*Buffy*] funnier. The hard part is getting the stuff that matters more' (Lavery and Burkhead, 2011: 31) Alongside the comedy, however, there is mention of the dramatic requirements of the episode, and especially the debate that takes place between Buffy, Willow, Giles and Spike about the relative merits of trying to kill Hus, the Chumash tribe vengeance spirit. The transmutation of Hus into a bear is a good illustration of the action/fantasy/horror aspect of the show, and I now want to offer an analysis of the episode drawing attention to the merging of these generic components. And it is worth noting that while I am going to be looking primarily at framing, lighting and, to a certain extent, at sound, these are the tools used to animate what is already absolutely explicit in the scripts: 'in almost all the episodes, the attempt to keep all three wells [comedy, action, horror] full at all times was something that we all strove to do. The juxtaposition of tones wasn't found on the set, but is built into the scripts' (Espenson, personal correspondence, 7 January 2008).

This building-in of generic diversity is not simply a formal trick in some episodes, it is a defining feature of the show's format, and to a certain extent a defining feature of a Whedon series. Indeed, I would go so far as to say that a defining characteristic of a successful Whedon format is the implicit anti-format it carries within it to the extent that every aspect of a show that becomes potentially predictable is open for revision. In the teaser to 'Pangs', a development from outline to second draft sees a simple fight between Buffy and a vampire called Kit become something different. The stage direction has 'A young, sweet-faced student-type, JAMIE' ('Pangs' second draft) looking nervous and worried. Buffy's arrival would seem to indicate safety for the boy, but Buffy punches him. The innocent victim has been re-imagined sufficiently by Whedon that an audience accepts that a young man could be in that role rather than the 'young blonde' *Buffy* sought to critique, but not content to simply reverse types, Whedon encourages his team to have the victim become the villain thereby affirming a trope from traditional horror (the bad guy is a guy) but only after having had the audience accept that the victim could be a man and might need a young woman to save him.

Having successfully asserted the show's major premise (Buffy hunts vampires and makes the world a safer place), and maintained its belief in modulating its own format, the rest of the episode works to do both of these things via the genre-busting espoused by Whedon.

The opening act revolves around setting up the threat to be faced by the team, and this itself is contextualised via Thanksgiving. A ceremony is taking place to commemorate the work beginning on a new culture centre that will celebrate America's 'melting pot'. The ceremony is being watched from the shade of a tree by Buffy, Willow and Anya and while Buffy and Willow debate the relative merits of Thanksgiving (Pateman, 2006), Anya is much more focused on the body of Xander who is one of the construction team. Anya's very expressive sexual desire, and her willingness to tell the others about exactly what fantasies she is having is cause for genuine humour and is effected via framing. While the three of them appear in long shot, framed together at times, the more usual construction of the scene is for Buffy and Willow to be in medium close up together with a cut to Anya in medium close up on her own, or with a small part of Buffy also in frame. The sense of Anya's partial isolation from the group is neatly manifested in the framing, but the framing also helps to provide her comments with a 'punch line' feel, as they are said with her on her own in frame, and our concentration focused entirely on her. A major shift away from this framing occurs when Anya contributes to the debate. Lamenting the thought that Buffy might not have a Thanksgiving dinner, Anya says 'Well, I think it's a shame. I love a ritual sacrifice.' Buffy tries to disabuse her of the notion that it is 'a one of those', but Anya persists: 'To commemorate a past event you kill and eat an animal. It's a ritual sacrifice. With pie.' One of the great comic additions, 'With pie' was included in the second draft and replaced the previous punch line, 'I'll bring sodas', from the original script.

What makes the line work so effectively is not simply the excellence of the writing, but the delivery and the framing of the delivery. For this brief part of the scene, director Michael Lange breaks up the earlier patterns of composition and has the characters organised like this, as shown in Figure 11. Here the medium shot composition of Anya on her own, or Buffy and Willow together, is replaced with a shot that has head and shoulder shots of Willow and Buffy at the extreme front of the screen with the backs of their heads to us, Anya half turned to camera, so we get a semi-profile, and, and this is the crucial thing, Xander in the distance, out of focus and just left of central. Anya's 'with pie' comment, which is funny enough in its own right, is said with the previous cause of the scene's humour, Xander and his sexual prowess, in shot but out of focus. The drama-debate frame of Willow and Buffy and the comedy punch line frame of Anya are replaced with a frame that allows both the drama-debate and the comedy to be united in a visual synthesis that is as good an exemplum of the overall style as one could hope for (see Figure 11).

The natural, outdoors lighting of this scene, is immediately juxtaposed with the darkness of the basement into which Xander falls, and the

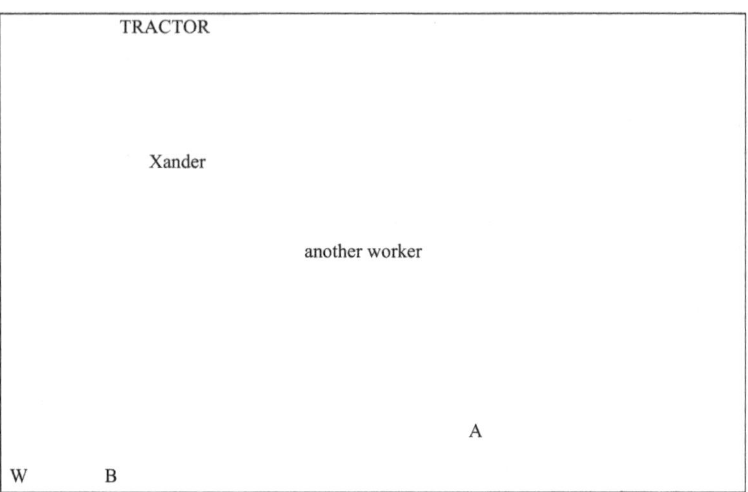

Figure 11 Diagram showing the relative placements of Anya, Buffy, Willow and Xander in the opening act of 'Pangs', season 4, episode 8, first broadcast 23 November 1999.

directional lighting as the sun streams in through the dust, and cuts a sharp left-right diagonal from top to bottom of screen. This lighting style, sharp diagonals casting shadows is used even in relatively domestic scenes such as the following one where Willow and Buffy are in their dorm and the shutters of the window provide muted shafts on the wall. Here a preferred lighting signature (stylised directional lighting and shadow) is used to light two very different genre components: one action-horror, the other domestic drama, but the continuation and modulation of style is what allows the show to maintain integrity and uniformity, even amidst its generic mixing.

As mentioned in Chapter 4, another common feature in *Buffy*, and also one that contributes to the integrity of the show, is the use of a line at the end of one scene to act as the link to the next scene. This link can operate in a number of ways, but tends to utilise a thematic cross-over that may then be ironised for comedic effect. As Buffy and Willow end their discussion, Buffy laments the fact that 'everyone has a place to go to' for Thanksgiving. The setting up of the image of familial unity and domestic warmth are immediately undercut by a cut to a scene of Spike, alone, frightened, wrapped in a tawdry blanket. This structural feature was written into the script and although the wording changed from draft to draft (Buffy mentions the 'comforts of home' in drafts one and two), the structure is identical. The shots of Spike evoke period drama, especially a David Lean style Dickensian view. The visual creation of the period-vision, especially in a later scene where Spike stands outside a derelict house watching a group of vampires feasting on their prey, allied with this structured juxtaposition (this later scene is set-up with Angel bemoaning his fate in having to stand outside of Buffy's life, looking in) demonstrates again how carefully Whedon's creation does not simply offer a smorgasbord of generic styles, but rather weaves these disparate elements together in a visually and narratively unifying whole.

As the commando boys of the Initiative chase Spike, one of them insults Riley, calling him a 'mother's boy' during a fake cough. Riley warns him that he might need to be quarantined, as we 'don't want anyone getting sick'. This is succeeded by a cut to Xander's basement and a close up of Xander looking very sick indeed. Again, the generic differences (action movie, night time commando fighters and bright directional interior lighting in a domestic space) are untied via the storytelling.

What is interesting here, is that the scene that unfolds between the sick Xander and the initially angry Anya, who has gone to his work place to see him digging only to discover he is not there, can be viewed very much as a comedy. Indeed, the sexual innuendo, domestic squabbling, loving resolution and basement situation all lend themselves very much to a sitcom style scene. And the scene is doing two things in terms of narrative. First it is establishing that Xander is very sick and second it is offering us and the characters a real sense that there is genuine affection between them. One of these is an episodically important story, the other is season-arc related (though these obviously intertwine). Deciding on which to prioritise is important, then, in terms of where the viewer's primary interest in the scene will lie. In the first draft, the move from the commandos was heralded by one of the characters observing that their commander (and psychology professor) can, when mad, 'get pretty scary'. This is followed by a cut to Xander's basement and the stage instruction, 'Anya storms in angry ...'. This clearly establishes the relationship as uttermost (while maintaining the narrative link between the two generically distinct scenes). The second draft has shifted the emphasis to Xander's illness with Riley asserting that Spike (or Hostile 17 as the Initiative have termed him) will be getting tired and weak, with Forrest responding wanly 'Yeah, well aren't we all.' We then cut to Xander's basement with Xander's ill visage and lethargic body being the centre of attention.

The move from Xander and Anya into the next scene is also introduced by juxtaposition of dialogue. Anya declares she likes whatever it is that is causing Xander's illness, largely because it has prompted him to call her his 'girlfriend' thus shifting the scene from sitcom to a beautifully modulated moment of drama as Anya is visibly affected by this assertion. Her comment takes us to the mission that Xander had fallen into. Its gloomy interior is broken by directional lighting and the appearance of a green 'miasma'. The discordant pan pipe music completes the horror genre, which is continued into the next scene which will be the climax of Act 1.

It opens with an angled close up on a pair of threatening looking scissors. Discordant strings play as we pan up to the curator's face, and then track back to allow the small space in the room to open up and let the curator step into it. This happens very quickly with the strings at moderately high tempo. A lamp offers practical lighting, which is supplemented by lights seemingly from outside the room cutting through the gloom. The curator is crouching at a glass cabinet. The shots have been either angled, fast tracking, or close up. Our view is partially fragmented. When we can see the full room briefly, the green miasma appears. As the curator crouches, it swirls inside the glass cabinet. The scene is derived entirely from horror shots, framing, lighting and sound. As the miasma turns into what we will know as Hus, the Chumash vengeance spirit, and he slits the curator's throat, we are unmistakably in the world of the macabre.

Act 2 opens in the same locale, with Buffy and Willow investigating the death. The lighting is similar, but the shots are much more medium long shots (as far as the space will allow) and medium shots. The framing dispels the sense of restriction and closeness, and the comic dialogue undercuts the content of the violence of the death. Only the persistent drumbeat and ethereal pan pipes provide much of link to the horror genre of the previous scene. However, as Willow asks Buffy to describe the artefact that was stolen from the cabinet, Buffy's response is 'pretty darn scary'.

From the earliest draft, this had been written as a Buffy voice over occurring between this scene and the next where we are in Giles's apartment. The seeming exposition, though, is a brilliant moment of comedy-as-edit where it transpires that Buffy is not describing the deadly Chumash knife, but rather her recent shopping trip. And this allows for the wonderful congruence of story, character and theme. The episode now develops into a search for Hus, especially in the light of Xander's illness being a consequence of Hus's spell. However, it is also a debate between characters who each stand in a different position relating to the moral dilemmas posed by Hus being a Native Indian. I shall come to the debate scene shortly, but here we have the beginning of Buffy's conflict – she wants to resolve the Hus situation, but even more, she wants a beautiful Thanksgiving. Her role as action-horror heroine is at odds with her desire to exist in an idealised family drama world, and this leads to great comedy.

The character-based and narrative-drive fusion of genres is matched by some beautiful framing in this scene that allows for the range of emotional and narrative levels to find an excellent visual counterpoint. This is achieved through having Giles's apartment provide two very different kinds of frame. The combined efforts of Carey Myer, production designer, Caroline Quinn, set designer, David Koneff, set decorator and Johnny Youngblood, on-set dresser, produce a room that has a frame within a frame. Looking through the living space to where the kitchen wall is, we see a rectangular area that could serve as a large serving hatch, or simply a be a glassless window (see Figure 12). What it does is allow the director to shift between long shots that have the lounge and kitchen wall in frame with the wall acting as an internal frame for the characters; and then to pan in to the kitchen itself, where a much more intimate frame is possible.

The long shot appears very staged, very still, very beautiful and grand; the shots in the kitchen have a greater sense of energy and fluidity and provide a sitcom and/or soap opera sensibility. Interestingly, the practical lighting from the downlighters on the kitchen cupboard veer between a sitcom-style wash lighting effect and a much more 'authentic'

Figure 12 Giles's apartment, *Buffy the Vampire Slayer*, 'Pangs', season 4, episode 8, first broadcast 23 November 1999. Giles's apartment with the frame-within-the-frame. As broadcast you would see the perfectly balanced composition, as well as the care of the colours (Giles's grey clothes that blend perfectly with the cupboards and wall decorations, for example).

British realist drama such as *Cathy Come Home*, or even an effect from the Dogma film makers.

As Buffy leaves, we are shown that Angel has been overhearing everything. He steps from his hiding place into the living area at the other end from the kitchen and the lighting once again becomes darker, with Angel's face cast in shadows, as he stands in front of dark coloured upholstery and furnishings. Giles is still in the light of the kitchen against a greenish wall. Each character's lighting suits their role on the show, yet ostensibly in the same space. Show format combines with generic code and character role to provide a seamless yet extraordinarily variegated palette of colour, texture and frame.

The final section of this episode I want to look at (though a whole book could be written on it alone) is a moment in Act 3 during the debate about what to do with Hus. I have written before about this marvellous scene in terms of the ways in which character and plot combine exactly to produce thematically consistent and subtle arguments that express not only a character's attitude to Hus, but tell us more broadly about their general relationship to history (Pateman, 2006).

As mentioned above, Whedon wrote much of this scene because Jane Espenson was never harsh enough. Notwithstanding that fact, one of the things that makes the scene so successful is the way in which Buffy continues to operate as a would-be idealised soap opera hostess while resisting her role as action-horror slayer. (Whedon frequently highlights the enormous tensions faced by the young woman Buffy Summers and the vampire slayer: its often tragic inflection is here given a sitcom twist.)

What is also interesting about this scene is the extent to which, because of the political sensitivities of the demon in question, and also because of the younger people's developing self-confidence and the concomitant side-lining of Giles who is no longer a watcher or school librarian, the whole scene is a version of the exposition scene. Giles's authority has not been entirely superseded, but it has been undermined enough that Willow will not simply accept his explanation of things, and, in this instance, Buffy's desire to produce a decent Thanksgiving meal means that she is not convinced by his position. Giles's exposition becomes a group debate; a format essential has become translated into something new, but something that retains the essence of the format (the giving of information) and also retains a formal staple – generic hybridity.

As a row rages between Willow and Giles, and a separate one is boiling between Xander and Anya, we have Spike offering his own incendiary comments. The house, it seems, is in a soap opera melee as each person's comment is offered in a head shot followed by another head shot, and a dialogue track that includes all the competing voices.

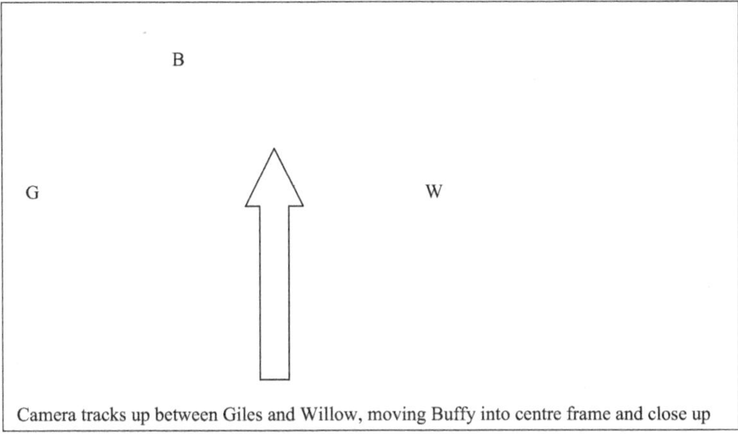

Figure 13 Diagram showing the movement of the camera as Xander and Anya row, Giles and Willow disagree, and Buffy just wants to baste in 'Pangs', season 4, episode 8, first broadcast 23 November 1999.

Amid this din, we see Buffy. She is standing, physically quite close to, but gesturally very distant from, the other characters. She is holding a bowl and stirring its contents very vigorously. She tries unsuccessfully to interject once or twice. She is pouting, visibly, even exaggeratedly, unhappy – more sulky child than upset adult. The lighting could cover either soap or sitcom and there is no music, just the arguments. A frame emerges that has Giles mid-screen on the left, Willow mid-screen on the right and Buffy in the distance, slightly to the left of centre and stirring her bowl. The camera is focused on her. As it moves forward the sounds of Giles and Willow continue but they are visually pushed to the side and then exterior of the frame as Buffy becomes central (see Figure 13).

The verbal violence of the soap opera and its attendant visual manifestation are lost and Buffy, in a voice that is of a petulant little girl, declares loudly, though not shouting: 'This is no good.' There is a beat, silence and then 'I have to baste.' She turns sharply to the left and exits the frame. The camera's tracking had produced a frame in which soap opera had been discarded and Sarah Michelle Gellar's acting allowed Espenson's script its full sitcom potential. It is a tiny, but marvellous, example of Whedon's desire to have, routinely, divergent styles and genres, and their attendant emotional and narratorial possibilities standing side by side, not only across scenes but within scenes too.

'Pangs' because it is ordinary, is also exemplary. It is an exemplary episode in two ways. The first is the way in which it illustrates the intermingling and cross-pollination of genres within any one *Buffy* episode; the other is its demonstration of the creative control that Whedon has over episodes that do not carry his name as either writer or director. From initial story idea, to plotting the beats, to minor suggestions to rewriting whole speeches, Whedon's contribution to every single *Buffy* episode is great. His creative control over *Angel*, as discussed elsewhere in this book was much less intense, in part because of the effort he was putting into the development of *Firefly*.

The Espenson-penned *Firefly* episode, 'Shindig' provides the audience with a view of one of the central planets, with greater wealth, strongly defied social etiquette and a well-delineated class system. Part antebellum South, the planet contrasts to the more 'wild west' of the outer planets and Mal's crew. In the episode, Mal offends Kaylee who wants to wear a pretty dress and, much more seriously, Atherton Wing, one of Inara's clients. Wing challenges Mal to a duel with swords and Inara tries to teach Mal how to sword fight. This scene allows for Mal's contempt of Inara's job but respect for her as a person to be established, as well as highlighting Inara's extraordinary capacity to be comfortable in almost any environment without ever, seemingly, adapting to it; while also always being somehow separate from it.

This thematic and character aspect – the ability (or otherwise) to inhabit differing cultures – is set up in the teaser section. The scene is in a pool hall, dominated by men and drab except for Inara who is 'the only color, the only elegance'. Mal and Jayne are playing pool with two men who, it transpires, are slave traders. The sci-fi element is maintained with the balls flickering, disappearing briefly then re-appearing, and the bartender pointing to a sign that says, 'Management not responsible for ball failure' (which provides an interesting counterpoint to Jowett's discussion of materiality in the show, see page 191).

Mal suggests that Inara might want to leave but she replies that it is 'entertaining, actually', which surprises Mal. She says, 'I like watching the game. As with other situations, the key seems to be handing Jayne a heavy stick and standing back.' Her poise and self-possession emanate with a quiet and absolute assurance. Even as a glass smashes near her and she heads for the exit, she has the composure to remark drily to the bartender, 'Nice place. I'll tell my friends.'

The scene is short, pithy, amusing and (re-)establishes Mal's penchant for violence and his malleable ethics (he steals from the men but justifies it because it is money derived from slave trading). Jayne's willingness to overlook anything if it turns a profit is also made clear. And Inara's capacity to be entirely at ease in a place while being noticeable out of place in it is also briefly and joyfully presented. This will contrast greatly with Mal's utter incapacity to be at ease, and his conspicuous inability to adhere to prevailing mores.

But the teaser as aired is the culmination of at least six different iterations and rewrites by Espenson. The first appearance is in the pre-outline:

> SALOON – NIGHT 1
> MAL, ZOE, KAYLEE and JAYNE enter a grubby-looking dive planetside. INARA accompanies them tentatively, not sure this is the place for her. Mal assures her it'll be a fine, well-behaved, high-class evening.
>
> CUT TO:
>
> 2 SALOON – LATER 2
> Huge fist-fight in mid-swing. A few quick shots and then we ...
>
> CUT TO:
>
> 3 SERENITY – CARGO BAY – LATER 3
> Our group straggles up the ramp into the cargo bay. Zoe, Mal and Jayne are bruised but exhilarated. Kaylee is laughing and a little drunk. Inara, her hem torn, follows behind. She takes no part in the revelry. She's not part of that world.

Here, Inara's separation from much of the crew is much more central to the teaser, and it is her lack of comfort that is highlighted. Also, Kaylee and Zoe's presence alienates her more emphatically than just being different from Mal and Jayne. While this establishes her difference (as the aired teaser does), it makes her vulnerable and lonely.

The second iteration, in the outline, offers a similar sense of her alienation from the crew and the activity of the ship. It explicitly locates her as existing in not just a separate shuttle, but a different world:

> SERENITY – NIGHT 1
> INARA is on her shuttle. Soft music plays. She wears a beautiful kimono in jewel tones. She kneels at a low table, copying a poem from a thin volume onto a piece of thick luxurious paper.
> She finishes, rolls the paper, ties it with a ribbon and exits ...
> Onto the catwalk over the cargo bay – noise and dirt. Dust hangs in the air. Below her, MEN are off-loading tractors –

there is shouting, revving, clanking. She makes her way along the catwalk.
She moves down the stairs, ignoring stares and catcalls from the men. One of them is coming up the stairs and he barely lets her by, forcing her to push past. He leers at her as she goes.
Downstairs now, she heads into the infirmary, where SIMON is treating JAYNE's hand. It was squished by a tractor. Jayne lets loose with lots of Chinese swearing.
Inara finds RIVER pressed against the glass, watching her brother. Inara tries to engage River. She gives her the roll of paper ... 'your brother told me you used to like poetry. I found this poem and I wrote it down for you.'
River thanks her and tears up the poem ... as if that's what you're supposed to do with them. She seems to enjoy it. Inara bites her tongue, tries to smile back.
MAL enters, in a brisk and backslappin' mood. He's loving all the activity on the ship. These are the sounds of profit and productivity and people. Mal tells Inara, now that the tractors are out on the surface, he can give her a ride if she wants.
Inara shakes her head, that's all right. She walks back toward the peace of her shuttle.

END OF TEASER

Apart from the shift in location to the ship, and the brief but important appearance of many of the characters that shows the isolation of Inara, the brilliant description of Mal's 'brisk and backslappin'' mood is a masterclass of brevity and precision. However, this was clearly not favoured, and by the time of the first draft proper, the location has shifted again.

JULY 8, 2002

TEASER

1 COUNTRYSIDE – DAY 1
MAL and INARA stroll along a picturesque path. Dappled sunshine, nodding flowers, that kind of stuff.

INARA
I've lost sight of the others.

MAL

(RELUCTANTLY)
We could catch up.

INARA
That's all right.

(THEN)
I'm glad you decided to keep
Serenity here another day.

MAL
I was waiting on a job, but no
luck. We'll move tomorrow. Reckon
there'll be something on
Persephone.

INARA
It does seem to be an excellent
place to find crime.

MAL
I just hope we're the perpetrators.

(THEN)
I never knew 'bout this part a'
Badwater. I mean, you figure, they
call a place Badwater ...

INARA
I love walking here. There's a
concept, Ahimsa. It's about
harmony, walking softly on the
earth, doing no harm.

Into this bucolic, contemplative moment storms Mal's gun-toting cowboy self, as he suddenly shoots dead a raccoon, commends his own shooting, saying, 'Head shot too! You know how hard that is with a pistol?' as Jayne lunges into the picture with a huge knife and the two men gut the animal and discuss eating it for dinner. Inara just walks away. Here, the shared enjoyment of the walk that seems to offer a point of contact for Mal and Inara is simply a device to highlight the actually much stronger shared purpose of Mal and Jayne. Again, Inara is not just separate, but weak.

By the second draft (15 July), we are in the pool hall that we see in the aired episode, but there is still quite some finessing to do to get the characters where Whedon wants them. In response to Mal's amazement that Inara is enjoying the evening, she continues:

INARA
I like watching people. And the
game is very exiting. Jayne seems
to be clearing the table.

ANGLE ON:
Jayne, sinking one of the few
remaining balls.

MAL
You're following the game?

INARA
We play billiards in my circles,
too, Captain. We just do it in
private homes. And we fill the
pockets with caviar.

Here, the explicit contrasting of her circles and the world she is in is perhaps unnecessary as the situation itself implies such a difference. It also could be suggested that it over-states the extent to which Inara has any circles in which she is completely at home. Her exit is also different from the aired version, with her self-apostrophising indicating, again, that she is somehow the victim of Mal:

Inara backs out of the way fast, tucking the money into her
gown. She ducks under a swinging pool cue and steps over a
fallen brawler.

INARA

(SOFTLY)
'Come to the pool hall, Inara.
Loosen up, have fun.'

While her poise is present and the scene shows her coping with and enjoying the evening, it does not have the calm self-possession of the final version (see Figure 14). The third draft (19 July) is largely as we see the final version, although her parting shot still has not been decided upon:

Inara, backed against the wall, jumps when a GLASS SHATTERS
near her head. She heads toward the door, fast.

INARA
I'll just pay for that drink next
time ...

Even by the fourth draft (25 July), which is the final one before shooting, the final line is in progress:

Inara jumps when a GLASS SHATTERS near her head. She heads
toward the door, fast. She passes the bartender as she
goes.

Figure 14 Inara in *Firefly*, 'Shindig', episode 4, first broadcast 1 November 2002. After many attempts, the teaser to 'Shindig' was agreed upon and Inara here wears red and sips a bright drink in the otherwise beige and dingy bar she finds herself in.

INARA

(DRILY)
Lovely place. I'll tell my
friends.

The teaser, so important in establishing the tone of the episode, has gone through several revisions in order to ensure that character is in exactly the right place for the rest of the show. The attention to detail, the importance of getting it right, the utter refusal to allow something to air that is not exactly as wanted must be a source of great frustration for the writing team, but also of great pride in their work.

Even at the level of naming minor characters we can see this process. Atherton Wing, begins as Asher Fizgerald, which becomes Atherton Fitzgerald, goes to Atherton Lee, before becoming Atherton Wing in the second draft. A similar transformation occurs in Espenson's 'Guise will be Guise' (A S2E6) where Wesley's love interest begins as Holland in the outline and first draft before becoming Virginia in the second draft.

Espenson says:

> Atherton Wing – It changed? I didn't remember that. Possibly a problem getting a name to clear? Maybe just me playing around to get a name I liked? Or sometimes you pick a name and then realise it's too similar to a character you already have established [Holland Manners, a senior lawyer at Wolfram and Hart].

> The girl in 'Guise will be Guise'–that I do remember. The first name I picked (which I thought was Georgia something) was considered (by David Greenwalt) to be too fakey. Like a romance novel name. He was absolutely right, and that's something now that bothers me in the writing of others–names like Alexandra Cathcart ... it's almost like they're drag queen names, you know? Over the top. But I had that joke that depended on it being a place name. ('You were in ___?') So then I tried another place name (that might be where Holland came in?). I think it was finally Joss who picked Virginia, just because we were running out of place name names. No other reason as far as I know.

A minor character in a relatively unimportant episode (story-wise) in a series that is often regarded as not having much Whedon involvement still has her name chosen by him.

This chapter has illustrated the laborious and challenging job of writing for a show where the show runner has such a clear and precise sense of what he wants, But I hope also to have shown just how much creativity, talent and skill the writers display, and, especially, the particular talents of Jane Espenson. The same level of commitment will, I hope, be demonstrated in the next chapter.

'Why'd this get so complicated?': Narrative and televisual analysis via *Firefly* 7

One of the mainstays of television criticism is an analysis of a show's narrative, usually linked to a hermeneutic enterprise. My own *Aesthetics of Buffy* is an example of this, and most essays and chapters on Whedon's work pursue this method. There are exceptions, of course, such as, pleasingly ironic for this example's purpose, David Lavery's (2002b) 'A religion in narrative' that describes Whedon's own stated belief in the power and importance of narrative from which Lavery's article draws its title:

> It's about the show, and I feel the same way about it. I get the same way. It's not like being a rock star. It doesn't feel like they're reacting to me. It's really sweet when people react like that, and I love the praise, but to me, what they're getting emotional about is the show. And that's the best feeling in the world. There's nothing creepy about it. I feel like there's a religion in narrative, and I feel the same way they do. I feel like we're both paying homage to something else; they're not paying homage to me. (Lavery, 2002b: n.p.)

Like many religions, it is not entirely obvious what the object of devotion actually is, though. Whedon has been working in an era of considerable change, and the technological, production, distribution and playback developments have provided significant opportunity and challenge to makers of televisual narrative art. In 2007, the *New Review of Film and Television Studies* published the important edition on what was dubbed 'TV III', which I shall have cause to return to. In the same year, Netflix introduced its streaming media content paving the way for even greater changes than the journal could have imagined, and fundamentally challenging the foundations of long-form televisual narrative drama by developing its own production wing, which in 2013 released *House of Cards*. The range of on-demand streaming platforms is growing and the 'dump' model (McCormick, 2017) changes consumption patterns enormously.

The challenges and opportunities presented by TV III and its successors, generate a number of important theoretical questions about that nature of televisual narrative. This chapter will address this theoretical set of questions first, and then discuss *Firefly* as an exemplary text that illustrates the limits of televisual narrative analysis.

As with much theory, the questions I am posing can seem to fall in to Monty Python's 'bleeding obvious' category, but from the seemingly obvious questions can arise very complex answers. The first, and most important, question about narrative is what its defining feature is. For Paul Ricoeur (1985) in his magisterial but often gnomic *Time and Narrative* volumes 1 and 2, the notion of mimesis is central. This incredibly awkward concept, however important, is a largely literary phenomenon (although there will be need to return to it later in the simplified guise of 'format'), and it is, it seems to me, the title of Ricoeur's book that offers us what, for audio-visual analysis, is the most prominent feature: time. Narrative happens necessarily through time. And it is time and its different relationship with narrative that I want to briefly sketch an idea about.

Broadly speaking, there are two aspects of time that are important to any analysis of televisual narrative. The first is the total temporality of the televisual narrative world. The second is the duration of the viewer's engagement with this world. The first of these is what scholars typically attend to (although even here there are enormously difficult theoretical questions that need to be posed); the latter is less frequently considered.

By 'the total temporality' of the televisual narrative world I mean all of the events, actions, interactions, words, images and sounds that constitute the progress of the televisual narrative world from the opening of the episode that encloses the world, to the ending of the episode that encloses that world. This poses some additional initial questions. First, should we think of each of the characters' own narratives as an individual expression of temporality? Second, if the episode uses analepsis and prolepsis should these be considered separate modes of temporality? (Lorna Jowett [2014a: 297–311] provides an exceptional account of the use of these techniques across Whedon's shows.) Third, given the story arc nature of many shows, should each episode be considered a closed narrative object, and if not, how do we account for the temporal interrelationship between episodes? In some ways, my discussion of 'Restless' in *Aesthetics* sought to address some of these issues, but more work needs to be done to allow the theoretical questions and the possible answers to them to inform our analytical/hermeneutic practice.

I will return to these issues when considering *Firefly*, but I want to briefly introduce the other set of questions around engagement duration.

In another book in this series, Dave Rolinson (2005) discusses Alan Clarke's dramas in the 1960s and 1970s. An obvious point to make, but a crucial one, is that if the drama were on BBC, it would run continuously for one hour, and in the moment of viewing, there would have been no expectation that one could watch it again. In other words, the total temporality of the televisual narrative work that Rolinson discusses is engaged with by the viewer for the full duration of its hour-long existence. If the viewer did not engage with the show for the full duration then s/he would miss parts of its world and would be unlikely to ever view them. The durationality was of necessity total and unique.

A similar show on a commercial network during the same period would have required a similar relationship with duration but with some differences. First, the total temporality of the televisual world would have been shorter to accommodate the commercial breaks. Second, these breaks, though not part of the total temporality of the world do constitute or contribute to the durational engagement with it. The paratextual nature of television flow has been discussed by, among others, Kackman *et al.* (2011) in their *Flow: TV in the Age of Media Convergence* but here the point is that duration of engagement and the total temporality are always different in advert-funded television. Notwithstanding this, and possible differences of content in the commercial breaks dependent on which regional provider you were watching, the structure of engagement in both cases (commercial and BBC) would be shared by the viewing audiences: a total, hour-long engagement for the BBC show; an interrupted engagement for the commercial show, but with the interruptions and their timings being the same everywhere. Again, the experience would have been experienced as a unique viewing experience insofar as watching the show again would have been impossible.

The importance of the relationship between total temporality of the televisual word and the duration of engagement becomes clearer when we enter the era of the videocassette recorder (VCR), commonly videos. As has been discussed by Alison Lury the VCR changes the nature of duration in two important ways. First, it allows the viewer to 'time-shift' (Lury, 2005: 107) it makes the act of re-watching possible thereby eradicating the sense of the unique viewing experience. It is not clear exactly how that knowledge of the iterability of experience affects the first viewing (which may still be a unique viewing, of course), but it must have some kind of affective impact. And, as importantly, the viewer is no longer bound to passively receive the unfolding information stream as it flows. S/he can pause and stop the temporality of the show (Lury, 2005: 108); s/he can even reverse or fast-forward it. The viewer now has some kind of control over the relationship with the temporality of the televisual world, at least to the extent of determining the durational mode of that relationship.

This control becomes even more pronounced with the advent of DVDs and then Blu-ray discs, and as Cathy Johnson (2007: 6–24) has asserted, the new technologies do not just create a new mode of consumption (based on an alteration of the relationship with time) but also produce new modes of production as the viewer's ability to manipulate durationality encourage producers to extend the possibility of the total temporality of the televisual worlds by, for example, referring to an event in an episode in season one of one show in the final episode of a different show representing the same imagined world (see Chapter 5 for a discussion of this in relation to *Angel*).

If videos and DVDs are technologies of information storage, there have been even more advances in the technologies of playback. These have led to whole new ways on interacting with total temporality to the extent of editing and splicing together favourite bits of shows, mash ups and so on. As mentioned, the growth of on-demand television series on platforms such as Netflix offers similar queries. Casey McCormick (2017: n.p.), for example, says:

> Therefore, I'm interested in two questions: how do on-demand native series take advantage of their distribution format to tell stories in new ways? And how does on-demand viewing change our experience of serial television, especially with regard to endings?'

While there is much to say on this matter, I want to discuss how the changing technologies of storage and playback, and their resultant influence on the duration of engagement, have another important impact.

Returning to our 1960 example, a defining feature of the relationship between the total temporality of the televisual world and the duration of the engagement with it would have been almost certainly limited to sitting in a specific space and watching the moving images on a static piece of furniture. The experience is likely to have been shared with family members (for those living in family units, which was a much higher percentage of the population in the UK than today) and the show being watched is likely to have been one of only two or three available. As such, the experience of the relationship between temporality and durationality would have been more commonly shared. This, too, must have an influence on how the show was received by an individual viewer.

The somatic experience (including duration) is often ignored by scholars as it seems to suggest too much subjectivity, too little scholarly distance. However if the eliciting of emotion is one of the drivers for Whedon in creating his televisual worlds, the contexts that might determine our ability to receive that emotion seem to me to be essential. This is not a plea for a criticism of uncritical personal enthusiasm, but it is a claim that the contexts of our reception (ever-adapting, as the duration of engagement has illustrated) are a legitimate component in, at least, how we frame our critical responses.

As an example, by the time *Buffy* was being aired, the changing demographic of the USA in terms of family structure; the proliferation of cable and subscription channels; the emergence of the DVD and web all had an impact on the duration and somatic experience of watching television. I had begun watching *Buffy* on BBC2 in its teatime slot with my girlfriend. It became a must-watch show very quickly, and the playing of Nerf Herder's theme tune always led to joyful semi-parodic head banging. The small flat I watched it in over-looked the sea, and the television was the central feature of the room (not a posh TV, but it was positioned such). We moved into a house with an upstairs bedroom, which I turned into an office with a desktop computer and dial up. By this point we were collecting the video box sets (we could not afford a DVD player) and my girlfriend began frequenting the chat rooms and discussion boards devoted to *Buffy* (and they were devoted to *Buffy* rather than to Whedon). My girlfriend discovered someone who recorded and then uploaded the episodes as they aired in the USA. Four segments, each about eleven minutes long would be uploaded. It could take up to six hours to download one segment with dial-up. Usually, two days after the airing in the USA we would have the episode on the desktop. It played in low resolution in a screen about 4 cm square. Any assessment I was making at that time about the total temporality of the televisual world was clearly limited by poor-quality images, but also heightened by the sheer effort that went into being able to see any episode. Soon we would invite a couple of friends around to watch with us. Glasses of wine in hand, chairs pulled as close to the desk as we could, we strained together to watch the show. In a very Whedonesque way, we had recreated through pastiche a twenty-first-century simulacrum of the 1960s living room – a found family shared viewing, all eyes fixed on a static object of furniture.

The duration of the relationship here was hugely extended, by virtue of the time it took to download. But that download time was part of the duration, part of the relationship, constituted the build-up and excitement. Equally, the duration of the relationship with the show itself was extended as we would pause, to pour wine, discuss ideas, ponder outcomes. I do not think these experiences are unique to me, and they are very important to my affective relationship and my critical relationship with the show. While it is easy to criticise some Whedon scholarship for being too fan-oriented, those initial relationships with the show, and the specific durational extensions mean that these aspects need to be acknowledged in the criticism – they should not dominate the criticism but they should be recognised as informing it.

Somatic experience as a function of durationality can have other, less sustained but equally important influence of affective and critical judgement. Arguing neighbours, a broken leg, thunder storms outside, sitting on a bus with earphones and smartphone, being in a lecture theatre for a class on a show, being fifteen, being forty-five, being straight, being gay, stroking a dog ... The list is, literally, endless but each of these small examples highlight an obvious truth: context matters and informs judgement. In a slightly different context, and developing a theory of television in the age of social media, Benjamin Brojakowski presents the notion of three mechanisms that cause enjoyment in the televisual experience. He (2015: 26) says, 'an example of a circumstance that reduces media enjoyment may be an unexpected phone call or email during a program. Conversely, communal viewing of a program may enhance the enjoyment.' Again, it need not determine judgement but to pretend it is insignificant seems to be an error. Equally, the opportunity to re-watch, fast-forward, freeze frame, zoom in ... all of these also influence out critical judgement. Re-watching became itself a central focus of Nikki Stafford's (2011) experiment on her blog *Nik at Nite*. Over the course of a year, every week a stipulated set of episodes (running sequentially from B S1E1 to B S7E22) would be re-watched by everyone who was part of the experience (and people came and went, but the numbers were high). Fans, writers, scholars would write essays on the week's episodes and others would then respond and a huge discussion took place. Clearly, watching an episode for these purposes and with the knowledge of this massive, informed, positive group has its own impact on the experience.

So, how might these sets of intersecting questions enable us to engage with *Firefly*? The purpose of this section is to show both how an analysis of the show might enable a discussion of the questions, but also to see the ways in which the questions can help us respond to certain challenges the show offers up.

In addition, there are other questions that we have not elaborated on here but that are implied in the durational relationship, such as the scheduling of the show on television (and all the attendant issues of producer/network tensions and expectations); its release on DVD, and (in the case of Whedon, in particular) engagement with fan communities.

Also, we need to return to the concept of 'mimesis'. In classical literary criticism, mimesis is such a central concept, in part because of its heritage from Aristotle, but mainly because of the largely linguistic nature of the object of analysis. Televisual narrative clearly does rely on words inasmuch as the script that informs the direction and acting is written (and this is very important, as I discussed in Chapter 6). However, the ability to show a tree, or play the sound of a car horn (and importantly a particular kind of car horn, the precise one desired for the story) means that the blander but more useful notion of 'format' is more appropriate for television texts. This term clearly extends well beyond the notion of 'imitation' or 'representation' that literary scholars use, as 'format' includes elements that are non-representational yet still contribute to the total temporality of the televisual narrative world. So, in thinking about format, we are describing the unique intersection of a range of production components that go into making a show. These include, but are not limited to: place(s), time(s), genre(s), mise-en-scène, character(s) and plot(s). Additionally, the format will include conventions from the genre or genres that the show is also using to orient its narrative. Confusingly, though, the format allows the conditions in which narrative can be created, but the created narrative will have an influence on the format in a recursive process of perpetual re-invention (however minor).

As an important caveat, my use of the term is intended to chime with common uses of it in the US creative context. There is a more legalistic use of the term that refers to intellectual property where 'first and foremost, a TV format is a show based on the format rights of an existing show that is a *remake produced under license.* In Europe alone, the income that broadcasters have generated from the top 100 format reached US$2.9 billion in 2013' (Chalaby, 2016: 1 emphasis in original). However, its use in this book is descriptive/creative not legal/IP.

For the remainder of this chapter, I will look at some aspects of *Firefly* to see how it helps us answer some of these questions, and how these questions help us assess *Firefly*. I will focus on: the format of *Firefly* and the impact this has on possible narratives; the importance of the pilot in establishing a particular format; the difficulty of assessing the episode to the season in terms of a total temporality of the season's narrative world; this will be related to the notion of the 'intended' sequence of episodes, which, in turn, leads to questions of the durational relationship between the text and the viewer and the possible impact of fan communities on the reception of the show.

When considering long-form televisual narrative drama, it is tempting to think of it as analogous to a novel, where each episode is equivalent to a chapter. However, as with the discussion of episodes of *Buffy* being withdrawn from broadcast after the Columbine shootings (Chapter 1), and the re-ordering of episodes in *Dollhouse* (Chapter 3), the analogy is less than helpful. The case of *Firefly* is even more extreme. If narrative is the representation of the unfolding of events through time and if, further, this unfolding has the double structure in long-form serial drama of the narrative in an episode and the collection of episodes and their extended overarching narratives, then it stands to reason that the order of the episodes is vital for an appreciation of the total temporal narrative televisual world.

A brief schematisation of the difference between the initial broadcast order of episodes on Fox and their subsequent ordering on DVD release and on the Science Channel in 2011 shows how divergent the ordering is (see Table 3).

The differences in the sequence are obvious. It is not just the case that they have different pilots and finales, but the ordering of the episodes themselves is different. Sometimes an episode that follows an episode on the DVD did the same when broadcast, but the differences outweigh the similarities.

I will discuss the dates of airing and its impact on durationality shortly, but for now it is the notion of 'intended' order that is of most significance. The idea of intention is, of course, a contested one. When used in relation to *Firefly* its most common meaning seems to be: the

Table 3 Comparison between the sequence of episodes of *Firefly* as broadcast by Fox, and the sequence as it appears on the DVD release

Aired sequence on Fox	Date aired	DVD sequence
The Train Job	20 September 2002	Serenity
Bushwhacked	27 September 2002	The Train Job
Our Mrs Reynolds	4 October 2002	Bushwhacked
Jaynestown	18 October 2002	Shindig
Out of Gas	25 October 2002	Safe
Shindig	1 November 2002	Our Mrs Reynolds
Safe	8 November 2002	Jaynestown
Aerial	15 November 2002	Out of Gas
War Stories	6 December 2002	Aerial
Objects in Space	13 December 2002	War Stories
Serenity 1	20 December 2002	Trash*
Serenity 2	20 December 2002	The Message*
		Heart of Gold*
		Objects in Space

Note: * = did not air.

order of episodes intended by Joss Whedon in order to offer the most coherent and satisfying combination of episodes into a unified season narrative. In the language of this chapter: Whedon's intended sequence of discrete total temporal televisual narrative worlds into a unified singular total televisual narrative world.

There is, however, a major flaw in this argument. Indeed, it is, I think, impossible to assert an intended order and if my contention is right, then it becomes very hard to assert a total temporal narrative world at the level of the season. As is well known, Fox did not like 'Serenity' as the pilot and forced Whedon to write a new one. The effect this has on the format is something I will discuss shortly, but the logical paradox it creates is also important. The initial pilot did a certain job in terms of setting the format up: its tone, palette, cinematographic aesthetics, space, place, time and so on. It established the story arc and developed the characters. It was made with a second episode in mind. The decision by the network to have Whedon and Minear create a new pilot means that a slightly different tone is established, the characters are more sketchily introduced and a new character, the villain, Niska is created. It also means the broadcast sequence is nothing like Whedon wanted, but the DVD cannot be what he intended either, as 'The Train Job' was not something he desired. The DVD has two pilots and/or an unwanted second episode. However, we cannot ignore the episode (as, for example, the pilot of *Dollhouse* being an extra, and not included as part of the canon) because it introduces a character out of keeping with much of the rest of the show. Keith deCandido is emphatic in his belief that the 'world building' work done by a pilot is simply not done well enough by 'The Train Job'. Indeed, it was done so badly that he (2004: 56) says, '... to my mind the thing that really killed *Firefly* was "The Train Job"'. Of particular concern for deCandido, is Niska. The problem is that, as pilot and 'world maker' (or format creator), the bad guy in this episode could reasonably be assumed to be representative of bad guys in later episodes. Niska is very much *not* like most of the series' other villains. Where future villains would enact a series theme of the separation within normal civil society between the haves and the have-nots, their villainy an expression of greed and exploitation within this context, Niska is 'just a brutal sadistic gangster' (deCandido, 2004: 58).

Niska makes 'The Train Job', for deCandido anyway, unrepresentative of the show: a bad pilot. I have discussed elsewhere how I disagree with this assessment, and I shall rehearse the argument presently, but the fact remains that it was unintended in the original idea but cannot be ignored because it offers us a character whose return later in the series is central to a story about a significant character in the show, the pilot, Wash. Also, the intended second episode was to have been 'Bushwhacked'.

If there is no genuine 'intended' sequence, and therefore no determined total temporality of the narrative world but rather an approximate collectively willed/deluded simulacrum of one, how does this affect the possibility of making large claims for the show in its entirety? In some ways, not too much. The remaining episodes on the DVD offer a coherent sense of character development, even if they are unable to really present the backstory that we will discover in the film spin-off *Serenity*. However, it is still the case that there is an aporia in the show that has always to place in some uncertainty a sense of the 'true' or 'real' narrative.

Before turning to the duration of viewer engagement, it will be useful to elaborate a little on the notion of format and narrative. As mentioned above, format both provides the conditions in which narrative can be produced, but is also (in part) produced through narrative. The format, once established, can be developed and expanded and this can happen through the stories told but much of the non-representational aspects have to remain as they were originally established. Too radical a departure from, for example, the extra-diegetic music, or costume palette, or camera techniques or interstitial editing techniques (such as *Angel*'s flash between scenes) will destabilise the format and as the format is what produces and grounds the world this is not usually desirable. Nothing as dramatic as destabilising the format occurs between the two pilots on the DVD, but we do see that, *contra* deCandido, 'The Train Job' does a better and fuller job of quickly and fluently providing as wide a range of the format possibilities relating to the representational components.

'The Train Job', written over a weekend after Fox had declined 'Serenity', had the exact same mission: it had to present the format of the show. It may be that it is correct to assert that the introduction of Simon and River and the representation of Niska were not effective in this 'world creation'. However, the teaser is incredibly effective at setting up the three most important visual codes – the science fiction (which 'Serenity' achieved brilliantly); the western (which 'Serenity' was less successful at); and the 'Chinese' (which 'Serenity' did almost not at all).

The episode opens in a bar. The initial shot is a moment of televisual narrative excellence. A Steadicam moves through the bar at knee height. Our first encounter with this new world is, quite literally, childlike. We experience the bar from a position of smallness and unknowing, open to the possibility that the movement provides us with. From this place of partial views, we witness the jumbled, hectic set-up of the bar. And immediately we see a hybrid world of many influences, different cultural

Figure 15 The opening sequence of *Firefly*, episode 1, first broadcast 20 September 2002. 'The Train Job' with its knee-level Steadicam and cultural bric-a-brac.

heritages, people and objects. We emerge from behind a chair leg, see a belly dancer dressed in red, patrons standing and sitting in muted colours, drinking alcohol, playing cards; a waitress or two move by with white-painted faces and kimono-style dresses; lanterns and bird cages hang from the rafters (see Figure 15). This is undeniably a saloon bar.

The setting of the saloon establishes an aspect of the format that can be returned to, thus providing for inter-episodic points of confluence and rhythm. Most notably, perhaps, 'Shindig' will open in a bar and include a fight. The explicit description of the bar as a 'saloon' in the pre-outline to Espenson's script for 'Shindig' makes it an unmistakably western locale. As such it launches us straight into a mixed canvas of styles and genres: we are in a place and of a time that is not our own and, therefore, likely to be science fiction; we are in a saloon and therefore gesturing towards a western; we are surrounded by cultural debris, the historical bric-a-brac of various cultures with a preponderance of Chinese and American. In seconds, the opening of 'The Train Job' has provided us with the formal and visual template for the format, and has therefore created the narrative possibilities of all of these aspects, too. This bric-a-brac provides another aspect that the pilot achieves that is the sense of what Jowett calls 'retrofuturism', which means that *Firefly*'s universe is full of material objects that are 'touched, tasted, handled; they are tangibly real' (Jowett, 2008: 105). I address some of the complexity of the idea of materiality in Chapter 6, but for now I want to look at a further aspect of the pilots and materiality, which is the establishing of *Serenity*, the ship itself as such an important object in space. As is true of most of Whedon's work, there is in the telling of stories, a desire to make the audience *feel*. This, I argue, fails in 'Serenity' because the *in media res* opening provides spectacle and chaos rather than character investment and affect. However, what both 'Serenity' and 'The Train Job' achieve is to make the ship integral and emotional. And this is down to not just the stories, the scripting, the camera work and the music: it is because of the object itself. As Loni Peristere (2007: 123), a visual effects supervisor of *Buffy*, *Angel* and *Firefly*, says:

> When Mal picked Serenity out of the sand, he raised her up and put her back together piece by piece and welded the steel into a solid machine to travel in. Joss wanted to feel that she had been kept together through hard work and maintenance ... So we kept adding pipes and pistons, heating coils and fly panels, all in the hope that her fans would see them, see her, and love her as much as we did.

This emphasis on materiality, on the objectness of things (the strawberry Shepherd Book offers as payment for travel, the beautiful items in Inara's shuttle, Jayne's hat and guns, the doctor's glasses) are all provided with a thematic and formatted introduction in this opening scene to 'The Train Job'. As the camera moves us in its childlike discovery, we approach a table. The belly dancer puts something in the hand of the person sitting there and the camera rises to show the person given the paper, and two others. The man nearest us (Mal) faces away, wears a coat of russet brown. The other two (Zoe and Jayne) have earthy greens and hints of brown and red. Their attire, in the hybrid saloon, signals the western motif in a way that ties the characters to this specific bar at this specific time, but also draws the show into the histories it was always hoping to. A game of some kind is being played, and drink is being drunk. Off screen a drunken voice demands silence for a toast and we shift to a medium-long shot (beautifully set up through the space next to some beaded curtains, thereby getting the sense of depth so crucial to all Whedon's shows) and we see more of the saloon – the lanterns, the Chinese-looking women, the red colours – and we hear a brief history of the civil war and the victory of the Alliance over the Independents. The scene is economical, it tells the history, it locates Mal in that history without us having to see the battle; it offers the chance for the first use of the phrase 'brown coats', and, in between, we hear Mal order a drink in Chinese quite casually, as though Chinese has, indeed, just been incorporated into the more general culture.

Mal being called a 'brown coat' means that the costume (and colour scheme) is absolutely related to his martial career, as the opening of 'Serenity' had also made clear but had over-determined the meaning; here the colour includes the martial but is not dominated by it. In fact, the costume has already been invested with the western before the military aspect is fore-grounded. As such, the colour palette is open to much more nuance and subtlety because it is not so dramatically over-determined.

A fight that occurs between Mal and an Alliance supporter tells us about Mal's character and his politics and leads to him being thrown through the saloon window. This moment of pure western is radically recast as a sci-fi/western hybrid by virtue of the window being virtual and flicking back into pretend presence soon after. The importance of this in terms of format creation is that the science fiction and the western do not sit side by side (as they arguably did in 'Serenity'); instead they become integral to each other – being thrown through the window signals both sci-fi and western. At that moment, the second pilot brilliantly establishes the format. As the fight moves outside and Zoe, Jayne and Mal are trapped against the edge of the sandy cliff (western), the ship *Serenity* appears from below and rescues them (sci-fi). Again, the scene is both, and thereby furthers the essential facts of the format's visualisation cements in the brief teaser. In addition, the teaser has been accompanied by a score that will develop through the remainder of the series. Even here, however, we can see the emergence of the 'specialised collection of musical symbols' created by composer Greg Edmonson that are also so central to the format creation (Goltz, 2004: 209).

I have written more extensively about the format of *Firefly* elsewhere (Pateman, 2014: 153–69, which features some of the above material) but it was worth indicating how the two pilots achieve different outcomes and, as such, affect the narrative possibilities that the format is seen to enable for the viewer watching this over the course of the truncated season. The format and narrative possibilities offered by 'The Train Job' might have the less impressive Niska; but they also have the excellent melding of the generic and thematic; the aesthetic and the political.

Whatever the best way of reading the 'intended' sequence, and of accommodating the format needs in this analysis, the obvious difference between the broadcast series and the DVD version is one of viewer control. To see the show as aired (unless you had a recording device), one would have had to have been in a room with a television at a particular time on Friday night for a succession of weeks. Even this is not entirely accurate, as there was a two-week gap between episodes three and four, and a two-week gap between episodes eight and nine.

The rhythm of weekly watching has its own contribution to how a show is received with all the obvious points of the rest of one's life intervening, but as Whedon said of *Buffy*, the aim is to make a show that people *need* to see, that actually orients their week, informs their living habits (as with my example of downloading the series from the USA). The durational relationship of the viewer with the show lasts a number of months, with the relationship being most affective when the total temporal narrative world of the show helps inform and influence these extended periods of time. One could argue that the sign of a truly compelling show is when the durational relationship with the traditional long-form broadcast model persist affectively even after the episode's temporal narrative world has finished.

A problem occurs, however, when this slow, but well-regulated temporal relationship is interrupted as happened twice in the very short run that *Firefly* had. Maintaining that affective commitment while the durational relationship is predictable and stable is part of the joy of being a fan of a show; having to modify the relationship through postponements and the interruptions of sporting or other events does not help. Arguably, the choices by Fox to shift the episodes around both in terms of the order they were broadcast, and then the broadcast dates themselves (especially after the well-publicised disagreement over the pilot) could have contributed to the fans' sense of protectiveness to the show. The outrage by fans (very early on calling themselves 'browncoats') at the treatment of the show led to protests (some arranged *before* any episodes aired because of the sense that Fox did not understand its product) and the small audience clearly had a big emotional response. However, while the very keen fans protested and sent postcards, the shifting of the episodes meant that more casual viewers had much less reason to maintain the durational relationship. In some ways, the format was not one that would easily capture the casual Fox viewer (Pateman, 2014) so there is something about the total temporal world itself that militated against a large audience; but equally, the necessary commitment to the durational relationship was made incredibly hard by poor decisions around scheduling.

The durational relationship of viewers with the DVD is, of course, significantly different. Here, the viewer can choose any order to watch the episodes in over any available time period, leaving seconds or months between episodes or even within parts of episodes. As McCormick (2017) notes in her discussion of Netflix, where whole seasons are 'dumped' in toto, the continuation into the next episode after the conclusion of the present one redefines the notion of an ending. Less dramatically, and with (slightly) more viewer intervention, the DVD shifts the relation between the anticipation of the episodic weekly watch to the (possible) joys of binge-watching: consuming whole series in a matter of hours. The total temporality of the fictional world remains the same, but the capacity of the durational relationship to be intensive, immediate and over in a day, as opposed to prolonged, anticipatory and lasting almost half a year, recasts the viewer's understanding of and relationship with the world.

Questions of televisual narrativity, total temporal worlds, durationality and so on are especially pertinent to discussions of *Firefly* because of its troubled production and broadcast history. They are also, however, applicable to, and important for, all televisual fictions and have been, at least, implicit in much of my discussion of the artistry and aesthetic choices in Whedon's shows in this book. They become more prominent again in the following chapter.

'I can bring back the world': *Dollhouse* – narrating the tabula rasa

8

As fans of Whedon know, the genesis of *Dollhouse* is as improbable as the show itself came to be. Eliza Dushku, Faith from *Buffy*, had been working in a number of low-quality film projects and Whedon began to meet with her to try and offer more positive career options (Pascale, 2014: 291). During this period, she was offered *Tru Calling* on Fox, which ran for two years (2003–5) and this led to a development deal between Fox and Dushku. During one of the lunches between Whedon and Dushku where Joss had intended to act 'all sage, saying things backwards like Yoda and laying out what I thought she should do' (Pascale, 2014: 291), he instead came up with a premise based on her experiences as an actor, hired out to be someone else's fantasy. Dushku jumped at the idea and Fox, presumably on the twin bases of Dushku's deal and Whedon's reputation, ordered seven episodes without even seeing a pilot (Pascale, 2014: 291). Production was delayed because of the Writer's Strike (see Chapter 3) but development began some months later.

Tim Minear was brought in along with David Solomon to act as executive producers along with other Mutant Enemy writing alumni Jane Espenson and Steven S. DeKnight while Whedon worked on his producing duties for *Cabin in the Woods*. Tim Minear, on a featurette on the season 2 DVD, recalls that the production was given the greenlight without any need for the pilot, and guidelines, restrictions or 'hoops' – simply an order based on the pitch by Whedon. This seemingly open and generous blank slate approach, he ruefully acknowledges, simply meant that all the restriction and guidelines would be imposed once writing had begun (Minear, 2009).

It is perhaps a little opportunistic to cite this as evidence of the inevitable impossibility of the clean slate, but the production history does offer a pleasing analogue to the concept, if nothing else. And it is a concept that Whedon has used as a narrative device to great effect in all of his shows. In *Buffy* there is the episode 'Tabula Rasa'

(B S6E9) where a spell goes awry, and the characters lose knowledge of themselves and each other, but retain language and high-level motor skills, desire and deductive reasoning. In the *Angel* episode 'Spin the Bottle', a supernatural event causes the team to revert to their teenage selves, losing all knowledge of their subsequent lives and each other. *Firefly* did not have space to develop the River Tam character, but the Alliance were clearly keen to erase her mind and the dangerous secrets it held. *Dollhouse* takes the conceit and has it as the basis of, and driving force for, the whole show's narrative – both in its episodic instalments, and in the overarching arc, as well as in its formal and structural constructions. This chapter will offer an account of the ways in which the tabula rasa operates as a device for characterisation that quickly recognises its own limitations and is replaced with alternative ways of conceptualising characters and/or people (composites, real, dumb shows, actuals and so on). It shall then look at the ways in which the cancelled pilot episode created a contractual need for a thirteenth episode for the first season that afforded a new kind of tabula rasa for the writers.

In the opening episode of the show, 'Ghost' (D S1E1), the head of the so-called Dollhouse, Adelle DeWitt is interviewing would-be and reluctant new recruit Caroline and is telling her that if she joins, her memories will be erased for five years and she will have untold adventures that she will not remember:

> *DeWitt*: Nothing is what it appears to be.
>
> *Caroline*: It seems pretty clear to me.
>
> *DeWitt*: Because you're only seeing part of it. I'm talking about a clean slate.
>
> *Caroline*: You ever try and clean an actual slate? You always see what was on it before.
>
> *DeWitt*: Are you volunteering?
>
> *Caroline*: I don't have a choice, do I? How did it get this far?
>
> *DeWitt*: Caroline, actions have consequences.

Apart from introducing many of the themes of the show in an exceptionally economical exchange (free will, appearance and reality, responsibility, creation and creativity) it also explicitly invokes the Anglophone translation and tradition of the tabula rasa as clean slate. Caroline's response strongly refutes the possibility of ever totally cleaning a slate, but nevertheless I would like to think of tabula rasa in its older form as a re-melted wax tablet. The reason for this is that it much more emphatically asserts the materiality of the object inscribed. A stylus breaks the surface of the

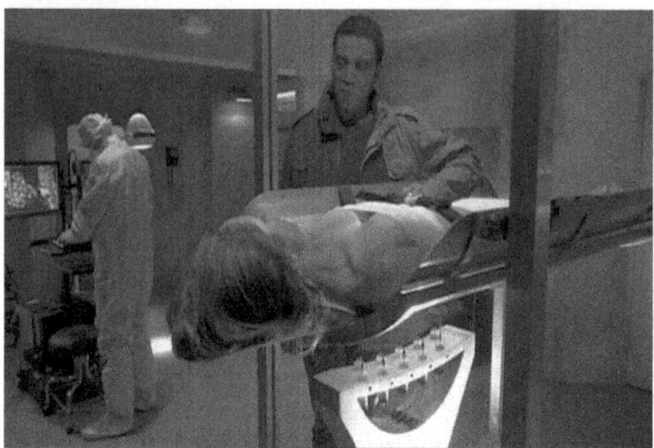

Figure 16 Caroline / Echo, *Dollhouse*, 'Epitaph Two: Return', season 2, episode 13, first broadcast 29 January 2010. In the end, despite the transference of minds and identitarian issues therein, it is Caroline's / Echo's *body* that is central to the potential for the ability to resist being wiped.

wax and creates grooves to produce the shapes. The melted wax may well erase the grooves, but they remain in the wax, a physical, if absent, intrusion. The image of chalk scoured on the surface keeps the body too much intact. While *Dollhouse* is fascinated by the mind, it operates on the body (indeed, in the penultimate episode Boyd – the incredibly deceptive founder of Rossum – explicitly states that it is Echo's [previously Caroline] body that will save the world, not her mind due to a unique compound in her spinal fluid that protects against the wipe technology [D S2E12]) (see Figure 16). Also, I will be discussing the body of the show (the corpus) and will wish to describe its formal and structural contortions in a way more suited to the wax tablet than the chalk slate.

This rather fussy distinction is not essential to my discussion, but it does help to ensure the bodily as well as the mental is kept in the foreground. One brief example of the importance of this, and of the problematic nature of the concept of the dolls overall, is from the episode 'Belle Chose' (D S2E3). The character Caroline that we were introduced to at the opening of season 1 became the doll Echo, a beautiful young woman who maintains basic linguistic skills, and motor skills enough to allow eating, washing, yoga. She and the other dolls are supposed to have had their own memories wiped clean and stored on devices so that they can be reinserted when the period of the contract has come up. Not only this, the dolls are not supposed to make any new memories in the dollhouse, living in a peaceful perpetual present without any motivation except to be placid and acquiescent. There is not meant to be any friendship or relationship building, knowledge acquisition, reflective judgement or planning. We have seen, however, that Echo has retained memories of her previous engagements, and we have also seen two other dolls, Victor and Sierra, developing emotional attachments for each other.

In 'Belle Chose', Echo has been hired by an English professor to be a student whose grades are poor and who seeks betterment through his instruction and sex. The stereotypes and hackneyed nature of this fantasy is one of the great narrative strengths and weaknesses of the show. In part trading on established forms to allow a mass audience to feel more at home in a show that is otherwise alienating and disarming, the stereotyped stories are 'part homage, part satire' (McCormick, 2012: 208). Victor, meanwhile, has been imprinted with the mind of Terry, the relative of a very wealthy family and a sociopathic young man who has been seriously injured by a car accident, and who has left a number of women imprisoned in his own macabre dollhouse. Victor has been imprinted in an effort to discover the whereabouts of the women. Victor, now fully inhabited by the personality of the sociopath Terry, down to and including speech patterns and gesture, escapes the Dollhouse and sets out to return to (and punish) the women. Successfully having discarded the tracking device embedded in the dolls ('imprint', 'inhabit', 'embed' – all bodily, material, 'waxy' verbs), Terry/Victor is at loose in the city.

In a plot device that will be discussed more below, Topher (the ethically ambiguous scientist responsible for creating the programs that become the imprints) reveals a new piece of technology that can be used to wipe the imprint from the mind of the doll remotely. Up until this point, the process has been clearly and firmly located in a chair that the doll reclines on, some (unspecified) electronic event occurs and the imprint is stored on a device, and the doll is back in her or his wiped state. The new technology allows for the wiping to occur at a distance. Unfortunately for Topher the wipe does not work, and rather than cleaning the dolls, the personality in one doll (Kiki/Echo) swaps with that in Victor/Terry. Psychopath Terry, now in Echo's body at a moment of intimacy with the professor stabs the professor in the neck. Terry, in Echo's body looks in the mirror and immediately sees and accepts that he is in a woman's body. Kiki, flighty, vivacious, uninhibited and very sexual, is now in Victor. Kiki/Victor is in a nightclub and dancing with great abandon, fun and flirtation. The very masculine body is inhabited by the personality of a young, sexually forward, white woman. Kiki/Victor straddles the DJ booth, writhes against walls and invites a young man to dance with her, resulting in the man (presumably from a homophobic distaste) punching Kiki/Victor. The scene has allowed Enver Gjojka to demonstrate his considerable versatility as an actor and mimic (a skill also played to brilliant effect in a later episode where he is imprinted with the personality of Topher who has had to go on a mission outside the Dollhouse, and the eccentricities of Topher [also played excellently by Fran Kanz] are beautifully captured by Gjojka ['The Left Hand', D S2E6, and 'The Hollow Men', D S2E12]). It has also allowed us to once again see the humanity of one-time FBI agent, now Dollhouse employee, Paul Ballard who steps in to rescue Kiki/Victor.

However, given the focus on Terry's mannerisms and physicality and on Kiki's very self-conscious awareness of her own body, and given the fact that the previous episode ('Instinct' D S2E2) had seen imprint technology affect the body 'at a glandular level', it is surprising that Kiki/Victor does not recognise the gender non-alignment. The viewing audience is aware of the narrative device but for the device to be effective it has to make sense within the world established and the failure of Kiki to recognise she is in Victor is problematic. In a show that is discussed frequently in terms of its post-human capacity, evidenced by its worrying representation of dolls as 'just bodies' (Jowett, 2014b: 136), the central narrative device seems to prioritise the psychological over the somatic. The 'post-human' here remains stubbornly part of the humanist tradition of the *cogito*.

This problematic encounter between personality and body has been discussed widely in relation to *Dollhouse*. Julie Hawk and Lorna Jowett approach the difficulty from, as it were, the other side and express concern over the seemingly essentialist assertion of heteronormative romantic love. Jowett discusses the romantic relationship between Victor and Sierra that transcends their doll states into both other imprints and into their pre-doll personalities once they are returned. For Jowett (2014b: 136), the dominance of the romantic narrative (and its culmination in a baby) poses the question of whether the baby is an expression of biological urge, heteronormative imprinting, or a pragmatic response to a post-apocalyptic world that needs repopulating. Hawk (2010: 18) is more determined in her view that the show asserts the 'go-to humanist value, sexual reproduction'.

The philosophical and political questions that the dolls pose are situated in the relationship and resolution to the questions of body and mind, imprint and 'real' personality, the effect of consciousness on corporeality and vice versa. The complexity of the issues raised may account for the relatively low viewing figures (the show asks rather than answers questions and the viewer has a lot of work to do in engaging with implications), but the impact on narrative is also a difficulty that the viewer has to contend with.

Season 1 of *Dollhouse* had two different problems to solve narratively. One related to the form of the show, the other to its content: both involved the difficulty of re-purposing an existing form. The first difficulty at first sight appears to have been a positive innovation from Fox. On 15 May 2008 the trade journal *Adweek* ran a story that said:

> Fox will premiere its new fall drama *Fringe* in a format that it is calling Remote Free TV, in which it will run only half the number of commercial and promotional minutes of a traditional show in order to try to maximise viewer engagement. (Consoli, 2008a: n.p.)

In addition, the new January starter, *Dollhouse,* would also benefit from the same innovation. The sales president of Fox, John Nesvig, explained the idea, 'each show will only contain five minutes of national commercial time per hour and each commercial break will include shorter commercial pods' (Consoli, 2008a: n.p.). The commercial viability was something that Nesvig was going to keep under review, while Peter Ligouri explained the rationale for the idea, 'we need to give viewers a new reason to come to network television, and we hope that this will give them less reason to change the channel during commercial breaks' (Consoli, 2008a: n.p.).

The idea seems sound enough and one would have thought that it would please a creative to have more space in which to tell stories, and would please audiences who would have more time to spend with their favourite character, and less time being interrupted by advertisements. Madeleine Brand, a host on the US radio station NPR (the same station that Whedon had appeared on singing 'Heartbroken' – see Chapter 3) in her show *Day to Day* broadcast on 11 March 2009 offered up the pros and cons. She introduced a segment about the idea by saying:

> The idea is that maybe viewers will actually watch the ads if there are less (sic) of them. Anyway, fewer ads means more minutes for the actual show. The writers will have to adjust and so will we, the viewers. Joel Rose prepared this report. (Brand, 2009)

The report by Joel Ross described the benefit to the characters in the new structure by offsetting the difficult task Echo has in fulfilling her mission by stating:

> Echo has one luxury other TV protagonists don't. Time – roughly, eight extra minutes per episode. *Dollhouse* has fewer commercials than most network TV dramas. That is supposed to keep more viewers watching during the breaks. (Rose, 2009)

The report has *Fringe* producer Jeff Pinker extolling the virtues of the plan for writers, 'It's a gift. We got to tell deeper, richer stories', but also explaining some of the difficulties that include each episode being roughly 10 per cent more expensive to produce. An additional eight minutes of air time requires that the writers also have a task which Pinker jokingly quantifies as a '[t]welve percent tax on their brain. It's impossible to quantify how much harder it is to tell a longer story', although he continues by stating that the new format's rhythm has been established and he believes his staff would find it hard to write a shorter script now.

Research conducted by Innerscope, a biometric engagement research company, used sophisticated eye tracking technology on randomly selected volunteers to assess the success of the primary purpose of the innovation that was to increase viewer engagement with the commercials. Some viewers watched episodes of *Fringe* with shorter pods, others with the standard pod length. According to *Adweek*:

> It found that viewers watching Fringe with shorter commercial pods had ad attention levels 31 percent higher, ad engagement levels 21 percent higher, unaided recall levels 250 percent higher and ad likeability levels 61 percent higher than viewers who watched the standard-length ad pods. (Consoli, 2008b: n.p.)

Brian Steinberg reported in *Advertising Age* that other metrics also supported the early view that the remote-free television was working, for *Fringe*:

> The initial read is that the idea seems to work. Brand recall of ads that appeared during the first episode of 'Fringe' was 32 percent higher than that of commercials appearing in traditional broadcast-TV programs, according to Nielsen IAG. The level of 'program engagement,' or audience attentiveness, for 'Fringe' was the second highest among debut episodes on broadcast TV in the past year (only NBC's 'Chuck' did better, IAG said). (Steinberg, 2008)

However, as *Brand Republic* announced a few months later, the experiment was cancelled by Fox because, although some companies paid up to a 40 per cent premium to benefit from the results listed above, this did not 'prevent a revenue shortfall' as the increased prices, 'were not high enough to match what Fox would have made selling more ads at standard prices' (Sandison, 2009: n.p.).

The commercial failure is, in the case of *Dollhouse*, a mirror of what could be argued to be a creative difficulty. Whedon was much less sanguine about the new format and in the same report where Pinker expressed qualified support for the venture, he says:

> These ideas don't come fast. It's actually a very hard show to break, and in our cases, increasingly difficult because they added about 10 minutes

> of screen time by pulling out commercials. The tonnage is overwhelming for writers. (Rose, 2009: n.p.)

What is noticeable is the sense of frustration with the story breaking process at all. The process is slow, difficult and overwhelming, and made more so by the additional minutes. One of the solutions that Whedon's team came up with, formally, was to have an extended teaser sequence. Whereas most Whedon shows have teasers that are typically a minute or two long, *Dollhouse* season 1 routinely has up to eleven or twelve minutes before the credits. This can no longer really be called a teaser, and this requires something of a shift in the storytelling structure as well as in the story receiving structure. Whedon's shows had always been very inventive at using the teaser to offer thematic and narrative hints about what was to come, and the inability to have this short introduction mean that the rhythm of the episodes had to be slightly different. This formal shift has implications for the relationship between the temporality of the narrative world and duration of the audience's engagement with it as described in Chapter 7, but what is of interest here in terms of narrative is just how hard the formal shift is when allied to a series structure that was – as implied in the quotation above – incredibly hard to get right.

As with any show, the negotiations between the network and the producer revolved around the overall tone and point of the show, its ability to produce arcs as well as stand-alone episodes, and the sequencing of the episodes to allow this. The network was more committed to the stand-alone episode where Echo's mission for the week was the principle point; Whedon was keen to develop the arc. The result was that the early episodes' efforts to establish the premise meant that 'we always look at the first bunch as a series of pilots' with the further contribution to the stand-alone feel being that, 'Every episode is a pilot for her (Dushku), because she's always playing somebody new. So it has been particularly challenging' (Whedon in Sepinwall, 2009).

A further challenge was getting the balance of the episodes right in terms of introducing the premise of the dolls as well as the purpose of the other characters. An episode that had been slated to be eighth in the series was bumped up to second as Whedon explains in the same interview:

> It had the kind of adventure and excitement that they absolutely wanted to see in the show. That had originally been episode eight. Obviously, we changed some things to make it work better as a second episode, but some of those decisions came through that way. And some of them was just, 'Which script is ready to shoot?' (Sepinwall, 2009)

Not only as a consequence of this, but also because of the foregrounding of the doll story, the other characters were not all as meaningful in the early episodes as may have been hoped. The role of Paul Ballard was queried in the same interview, which prompted Whedon to recognise that the emphasis on the doll stories had not allowed much development or interest in the others, 'Things are going to get very strange and very ugly for everybody as soon as I can make it that way' (Sepinwall, 2009). The difficulty of establishing the premise (the format), providing the network with the anthology-style episodes they wanted, while also retaining the Whedonesque hallmarks of complex characters in developing story arcs is clear.

The challenge of having a main character as tabula rasa, filled with other personalities on a week-by-week basis, is not only related to the question of garnering audience sympathy for the doll, it is also to do with establishing convincing and compelling subsidiary stories and/or arcs. Season 2, with the staff aware of just how likely cancellation was due to the incredibly low viewing figures in season 1 and its surprise renewal, thrilled in a massively expansive story arc that was also propelled by the events depicted in 'Epitaph', of which more below. Season 1, however, for the reasons described above struggled, and in some measure this is because of the disconnect between the A and the B stories.

A common feature of Whedon's shows has been the strong relationship between the main story and the subordinate story. In *Buffy*, the quest to discover the monster and thwart its plans always has a secondary story running either offering thematic texture or character advancement. Famously, in 'The Zeppo' (B S3E13) Xander's story of trying to discover his role and purpose in the group was elevated to main story, while the terrifying hellbeast trying to break in through the Hellmouth was mere background. The ability to invert the A and the B story was possible because an audience who had watched the show for a while would be aware of the importance in Whedon's shows of the dual story structure.

In *Dollhouse*, the monster-thwarting part of the story is Echo's mission. However, Echo does not exist as a character in the earlier episodes so the story really is about whoever is inhabiting her body for the duration. The viewer sees and remembers the corporeality of Echo, but engages with the hybrid imprint. It is not the same as in a show much referenced in relation to *Dollhouse*, *Alias* (ABC 2001–6) where the same character enacts different personae; and nor as in the show that Whedon liked to refer to, *Quantum Leap* (NBC 1989–93), where the main character's consciousness is dumped in another's body and he has to figure out how to avert the crisis. In *Buffy*, the discovery of the monster involved teamwork, sometimes conflict, resolution and growth. Here, although the handler might be keeping an eye from a distance, there is no one to act as a team, and the story of Echo's imprint has to stand alone and engage our sympathies. As Whedon said, it is a pilot each week, and that almost by definition, does not allow for the *development* of our relation with the characters.

The supporting characters are not, for the most part, on the same mission and if they are and they are dolls, then the same difficulty occurs. The tabula rasa character allows for inventive and clever stories, but does not invite much in the way of emotional engagement. The slow reveal that Echo is retaining aspects of her imprints does mitigate a little against this, but the first season did suffer from the very thing that grounded the format: the tabula rasa. To solve this, the tabula rasa was rejected in favour of the 'composite' character wherein all the imprints that Echo had ever been co-existed in her brain and she was able to move between and emerge from them.

The fact that we now have a character (one with many discrete personalities, but a single character) offers new storytelling possibilities and season two is a much different and more enjoyable show as the various different strands that would have unfurled over the next four seasons are concentrated into this single one. Moreover, as McCormick eloquently explains, the whole of season 2 is written in the shadow of the future that was shown in 'Epitaph', the unaired but released-on-DVD episode. Region 1 and 2 box sets went on sale on 28 July and 7 September 2009. The first episode of season 2 aired on 25 September in the USA. It is, therefore, a reasonable assumption that many viewers would have been watching the second season with the knowledge of the techno-apocalypse to come. It is equally as plausible though to assume that many viewers would not have had this knowledge, which poses a further set of theoretical questions about the relationship of the production agreements that determine how many episodes will be made and/or aired, and the experience of watching a show on television as broadcast. The interpretive capacity of a viewer who had not seen 'Epitaph' is clearly significantly limited in comparison to the viewer who has, if we assert that the temporal totality of the televisual world includes episodes that were not available on television. McCormick is unambiguous on the subject. Using different language than mine she (McCormick, 2012: 211, original emphasis) asks, 'If "Epitaph 1" never aired, does it count as part of the text? *Of course it does.*'

Produced by Whedon at 'half the cost' of a normal episode (Whedon, 2009) and created to fulfil the thirteen-episode CD distribution deal 'Epitaph 1' is an astonishing end to the season. Set ten years in the future, we are introduced to a whole new set of characters in a world recognizably the same as that of the series, yet blasted, defiled and semi-destroyed. The present of the episode (the future of the story) is shot in video, and is contrasted with the past of the episode (the present – largely – of the series) that is shot on film and features some scenes taken from the unaired original pilot, called 'Echo'. This pilot, like that of *Firefly*, had not been to the network's liking and, as the production process was halted and Whedon re-thought about how to make the episode work. Whedon was unusually sanguine about the process and the network's reasons for asking for a new pilot. Later he was less forgiving, but for now he publicly assented to the network's position. Unlike my claim about *Firefly*, I think the network got this entirely wrong. Whedon said that the original pilot had the 'feel' of the show but failed to introduce its 'structure'. This is accurate but unimportant as the structure that was created for the first six episodes was precisely why viewers found it so hard to engage: the original pilot had mythology, complexity, interesting actual characters. It may have done nothing to induce more people to watch, but it would have made those who did feel much more strongly positive than in the event the aired plot did.

Because thirteen episodes had been shot but the unaired pilot was not part of the series and so not contractually suitable for the thirteen-episode DVD deal, Whedon's offer of a half-price season final replacement was met warmly. Into this post-apocalyptic (thought apocalyptic) world of 'butchers' and 'dumb shows' (people who have had their identity wiped by the radical expansion of the capacity and scale of the wiping and imprinting technology of the Dollhouse; and those who have been imprinted with a voracious desire to kill), the viewer is thrust. It is audacious, compelling, disarming and, as McCormick (2012) notes, establishes a narrative structure wherein the whole second season needs to provide answers or clues to the reasons for the shift from individual dolls being imprinted in a chair, one at a time, for defined purposes with a clear architect, to the mass and seemingly random wipes and imprints of the season one finale. In a sense, the show morphed into detective story where each episode provided clues to the questions of 'whodunit', 'why?' and 'how?'.

Certain of cancellation at the end of season 2, the show had the freedom to be as inventive, expansive and mythology driven as it wanted. Luciana Hiromi Yamada da Silveira (2010: 154) argues convincingly that awareness of the cancellation meant that the 'viewership was defined and aware of (or at least ready for) the show's plot and intentions and ... that the rest of the story would have to be told in a very limited number of episodes'. As she continues, the storytelling changed and became both much denser in terms of the mythology of the show, and much more rapid in terms of the setting up and resolution of plot points that could 'easily have played out over the course of a normal season' (2010: 154). Given the wide range of stories and arcs that the writing room had at their disposal, the series shifts again. No longer the stand-alone anthology style of the first six episodes; nor the unravelling of the Alpha and Ballard plot lines in the second half of season 1; the second season is a breathless collection of mini-seasons collected within the overarching 'whodunit' trajectory of the story with time for some detailed character development, especially in the stories of two of the dolls, Victor/Anthony and Sierra/Priya. The episodes devoted to their story development, 'Belonging' (D S2E4) and 'Stop-Loss' (D S2E9) also develop other characters – especially Topher, and also the Rossum corporation's activities in a fashion that is narratively satisfying and mythologically textured, unlike much of season 1. The relationship between the two speaks both to a kind of emotionality that transcends the attenuated humanity of the dolls, while raising the spectre, as mentioned earlier, of a conservative re-assertion of heteronormativity. It is difficult to ignore the gendered and biologistic aspect of this relationship, but a slightly different response to it would be to adopt and adapt Elizabeth Barnes' (2007) notion of 'sentimental ontology' that she develops in her discussions of *Buffy*. In it she says, 'where material bodies fail as an index to identity, I would argue, feeling comes to take its place. Though itself no definitive marker of *biological* humanity, feeling in *Buffy* does become the basis of humanity in spirit, a spirit that even vampires may (re)acquire' (2007: 63, original emphasis). Whedon's emphasis on emotion, on feeling, on audience identification with characters does support a view of the relationship between the two that is as much about a celebration of sentimental ontology as it is about heteronormative conservatism.

The concept of the tabula rasa that had provided the technical difficulty of the first few episodes – having a new character each week played by the same actor/doll – is replaced with a composite wherein the actor/doll has simultaneous access to a plethora of personalities and skills. The notion of the composite character is introduced in season one where Alpha, one of the dolls, has somehow evolved to exist with all of the imprints that have been planted in him. Able to access any personality within him at any time, but unable to form a coherent sense of self, he becomes dangerously violent and commits acts of murder against individuals in the Dollhouse as well as, in season 2, against anyone who booked romantic engagement with Echo. By the time of this episode, 'A Love Supreme' (D S2E8), Echo, too, has been able to harness the imprints within her. For reasons unexplained, she is better able to manipulate the multiple imprints and is able to forge a coherent identity as Echo. Both she and Alpha are said to have evolved, to have become a human-technologically enhanced hybrid. This is unlike most of the rest of the dolls, although we do see that, in the doll state, the supposed tabula rasa is capable of development and the exercise of some emotional functions. These developments have occurred in other Dollhouses we are told, and suggests that if cared for, nurtured and provided with a safe environment in the doll state, emotional and intellectual growth will occur. This is stark contrast to the 'Dumb shows' of the two Epitaph episodes. These people, wiped of their personality and left doll-like with no safety, care, guidance or structure are literally at the mercy of the butchers, those who have been programmed to murder them. The remaining 'actuals' – those for reasons not entirely clear unaffected by the wipes – that we see in these episodes are trying to reach safety, away from the mayhem.

In Epitaph 1, the term 'actuals' is used by the new characters we are introduced to, and it remains a term largely descriptive of this group, of whom Zone, played by Zack Ward, and Mag, played by multi-Whedon collaborator Felicia Day, are the prime focus. However, the staff of the Dollhouse whom we have been watching for the period of the show are also (mostly) actuals, and just as we witness in Echo's composite identity and (in Epitaph 2) Alpha's slow progress to ethical maturity, so too we see the journey of one of the more morally unmoored actuals, Topher Brink.

In a show that can easily be read as a meta-commentary on Whedon's personal relationship with globalised media corporations, Topher is also easy to place as Whedon's 'diegetic surrogate' (Lavery, 2014a: 125). Indeed, Whedon himself makes the link, 'That Topher – what's wrong with him? He just creates these character people and then he just puppets them around, and he thinks it's ok to do that. Who's he based on? What monster?' (Lavery, 2014a: 125). And as Andrew Zimmermann Jones makes clear, for the first season, Topher is a monster or – which may amount to the same thing – he has no empathy, no capacity for emotion and has 'no moral reaction to anything' (Jones, 2010: 81). Given the lengths to which Whedon has gone to assert his personal investment in, commitment to and passion for his shows and the characters who inhabit them, the relationship between Topher and Whedon seems less surrogate and surely more satirical. Written in the aftermath of the Writers' Strike (see Chapter 3), *Dollhouse* implies personal and ethical impotence in the face of global capital and its corporate standard bearers. He wrote a letter to the WGA membership saying, 'I have been mugged an embarrassing number of times ... and the only mugger who still hurts my gut is the one who made me shake his hand. Until there is a deal – the right deal ... let's keep our hands in our pockets or on our signs. Let's not be victims. Let's never' (Pascale, 2014: 295). Topher is the satirical alter-ego of this impassioned artist. He is the sociopath mad-scientist as creator: interested in the form, the structure, the technique, the act of creation – not what is created; and certainly not the instrument through which the creation is manifested: the dolls. If we are to allegorise, maybe Topher is the Network exec, the studio boss; maybe Topher is the self-seeking writer-for-hire functionary. But he is not, I think, a Whedon surrogate.

And this is important for this book's thesis because, among what I have been arguing, is that Whedon's shows insist upon the possibility of change. Buffy is fated to die and does die, but Xander brings her back to life; Gunn refuses Skip's description of the inevitability of all that has happened to that point in *Angel*; Zoe refuses to wait for Mal's signal in 'Out of Gas', and Topher discovers empathy, compassion and ethical insight. Change, whether of a fictional, fated demise; inevitable historical unfolding; hierarchy and obedience to protocols; or personal state of being are vital to Whedon's shows because they are the artistic corollary of his politics. Topher cannot be Whedon at the beginning, because, in some sense he needs to be much more like him at the end. It would be over-stating the case to say that Whedon is seeking to save the world, but his characters (Buffy, second season, ethically improved but emotionally traumatised Topher) do. And they do so because the can, because they choose like Mal 'to misbehave'; Anne working with homeless kids and runaways in *Angel*, when asked by Gunn what she would do if she discovered it was all pointless, answers that she would 'get this truck packed before the new stuff gets here' (A S5E22, 'Not Fade Away').

Topher's growing awareness of the dolls as people (prompted by the imprinted Dr Saunders in the body of the doll Whiskey choosing not to like him), and of his own emphatic culpability in the creation of the technology that has destroyed the world, creates extreme mental torture for him. He breaks down, is further broken by having to watch a person get shot every day in front of him while working captive for the Rossum Corporation (see Figure 17).

Eventually, the skills that led him to carelessly allow the world to teeter on the edge of utter annihilation provide him with a chance to offer the possibility of rescue. This, however, will require his death as he sets the charge to produce the pulse. Mentally shattered, blasted to smithereens, Topher's journey to salvation has been grim, destructive, terrifying and essential; change – personal or political – is hard, maybe even unbearable. But the alternative is worse. There can be no blank slate; but there can be compromised new beginnings.

Figure 17 Topher, *Dollhouse*, 'Epitaph Two: Return', season 2, episode 13, first broadcast 29 January 2010. Topher's ethical rehabilitation is aided by the torture of being driven mad by having to watch innocent people get shot in front of him every day that he failed.

Topher's act of sacrifice, like Buffy's, like Wesley's, is a fictional realisation of one of Whedon's profoundest beliefs, which is his atheism. He has said, 'I am an atheist and an absurdist ... The morality comes from the absence of any grander scheme, not from the presence of any grander scheme' (Pascale, 2014: 263). Topher sacrifices himself, not from an overarching religious belief, but because of his understanding and empathy. *Dollhouse* may well present a vision of a post-human future, but Topher's act is an assertion of a certain kind of humanity, of a certain humanism. In 2009, Whedon was awarded the Outstanding Lifetime Achievement Award in Cultural Humanism from Harvard University's Humanist Chaplaincy and the Secular Society. In his acceptance speech, he made the following observation:

> The enemy of humanism is not faith ... The enemy of humanism is hate, is fear, is ignorance, is the darker part of man that is in every humanist, every person in the world. That is what we have to fight. Faith is something we have to embrace. Faith in God means believing absolutely in something that has no proof whatsoever. Faith in humanity means believing absolutely in something with a huge amount of proof to the contrary. We are the true believers. (Pascale, 2014: 325)

As Emily Nussbaum (2009) observes, the ways in which Whedon's faith in humanism and fight against hate, fear and ignorance has shifted its political focus over the years. While in *Buffy* the feminism was about, in part, exposing 'sexual false consciousness', his later works are much more profoundly about the exploitation of individuals by huge corporations or organisations. While the role of the Watcher's Council and Wolfram and Hart in *Buffy* and *Angel* had begun this investigation, the role of the Alliance in *Firefly* developed it further, and the expression of it in *Dollhouse* offers an angry, radical cry of 'political anger' (Nussbaum, 2009). *Dollhouse* keeps but complicates Whedon's feminist politics of representation, and asserts both individual responsibility as well as collective action in the face of overweening power and abuse.

Coda: *'I'm not done baking'*

Whedon has been working in mass mediated art for around thirty years. Assuming nothing unexpected happens, he could well be working for another thirty. What that work will look like, and how his vision will develop, is as yet unclear. At the time of writing, what is clear is that the televisual Whedon future is being carried on by Jed and Tancharoen. *S.H.I.E.L.D.*, despite having viewing figures of just over 2 million for the final episode of season 4 (and struggling to reach over 5 million since season 1), has been renewed for a fifth season. ABC's and Marvel's parent company, Disney, presumably feel the franchise overall is worth the investment, and will doubtless reap lucrative benefits through syndication.

Whedon, himself, has been announced as the writer, director and producer of a stand-alone Batgirl movie for DC, the title of which has yet to be announced. *Variety* printed the exclusive on 30 March 2017. Barely six weeks later, he took over another DC film, *Justice League*, when its director (and DC stalwart) Zack Snyder withdrew after the death of one of his daughters. Whedon is to be responsible for post-production and some additional scenes. It is unclear what his credited involvement will be billed as.

In between these massive, global film project announcements, Whedon directed an advert for Planned Parenthood, a group that seeks to offer advice and support to people regarding reproductive choice. This marks a further turn towards public political work that has included the Mitt Romney zombie video, the ad in support of Hilary Clinton as well as his on-going work with Equality Now. He also uses Twitter to engage in political debate. The anger described by Nussbaum is evident in these tweets, and some have produced significant backlash for what some perceive as their misogyny and promotion of rape culture. An attack on Paul Ryan that claimed to find him being raped by a rhinoceros 'funny', and another where he seemingly belittled teenage cancer survivors in order to mock Ryan and Donald Trump, caused particular disquiet and anger in some areas of the press. Whedon posted an apology and deleted the original tweet. He said, 'So I tweeted something that inadvertently offended everyone except the people I was trying to offend. I'm sorry. I'll be quiet for a bit' (Whedon, 2017).

Whatever the rights and wrongs of these tweets, it is clear that the politics that has animated his art over the last thirty years is becoming more central to his public profile. He has never been shy of expressing his views clearly and openly, but the last few years have seen an increasing use of social media as a vehicle for his views.

It is plausible to hope that as he continues to produce multi-million dollar movies as well as smaller independent film projects; as he works on existing comic book franchises and possibly develops new ones; as he uses his position of cultural centrality to voice the concerns of marginalised groups; he will also return to television. Many fans and scholars are very eager to see what new televisual stories he has left to offer, before he is done baking.

Appendix 1: Jane Espenson correspondence

Below is an edited and slightly re-ordered collection of emails from Jane Espenson. They all respond to various questions I asked her during a few months in 2008. Neither an interview nor a straightforward Q&A, this correspondence developed organically over those few months and offers some fabulous insight into Whedon's working practices, the creation of some of his shows' most popular episodes, and the workings from *inside* the Mutant Enemy writers' room. It is also a testament to Espenson's good grace, benevolence and generosity. Thank you, Jane.

The clarity and precision of her writing means that my emails are unnecessary as it is nearly always clear what she is responding to (and where it is not I offer a brief explanatory parenthesis). I have dispensed with the introductory and concluding formalities after the first email. Even in these exchanges, Espenson's skill as a writer and comic is manifest.

---

2 January 2008

Hi Matthew! I got your letter today about the book you're going to be working on. It looks like a great project. Thanks for the praise of 'Pangs' and 'Storyteller' – they're also two of my faves. I'd be happy to talk with you if we can set up a time for a phone interview, or – even easier – if you wanted to email questions for me to answer. What would work best for you? Jane Espenson

5 January 2008

Hi

I'm passing your question about an 'archive' along to Joss [I asked if there was an archive of all shooting scripts], but I don't think there is anything like that. I have a fairly complete set of *Buffy* scripts, and a few call sheets, and I think other writers kept stuff, but I haven't heard of anything beyond that. I'll let you know if I find out different.

[I asked about 'Pangs]

Buffy was a very top-down show (as opposed to, say, *Battlestar*, which is more group-driven). Every *Buffy* episode came very much from Joss's brain. 'Pangs' was not an exception to this. It was almost a case of watching Joss break the episode, in fact. He was, of course, very much involved in the *Angel* episode that accompanied 'Pangs', so he made sure to construct 'Pangs' specifically so they would work together. If both eps have, in essence, one writer, the co-ordination problem disappears.

This was an episode in which he had an extremely clear vision and I was just there to carry it out. He determined every scene and every act break. He also extensively rewrote act three ... the yam recipe that Giles is working with is Joss's personal recipe, for example.

BUT ... I am very proud of the personal touches I managed to insert. I only had a few days to write the episode, and I started by doing some short-and-intensive Chumash Indian research. It was when I found the list of ways that the Chumash had suffered (cut-off ears, syphilis, etc), that Joss realised those could help shape the story. Spike getting shot with arrows was not part of the original plan, either, but was something that came out of my first draft. And, of course, the dialogue was largely mine. 'What's a ricer?' 'You made a bear, undo it,' 'Sorry about that Chief,' 'A yam-sham.' (However, the iconic Spike speech about the plight of the Indians was pretty much all Joss – I never wrote a version that was quite harsh enough).

In terms of how I got the assignment to write 'Pangs' – I think it was just my turn in the rotation. (Looking at the list ...) Joss was already slated to write ep 10, and Marti had already written two eps. Doug had just written an ep. It would've made sense to give 'Pangs' either to me or to Fury. I suspect I wanted to write 'Something Blue' instead, if that episode was already being planned. I remember being envious of that episode, since I adore writing out-of-character stuff. I certainly didn't lobby to write 'Pangs' (the way I did 'Superstar'). It was just handed to me.

Lucky me!

7 January 2008

In terms of scripts – they're exactly as they are in the *Buffy* script books you can get at the bookstore – those are essentially photocopies of what I have. So you probably don't need to see those, assuming you've bought the script collections. I looked through my stuff today. No call sheets, it turns out. All I have is a production schedule from 'Superstar'. I have a lot of early drafts and outlines on my computer, but they were all written in Scriptware. I've written to that company to find out if they still make software that can open the files.

The squabble-scene sequence you're talking about was in act three, which is the act entirely rewritten by Joss, so I can't speak to any specifics. (I wrote most of the dialogue, *except* in act three.) But I will tell you that the shifts in tone were something that was implicit in the series. Joss liked to point out that even the title, *Buffy the Vampire Slayer* had three parts: comedy, horror and action. In almost all the episodes, the attempt to keep all three wells full at all times was something that we all strove to do. The juxtaposition of tones wasn't found on the set, but is built into the scripts.

In response to a rather arch question about style. I don't really know what a David Lean-esque style is, but the script does call for Spike to be looking in on a family scene set 'in a pool of golden lamp light' and for him to be 'a picture of misery and longing'. We absolutely wanted him to be cold and small and pitiful. We didn't see this causing any problems – he was, in this episode, powerless, and a lot of the comedy came out of the contrast between that and his normal fearsomeness.

You ask if Spike's argument, 'not only spoke to his vampiric relish for strength and violence, but also to William's position as a member of a benefiting class at the height of Victorian colonial conquest?' Nope. This was a season four episode. 'Fool for Love' was season 5. We didn't realize until we were breaking 'Fool for Love' that Spike was not, in fact, working class.

Hope I'm not puncturing too many illusions! We knew a lot of what we were doing at the time, but some of it was just luck and happenstance!

Keep askin!

8 January 2008

Ooh! These are some good ones. I've got some good answers for these. First, yes, you could see early drafts if I could get them open. So far, no response from Scriptware, which is a bad sign. Perhaps they're totally defunct?

A writer absolutely needs script-writing software. Absolutely. For a while, every show declared what program *that* show used. But now everyone seems to have settled on Final Draft. It's essential for the writers' assistant who has to, yes, keep track of revisions. But it goes way beyond that. See the stars in the margins of some scripts? Those indicate WHICH lines have been most recently changed. The program puts those in automatically. It also stores *your* show's format – does your show use (more)s and (continued)s, how wide is your dialogue field? Even notations on the page about what color that page should be (to indicate which draft it is) – that's all done automatically and with uniformity from writer to writer. Also, the ability to do dual dialogue and things like that ... that would be hard to do well and quickly without the assistance Final Draft gives you (although I have severe quibbles with how Final Draft handles dual dialogue). Even the fact that the program fills in the characters' names after you type the first letter of the name becomes a help that every writer leans on. Then you hit return, and you're ready to type dialogue without having to hit another key. Hit return again, and you're back at a character slug line. You can type pages of simple conversation without having to even look at the screen. Great stuff.

You ask, 'Can a writer or an actor significantly influence where a character will go?' Yes. Absolutely. Joss was open to this, very much so. Sometimes an actor had an influence without doing anything but be himself. Doug Petrie went to a casting session where he watched Tom Lenk try out for the role of Andrew. He came back with the suggestion that we rewrite the character to fit Tom Lenk. We did so. Other times, as with Spike's background, it would be an actual verbal suggestion. It was one of the writers (probably Doug, again), who suggested making Spike upper class. I remember Joss responding almost instantly to that. An actor might also come in with a suggestion like that, and Joss would be open to it if he agreed with it.

Sometimes a character movement might be smaller. I wrote a line for Tara in 'I Was Made To Love You', that went something like 'she practically had 'made in China' stamped on her ass.' Joss hesitated over it, and considered having me cut it, but ultimately was okay with my pushing the character that way, and left it in.

So, yes, there were lots of forces acting in a world-to-Joss direction to influence character. But far fewer than on some other shows. *Battlestar*, for example, encourages a great deal of actor and writer influence over character.

About writer input you ask, 'is that something that is fun to work with as a writer, as it keeps the possibility of change and development high?' Yes. All writers' rooms are collaborative. On sitcoms they are WILDLY so. Many TV writers are not feature writers because they love the room so much. Some shows (always dramas), don't have rooms. Each writer works one-on-one with the show runner (*House* works this way. So did *X-Files.*) But even then, it's cooperative, collaborative. Every writer wants to be able to influence their show, to help make it the best it can be. The room is usually how this is done.

You ask about 'Band Candy'. That was an unusual situation. I pitched that episode. I mean that this was an idea that I had and brought to Joss. Some episodes came about in this way, although not as many as you'd think. I think this was the only ep I ever pitched that Joss took. Luckily, I pitched it at my job interview. The original idea was coffee – Giles and Joyce were going to be regressed to teens by drinking magical coffee. That turned into candy as we worked on the idea.

Strangely, the show I had worked on immediately before *Buffy* was *Ellen,* at which we had also done an episode about selling band candy. The stories, however, were unrelated.

I already knew I liked writing Out-of-character stories. They were a lot of what I pitched at the various *Star Trek* shows, which did these types of episodes well. I pitched 'Band Candy' specifically because I knew it would be fun writing the adults as teens. Luckily, Joss liked the core story about realizing we all NEED our adults to be adults even as we chafe under their advice.

Who was the most fun to write as a teenager? Well, I have some regret on that point. I assumed that Snyder was about the same age as Giles and Joyce, when in fact, we were playing him as about 10 years older. I should've given him earlier cultural touchstones. Let Joyce talk about Barbarino, Snyder should've been all about Elvis. Sigh. Regrets.

I think writing Giles as a teen was the most fun, because it was a chance to see 'Ripper,' his youthful persona.

I WAS there at the filming of 'Band Candy', which was unusual. 'Band Candy' and 'Superstar' were the only two, I think, where I attended the whole filming. The actors were having fun, although since it was my first episode, I had nothing to compare it to. I think Giles and Joyce were really enjoying themselves. And Armin Shimerman became someone I consider a friend. I think he really had a great time.

Okay ... this is fun!

9 January 2008

Dual dialogue is just the name for side-by-side dialogue used to indicate two people talking at the same time. The problem is that Final Draft treats the block of text within the dual dialogue as sort of impenetrable lump unaffected by search-and-replace, for example. And once a chunk of dual dialogue is marked as 'revised' – gets those asterisks next to it – they don't automatically disappear when you move onto the next draft. Clearly a bug in the program. Very irritating. Wish they'd fix that.

Buffy's 'Mommy' line was all Joss. In fact, he wrote the whole Buffy-finds-Joyce scene, since we all viewed it as more a part of 'The Body' than a part of my episode.

Giles's Englishness is interesting. Doug and I used to talk about it. He pointed out that it wasn't like writing a character in a novel, where word choice, grammar, references, etc were the only way of reminding the audience that a character is English. Giles was going to be clearly English no matter what we wrote for him, because Tony's accent did that FOR us. That being said, though, we all enjoyed getting to try out Britishisms for him and Spike. I was pleased to get to use 'berk,' which I knew was an English insult in, I believe, 'A New Man,' and Joss got a reference to 'Jaffa cakes' in something else ['End of Days', B S7E21]. Part of the fun of writing scripts is finding ways to make lines unique to one character – writing them so that only that one character would sound right saying that line. Maybe leaning on something as bald as English references is a cheap way to do it, but it's irresistible. Also, we had a safety net because Tony would be able to catch anything we got wrong. In fact he changed some insult I'd written in 'Band Candy' to 'dozy cow,' which sounds very British to me.

You mention the 'bloody colonials' line from Pangs'. That was Joss, and it surprised me when I read it after his rewrite. I wouldn't've written that for him – don't know why, but I just never would have. But I see, now that you point it out, that it is a reaction to Buffy criticising his choice of words, similar to the way he spoke to Maggie. Hmm ... I don't know that I see this as a rejection of political correctness. I see it as Librarian's Pride, instead. Giles is proud of how he speaks, and is a bit defensive when called on an infelicity of wording. Whether he actually spoke properly or not is, to him, beside the point. He said it, and as a man who is proud of his speaking ability in general, he'll stand behind his words, right or wrong. I'm not sure he is unimpressed by linguistic pieties – he'd be the first to roll his eyes at some of the kids' grammar-mangling. He just doesn't like to have his own errors pointed out and would prefer to believe they don't exist. I'm reminded of an exchange I wrote in an episode whose name I forget ['Listening to Fear', B S5E9]. It went something like this:

> *Xander*: Why are we even doing research about some snot monster?
>
> *Giles*: Because it's a snot monster from outer space! Forget I said that.

It was something like that. Perhaps the 'forget I said that' was implied, not actually said, but I remember that the moment was all about Giles blurting out 'snot monster from outer space' and then reacting with shame at what he heard himself saying.

We're touching on something neat, here. Giles as flawed and testy and defensive. That's one of my favorite colors on him. It's fun to give paragons flaws, and I think it's one of the things that makes a show feel real and deep. It's why I love *Battlestar* – the villains are so adorably touching and the heroes so deeply flawed that in the end you can't tell who's who. *Buffy* did the same thing. Giles killed Ben because he was dark enough to be able to do so. And Spike was redeemed. And Willow fell. And Buffy blamed her friends. We were able to make those moves because all the characters had good and bad traits right from the start.

Thanks for asking all these great questions – giving me an excuse to write something!

10 January 2008

'Superstar' came out of Joss's head. He came in one morning, talking about a teaser that had come into his head fully formed. He described the teaser that you see on the air, line-by-line. I begged to be allowed to write the episode, and he let me take it. When we were all in the room for the break, it was Doug who suggested the alternate credits. There were actually more shots indicated in the script for the credits, but due to time/shooting constraints we didn't get all of them. I especially wanted one of Jonathan kissing a girl in a swimming pool, but it didn't happen. The images that were shot were the ones easiest to do on our stages. I regret that I didn't push for a shot of Jonathan kissing someone, somewhere – seems like an omission.

I don't think Joss thought of the episode as a reward to Danny for his work in 'Earshot', I think he thought of it more as a way to make the most extreme and illuminating alternate universe – who would be the LEAST likely person to replace Buffy in her power position? Joss's most common refrains in the room were, 'what's this episode really about?' and 'what's the Buffy of it?' As you can imagine, then, the effect on Buffy was always considered primary.

Buffy's passivity was fun to write. A lot of the credit goes to Sarah, of course, who played it so well. It wasn't a huge or tricky rethinking of the character. I just wrote lines that made it clear she was unsure of herself.

I picked Jonathan's song. Huh. It never occurred to me to even think of another genre. I wanted something swoony and romantic. An old standard seemed like the way to go – a bit of Frank Sinatra, you know?

Was Jonathan tailored to Danny? Well, probably somewhat in the way that all actors lead you down certain paths as you pursue what they do best. I didn't become friends with Danny until after this was shot, so I didn't really know him and only had what I'd seen on screen to go on. Which wasn't that much. So I pretty much just wrote it and hoped he could do it, because we were really asking for a totally new character from him. But Jonathan in general was probably shaped by what we'd seen him do well. I know I wrote a line for him in a later episode ['Storyteller', B S7E16] in which he and Andrew were in Mexico, 'We'll look it up tomorrow in the dictionario.' I totally wrote that because I could just *hear* him saying it. (oh, and BTW, it's Tom Lenk, not Lenck – the longer spelling was a typo on an early film he did.) The interesting thing about Danny, of course, is that in real life he's much more like Superstar Jonathan than Nerd Jonathan – very confident and accomplished and popular.

The Riley supporting Buffy thing was totally plot, not an attempt to firm up audience interest. We knew that Riley was unlikely to be a fan favorite from the beginning because he was replacing Angel. There was certainly no panic or surprise on that score. We were aware of fan reaction but wouldn't really have been concerned by like/dislike of a character. If there was massive disinterest in a plot line that might've been more likely to shake us up. But, ultimately, I suspect Joss would only pay attention if something the fans were saying confirmed a small nascent fear of his own about a story. If he loved a character or a story or an attitude, he would never change it because of a popular vote against it. He had the good sense to trust his guts. TV is not a democracy.

19 January 2008

Yes, Joss knew the etymology, so we knew that. But American censors don't! ['berk' from the rhyming slang 'Berkley hunt']

Found my old computer and it did reboot and I've managed to convert ALL my old *Buffy* files to Final Draft!!! So now I have access to all of them. The formatting has been slightly degraded (some lines aren't centred, page breaks disappeared, lots of stage directions have been make to look like dialogue) but they're remarkably intact overall!

Now, theoretically, I can make PDFs of them so you can see them. (Or you can get Final Draft, which would make it easy for me, but substantially harder for you.)

What would you most like to see? I'll try making a pdf of my first draft of 'Pangs'. I'm attaching it here. Can you open it? Remember that the formatting is weird.

20 January 2008

As far as I'm concerned, you're welcome to everything. The scripts do belong to FOX, so they're the ones to ask, I suppose. For an academic work ... I have no idea.

If you were able to open that last file I sent, then this is easy – I can easily make that sort of PDF. I guess I'll just do it alphabetically? I'm attaching the materials for 'Afterlife', my first script alphabetically. I've tried to clean up the formatting as much as I can, although I'm sure I missed many things. The asterisks really mess up some of the lines, but they are an accurate marking of what changed draft-to-draft, so I left them in.

I'm attaching my original outline and four drafts. Take a look at 'em – do they look okay?

20 January 2008

Oof. It's time-consuming, cleaning up the formatting. I may not always bother to do it.

21 January 2008

Hi

Oh, did I send you Final Draft files? I meant only to send pdfs – no need for you to get Final Draft. I'll go back and make sure I've sent you the right stuff. Attached here are three drafts of 'Checkpoint'. Some of the scenes were written by Doug – I can tell you which ones if it matters. I don't seem to have an outline for 'Checkpoint', which makes me think Doug probably wrote the outline.

You ask about the titles and responsibilities. This is both complicated and simple. The simple part is that the show runner is king. Yes, the network (and to a lesser degree the studio) can veto his stories and demand rewrites, and, theoretically, even step in and re-edit an episode. But on *Buffy* we were left remarkably alone. And in our little world (a separate little facility of three soundstages and a small office building at 1800 Stewart St in Santa Monica), Joss was the ultimate authority.

'Producer' is a very vague title. Often, it refers to non-writers – Gareth Davies was a producer on *Buffy* – who makes sure the budgets are being met and that the directors are completing their shooting days, etc. He was never in the writers room, had no input on stories, although he was instrumental in finding ways for the show to look as good as it could without blowing all our money in the first week.

'Producer' can also be part of a purely decorative title. Fran and Kaz Kazui had automatic producer titles on the show as the part of contracts having to do with the original movie. None of us ever met them. They had no involvement in the show.

To complete the confusion, 'Producer' is also one of the levels of titles given to writers employed on the staff of a show. You start out as 'Staff writer.' Your contract specifies that if you're brought back for a second year, you're automatically bumped up one level to 'Story editor.' There is no editing of stories involved – it's just the next title up for a writer on staff. Same duties: write scripts. Next level: Executive Story Editor. Same duties. Then Co-Producer. Then Producer. Then Supervising Producer. Then Co-Executive Producer. New responsibilities may or may not be added as you rise up this inevitable (and contractually specified) ladder ... you may start to go to editing sessions or get more involved on stage, or you might sometimes be asked to rewrite your colleagues' work. but generally, you're just a script-writin' machine! (Yay!).

As you can probably tell from the list ... 'Co' is a lesser step. If your show wins an Emmy, for example, the statuettes go to everyone with the title 'Producer' and higher. Co-Producers do not get statuettes (they get plaques, I believe). As I was told when I was a co-producer: 'Co means not'.

I have been watching *Torchwood* – I love it. Great stuff. Haven't seen James' ep yet, but I can't wait.

21 January 2008

A quick and easy one. You'll see that this one ['Conversations with Dead People'] was written in completely separate segments. I remember that Drew Goddard also did a bit of work on the Dawn story, rewriting me a bit as we approached shooting, but that would be after these drafts here, which are the only ones I seem to have saved. This segment is a good example of material lost for practical reasons – we couldn't use the front exterior of the house, and we didn't have time for as many pages as I wanted. I have some regret, because I really like my second draft.

21 January 2008

This ['Doomed'] is another shared-credit one. You can see that I was responsible for act two and the top of act three. This is one that had to be written extraordinarily quickly, I believe – a weekend, if that. There was never more than one draft from me. Someone (Joss? Marti?) must've taken the combined contributions and quickly polished it before shooting.

22 January 2008

This one ['Doublemeat Palace'] has an outline and four drafts. There are large changes between the first and second draft. This is an unusual example of plot changes (in the B story in this case) after the outline. There are also more changes in the A story than was usual.

This episode was problematic from the beginning. It relied on a tone, rather than events, to try to create a sense of forward motion. Many people regard this as one of the weakest Buffy episodes ever. It was also written (and, especially, rewritten) very quickly.

22 January 2008

Hi again

Here is 'Drowned,' another script co-written with Doug Petrie. I have very little memory of this one, and I don't recognise a lot of the writing – this one feels like it's got a lot of Doug in it to me – there are only a few scenes that I can positively identify as my own. And, as with another that we discussed, I don't have an outline, so Doug must've written that. This one really doesn't feel very much like mine.

Notice that 'Tucker' became 'Andrew' over the course of the rewrites, and that the Andrew character doesn't yet fully reflect the ultimate characterization.

22 January 2008

Here is 'Earshot'. It appears I only did 2 drafts. Differences between the second draft and the aired version reflect Jossian rewrites – for example the replacement of my 'Catcher in the Rye' classroom scene with Joss's 'Othello' classroom scene.

You'll see that we reformulated how Buffy's mind-reading would be presented between the 2 drafts. Originally, all thoughts were to be in her own voice (to protect the identity of the killer), but we changed that when it became clear it was cumbersome.

22 January 2008

Attached is 'End of Days', another co-write with Doug. He wrote all the big actiony bits, I wrote all the funny Andrew/Anya, Willow/Giles, Xander/Dawn stuff.

I can't access the *Torchwood* link, because it's restricted to people logging in from the UK, but we get Torchwood here on BBC America, so I'll see it eventually.

'Conversations' – I don't recall now what the reason for the changes was other than that the story needed to be shorter and simpler, easier to film very quickly. All the special effects I originally requested would have been very expensive and time-consuming. I suppose it's possible that Joss also felt a battle against the darkness instead of an appeal to dead-Joyce (a summoning) might be more appropriate to support the interpretation that Joyce might be The First – but that's just conjecture.

'Doublemeat' – Joss made me watch a movie called *Parents* starring Randy Quaid, and instructed me to capture that tone. I don't remember if he had me watch it before or after the first draft. Anyway, he was very unhappy with my first draft. I didn't really get why until I reread it before I sent it off to you ... NOTHING HAPPENS! There's no tension, sense of danger, sense of WHY these scenes are worth watching. The changes that I made adjusted the tone so that, hopefully, the strange heavy sense of wrongness makes the audience curious, but I see now that I probably should've gone further. At the very least, I should've made the scenes much shorter, made the whole thing 'cuttier' – lots of little weird shots of meat, and so forth. This episode just never got weird enough, I think, now that I look at it again. I don't think the problem was the story, really – Buffy takes on a very ordinary job, and her dislocation makes her think something horrible is going on there ... then it IS, but it's not the horrible thing she thought it was ... That's a fine story, and we used it to good effect to bring the overall arc down to earth – the reality is that Buffy needs to support her family, and that she CAN never aspire to a real career, and that the affair with Spike had a lot to do, early on, with trying to dissociate herself from the real facts of her life. That's all good stuff.

'Earshot' – it was awkward, writing the first draft with everything in Buffy's voice, because I had to worry about how we'd know who was saying what, and I had to worry about whether or not the jokes would really 'land' that way – Cordy having no subtext is obviously funnier if both the words and the thoughts were in Cordy's voice, for example. The idea of cacophony in her head was just not happening, too. I think it was pretty obvious to us that it didn't work. Me – because it had been hard to write, and Joss, because he could visualise the final product.

[In response to a query regarding Angel and Firefly drafts] I'll see what I can do about timing those drafts!

23 January 2008

'First Date' – this one has an outline and a revised outline. I don't know why there's a draft between the first and second drafts, but there is.

I'm especially proud of the Chao-Ahn joke run in this script, since it was something I came up with all on my own without Joss input, but it made it to the screen exactly as I wrote it.

BTW, the idea that Nikki was the principal's mother was not something we knew when we started featuring the principal. That was something – and this was very unusual – something that the staff came up with and brought to Joss. Sort of: Hey, wouldn't it make sense that Wood was the kid of that Slayer we saw Spike kill? We were stunned to realize that the timing worked out just right.

23 January 2008

There's a lot going on in the first half of the alphabet, huh? We're only up to 'Gingerbread'.

This is the script on which I was the most rewritten. Only the second ep I wrote for the show. I did three drafts, then Marti took over. If you look at the shooting draft and subtract me, that's Marti.

The name SPAM was changed to MOO because SPAM is a trade-name, and we couldn't use it. Probably just as well, since the now-ubiquitous use of 'spam' to mean junk email has weakened the impact of the word. (And, presumably, the trademark.) I made a long list of other possible acronyms that could replace SPAM, including POO (Parents Opposed to the Occult) and MAW (Mothers Against Witches) and lots of others. Joss selected MOO from the list.

This script contains one of my proud British speech pattern moments. Giles says, '... I'm afraid they may have done' without a direct object, which a US speaker would never do. I've always been amused to hear Brit speakers do that, and I was pleased to get to use it.

I'm particularly pleased with the Giles/Cordelia moments in the script. Those two were almost never alone together and I adore taking pairings like that and exploring them – Like the Spike/Andrew scenes in another episode. I also especially love it when an adult, especially a nurturing teacher type, doesn't like a child on the basis of their personality. There is too often an assumption on TV that you either 'like kids' or 'hate kids' without acknowledging that kids have personalities that can be evaluated one-by-one.

Oh, another thing about 'Gingerbread'. I originally wanted the dead kids to be different than other dead kids from tv and movies – I didn't want them to be stoic and dreamy and creepy, but instead energetic and inarticulate like real kids, but Joss pointed out that dreamy dead children are always chilling. He was totally right on this point.

Also, this story has a shared credit. Thania is a writer who had pitched a witch-burning episode as a freelancer the year before I joined the staff. They never did the story. Then I suggested that we do a book-burning episode and the two stories were combined. Since we used ideas she had brought in, she was given the shared credit. I didn't actually meet Thania until 2007, when we briefly shared a writers' room at *Eureka*. Now I see her out on the picket line, of course.

23 January 2008

This ['The Harsh Light of Day'] is one of my favorite scripts ever. I love this one.

You'll notice a big change in Parker between the first and second drafts – Joss pointed out that his insincerity was too clear in the first draft, so I tried to write him more genuine after that.

My only regret with this one was that I think the central notion that Buffy was acting out in response to Angel's absence got lost. Many fans felt that she had forgotten Angel too quickly, when in fact, this episode was intended to demonstrate how she had NOT moved on at all.

This episode was another case, like 'Superstar', in which we wrote an extended role for an actor who had previously only had a much smaller part (Mercedes, Harmony). We gambled that she'd be able to do this and she was much better than we'd even hoped. Her Harmony added so much to this ep.

23 January 2008

The file that appears to be the first draft of 'Harsh Light' is actually (obviously) incomplete. I'm not sure why I saved it, but it represents a script at half-way through the writing. As you can see, I don't write in sequence, but jump ahead to capture small moments out of order.

24 January 2008

The first draft here ['Life serial'] is just my stuff, then Fury's material is added to it for the other drafts.

I really loved my first, much-too-long take on the mummy hand loop, although my first attempt at the kitten-poker sequence is inexplicably long and dull. Note that 'Clem' didn't yet have a name at this point.

24 January 2008

Here is 'I Was Made To Love You'. Notice that it lacks the final scene, which was never included to try to keep it from leaking out. I know I wrote a version of it at some point, but mine was not used, obviously, in favor of Joss's, as was correct.

You'll notice from the dates that this one was rewritten very quickly – it must've been on a very tight schedule. You'll also notice that lots of the first draft stayed as written, a nice side-effect of lack-of-time!

The idea of Ben appearing in Glory's dress was something Joss came up with in the room. I don't think I'd've been brave enough to go there without his okay.

We had no idea at this point that we'd ever see Warren again. Great luck on the casting.

This is one of my favorite kinds of episode – simple story, simple theme, little action, lots of room for jokes.

24 January 2008

After Joss agreed that Robin was Nikki's son, we worked it into the plots just as if it had always been there. So, Joss was fundamental in the breaking, as usual, and laid out the course the events would take. We just suggested a backstory fact that fit what we'd already established.

24 January 2008

Joss was the show runner on *Angel*, but with varying degrees of involvement. The show was gradually turned over to Tim Minear to run, but with Joss retaining veto power.

Harmony – really fun character. I loved writing her. You need extreme characters at the edge of your show, and as they become more and more central, they get more nuanced and subtle and less extreme. So you need to bring in new, more extreme, characters at the edge again. Cordelia became a real person. Harmony was able to step in and take over the old vacuous place she'd left behind.

24 January 2008

I love Giles's hokey-pokey. Joss suggested adding Buffy saying 'That's what it's all about'. Genius!

There's no comparison between writing Buffy and Buffybot. Buffy is hard to write, because she's a real person and can say or think anything. Buffybot – that doesn't even really require writing skill, although it's a lot more fun because it's so easy. I just wrote her as I'd written April. When a character has no subtext and can simply say what they're thinking without effort, it's as easy as writing an outline. Dialogue gets hard (and interesting) in all the other cases in which you *know* what the character is thinking and feeling and now have to figure out what they could possibly allow themselves to say, figure how much they even understand about their own thoughts, figure out what they'd be willing to expose of what they're thinking, figure out what their vocabulary will even allow them to express ... all while making sure that the words they choose will reveal enough so that the audience know what the character is thinking and feeling. That's the really fun stuff.

As I say often in my blog, emotion leads to inarticulateness, so when it's most important to understand what a character is feeling, is when they're lease capable of expressing it. A wonderful puzzle.

24 January 2008

[In response to a question about the sequence of writing a script, and whether it is sequential or aimed at a clearly articulated later scene.] Oh yeah, that happens all the time. It's very common to have a moment near the end of the script in mind, in perfect detail, and then have to work out how to break the story so that you can arrive there. I think that's just true about story, not necessarily needing to even bring tone into it. (Luckily, in TV, the tone is generally in place already. Other than perhaps 'Doublemeat Palace', we had a *Buffy* tone in place.)

So, certainly that happens while the story is being broken. Then when you're writing it ... I used to think that I was just doing the fun and easy scenes first – The two-person conversations where they're just sitting and talking without action. But the fact is, that those scenes are also usually the ones with the most emotional revelations. So I'm also making sure that the emotional pay-off moments are hammered down. The big complicated scenes with seven people interrupting each other with their own agendas are fun to write, but require so much thought that they're usually left alone for a little while, although I might just write a sub-section of it where a big realization happens or something – just a line or two. The last thing I write is action. It's the hardest, and the most visual, and it generally doesn't advance the story as much as talkin' does. Bleah. Action is hard.

And, you're right, laying out the season is very much the same way. Yeah, we have signposts we're aiming at, generally having to do with the main arc of the year ... you know, Buffy will come back to life here, The Mayor will turn into a snake there. we also have things like Buffy's birthday that we tried to keep consistent from year to year. Some episodes had very specific things that had to happen during them. Which meant that the eps preceding them had to help make those events seem spontaneous.

The most extreme example of this was the musical. Joss wrote it long before we wrote all the episodes leading up to it. So we had to make sure that everything led up to it perfectly ... Buffy, Willow, Giles ... everyone had to be in the exact right place to launch into that episode. I remember that being very tricky. Marti was our leader during those episodes (because Joss was off writing songs, etc), and she did a great job. See, usually, you can move stuff around a bit, and pull an event forward if you need it, but we couldn't pull anything out of the musical and use it before we got there. Very difficult.

25 January 2008

Joss came up with the moment [in 'A New Man'] where Giles seemed to have exited and then returns, interrupting Ethan's evil soliloquy – that's the moment everyone remembers. I just transcribed it exactly as Joss acted it out.

Lots of Brit-speak in this one. I just went with what felt like stuff I'd read. You asked in another email if all shows attempt to get things right like that – I believe they do. Generally the show runners and the writers want things as flawless as they can be. The only enemy is time.

I like 'A New Man' a lot – the sequence with Spike crashing the car was shot, but was cut for length, which is too bad. But lots of fun Giles/Spike and Giles/Ethan stuff remained. I got to do my favorite thing again – take two characters who are rarely alone together (Giles and Spike) and put them in close quarters for a while.

I can't believe how many times I've written characters complaining about how slow a car is. Wow.

25 January 2008

I wasn't downstairs at *Angel*, so I was never sure how much and when Tim replaced Joss at *Angel*. I think they were breaking stories without him by the end, but that he was very satisfied with what they were doing ... I just don't know. Certainly Joss's involvement was much stronger at the beginning.

Tim also had a lot of control over *Firefly*, but that was just a baby, so, again, Joss's influence would've been at its strongest. Certainly I never got notes from Tim that were independent from Joss. I think you can take *Firefly* as pure Joss.

Anya was, in a way, a Cordy replacement. She certainly filled a similar niche exposition-wise. We never thought of Andrew as replacing Xander. I guess the case can be made that as Xander matured, there was use for someone more immature.

25 January 2008

Oh yeah, the Giles-menaces-Maggie moment – that was another one that Joss acted out with tremendous zeal in the writers' room. I just wrote it down. I love that moment, but I knew as soon as he did it that I'd spend years having to say, 'Thank you, thank you. That was Joss.'

25 January 2008

Here's 'Pangs' again. With better formatting this time.

We got to pet the bear on set. Sweet little guy. He never really looked as fierce as we hoped. We used to do impressions of his hurt little face as the potatoes hit him.

26 January 2008

We didn't do it to his face.

We were making fun of ourselves for having cast such a sweet-looking bear.

26 January 2008

Here's a bunch of different versions of 'Replacement'. Note the title changes and the change in the way 'Xander' is identified in the script – this was an attempt to help with the mislead that Xander had been copied rather than split in two.

Notice that although this appears to be a Xander story – Xander has the A-story, the Buffy story concludes the episode and is, in a way, deeper – Buffy is worrying that Riley prefers the non-Slayer parts of her, when in the end we learn that the problem between them actually comes from her not loving him. A powerful, deep little story. Joss always asked 'What's the Buffy of it?' when we were trying to break a story, and this is a great example of how even an apparently Xander-centric story has a strong 'Buffy of it.'

More British in this one. '... great tall robe-y thing.' That, also with 'come over all demony' from 'A New Man,' makes me realize that the only Britishisms I know come from *Monty Python* and *Blackadder*.

26 January 2008

Even then, the titles would get out on the web, so we wanted to make sure that the big secrets of the episode weren't revealed by the titles. The options with 'half' revealed that Xander was split, not copied.

Most of the time, though, when a title changed, it was just because the author of that episode had a better idea as they were writing. Some titles (including 'I Was Made to Love You') were dictated by Joss.

26 January 2008

Here is 'Same Time Same Place', which I remember as having to be written very quickly.

The thing about the sign being too pale came off something that happened on my very first show, *Dinosaurs*, in which, for some reason, every time there was a sign that needed to appear on camera, it was rendered in something unreadable, like yellow-on-white. At least, that was the perception of the writers at the time – I joined the staff at the very end of the show's run and mostly just heard the sign stories second-hand.

I really ran with the idea of paralyzed Dawn in this one ... just the kind of comedic situation that I most love. And the Anya/Willow spell scene is one of my all-time favorites, too.

Gnarl was played by Camden Toy, who also was one of the Gentlemen in Hush. He moves with creepy menace ... just perfect.

26 January 2008

I forgot to mention that the outline for 'Same Time' is actually not the outline. I always take the outline file and expand it into the first draft. Sometimes I forget that I haven't retitled the file yet when I save it. So the file that's labelled as the 'Same Time' outline is actually the first step in the first draft.

26 January 2008

[In response to a question about the input of actors and others into the stories] Depends on the show. *Buffy* had very little director or actor input. Joss wanted it how he wanted it. *Battlestar* is totally collaborative, on the other hard – tons of input from everyone involved, often to the extent that major plot elements are changed after the writer gets to Vancouver, or even changed on the set! That did not happen on *Buffy*.

26 January 2008 JE

[In response to a question about a brief scene between Willow and Anya in 'Sleeper'] Haw! I had no idea I was doing so much! I just liked the idea of calling back the other girl-girl spells (floating the rose, etc) that we'd seen Willow do, so the '... sexy' thing just seemed like an observation Anya could make. Then, once the ball is rolling with that first line, then you just figure how Willow would react, then you decide how Anya would react to that – like playing checkers against yourself. Or draughts, even. Those characters existed as such fully-realized people that it was easy to just let them talk. If you have that going for you, and you remember what the scene is supposed to be driving toward, then it lays itself out pretty naturally. Two-person scenes tend to be easy. The hard scene in this script was the tricky Spike-in-the-basement scene where Spike's lines had to make sense twice. Then the scene had to be cut way back in the editing room, and that was a HUGE headache, because if you cut something in one iteration, it had to be cut in the other one, too. What a mess!

27 January 2008

'Triangle'! Another one I like a lot. The troll was wonderful to write for. And I'm very proud of Spike's interest in the fried onion appetizer. And I love that he tries to be helpful with the location of possible babies – 'what do you think – hospital, maybe?'

30 January 2008

[In response to me asking for specific scripts on my birthday!] I can't recall if it's today or tomorrow that's the big day. But here are the Superstar and Storyteller files anyway! Hope they make things festive!

6 March 2008

[Response to a request to meet up. Which subsequently happened the day after President Obama's election in 2008.] Sure, we can coffee in November – no problem.

I'll look for my *Angel* and *Firefly* drafts when I'm at home tonight. Shouldn't be a problem.

11 March 2008

Here they are, but they're very rough ... I haven't look at them or cleaned them up ... who knows what's in there. By the way, please don't reproduce script pages in the book unless you give me a chance to clean them up – these don't reflect how the originals looked!

26 April 2008

[In response to a question about television as art] I'm in Vancouver and I'm totally swamped in work. But I don't think I'd have much more to say on this topic, even with time. All I know is that the writers (which includes Joss of course), were very much thinking of the show as art, or literature, with something larger to say – there was no expectation of changing the world, but maybe a hope of illuminating some things?

2 May 2008

[In response to the change of a record from Pink Floyd to Velvet Undergound.] I recall him dictating that 'classic album' exchange. ... even the choice of album was something that came directly from him. In order for the idea to be cut and then make its way into the produced episode, it would almost certainly have been either Joss, or me, changing my mind – not, on our show, the director. Gotta be Joss or me. I simply don't remember which, but I'd guess it was Joss.

2 June 2008

[Feeding back on a conference paper I was drafting] Love it!

My only question – you refer at one point to the scene existing in the first draft in outline form. I mean, you quote the first draft, but the scene doesn't have any dialogue in it yet. I would not have turned in a draft of the script with just a summary of the scene – if it was like that in the draft I sent you, then it must've represented an incomplete stage of the process, not the first draft I turned in.

Other than that, it is lovely! Great clear point, well made! I get what you've been driving at!

2 June 2008

Hi

Yeah, I just looked at the file I sent you that's labelled 'first draft' – it's clearly in progress at this stage – some of the scenes are written and others are not – they're still in outline form, perhaps slightly augmented with additional thoughts. This is not the actual 'first draft' and shouldn't be referred to as such. You can refer to that scene as representing a 'revised outline,' if you want, but it looks to me as if the original first draft for 'Harsh Light' has not been preserved.

23 November 2008

Re: 'Pangs' – I remember that those things were changed, but I don't remember why. Sorry. I think the change from Anya to Xander may simply have been something Joss requested without explanation, but I'm not sure. The change to Hus might've been literally to lose a page in length in the script – changing to a shorter name sometimes is enough to pull up a script when you're trying to lose a crucial bit of length, believe it or not. The woman curator – I have a vague memory that I was surprised when I saw the footage, but I can't be sure.

Atherton Wing – It changed? I didn't remember that. Possibly a problem getting a name to clear? Maybe just me playing around to get a name I liked? Or sometimes you pick a name and then realize it's too similar to a character you already have established.

The girl in 'Guise will be Guise' – that I do remember. The first name I picked (which I thought was Georgia something) was considered (by David Greenwalt) to be too fakey. Like a romance novel name. He was absolutely right, and that's something now that bothers me in the writing of others – names like Alexandra Cathcart ... it's almost like they're drag queen names, you know? Over the top. But I had that joke that depended on it being a place name. ('You were in ___?') So then I tried another place name (that might be where Holland came in?). I think it was finally Joss who picked Virginia, just because we were running out of place name names. No other reason as far as I know.

Hope that helps!

Appendix 2: Definitive guide to Whedon output week-by-week

This list provides a week-by-week list of television shows and comics executively produced by Whedon as first broadcast or published in the USA; film premieres where Whedon is a credited writer, director or producer during the same period, and comic books for which Whedon has written, as well as political videos.

The list is organised by the following pattern: date, season/episode (if relevant) title, network or publisher.

Buffy is in normal type, *Angel* in bold, *Firefly* in italics, *Dollhouse* is in normal type, *Agents of S.H.I.E.L.D.* is in normal type, films appear in square brackets, and comic books in round brackets.

Key: * = Whedon writer/co-writer credit; ** = Whedon writer and director credit, ^ = Whedon director-only credit, <> = film producer credit, ++ = a writing or directing credit for Maurissa Tancharoen and/ or Jed Whedon.

(1997)
(*Buffy* Season 1)
10 March, S1E1 Welcome to the Hellmouth. The WB*
10 March, S1E2 The Harvest. The WB*
17 March, S1E3 The Witch. The WB
25 March, S1E4 Teacher's Pet. The WB
31 March, S1E5 Never Kill a Boy on a First Date. The WB
7 April, S1E6 The Pack. The WB
14 April, S1E7 Angel. The WB
28 April, S1E8 I Robot, You Jane. The WB
5 May, S1E9 The Puppet Show. The WB
12 May, S1E10 Nightmares. The WB*
19 May, S1E11 Out of Mind, Out of Sight. The WB*
2 June, S1E12 Prophecy Girl. The WB**
(*Buffy* Season 2)
15 September, S2E1 When She Was Bad. The WB**
22 September, S2E2 Some Assembly Required. The WB
29 September, S2E3 School Hard. The WB
6 October, S2E4 Inca Mummy Girl. The WB

13 October, S2E5 Reptile Boy. The WB
27 October, S2E6 Halloween. The WB
3 November, S2E7 Lie To Me. The WB**
[*Alien Resurrection* premiere: 26 November]*
10 November, S2E8 The Dark Age. The WB
17 November, S2E9 What's My Line I. The WB
24 November, S2E10 What's My Line II. The WB
8 December, S2E11 Ted. Writer. The WB*
15 December, S2E12, Bad Eggs. The WB

(1998)

19 January, S2E13 Surprise. The WB
20 January, S2E14 Innocence. The WB**
27 January, S2E15 Phases. The WB
(January, *Buffy*: The Origin#1. Dark Horse)
10 February, S2E16 Bewitched, Bothered and Bewildered. The WB
24 February, S2E17 Passion. The WB
(February, *Buffy*: The Origin #2. Dark Horse)
3 March, S2E18 Killed By Death. The WB
(March, *Buffy*: The Origin #3. Dark Horse)
28 April, S2E19 I Only Have Eyes For You. The WB
5 May, S2E20 Go Fish. The WB
12 May, S2E21 Becoming I. The WB**
19 May, S2E22 Becoming II. The WB**
(May, *Buffy*: Angel #1. Dark Horse)
(June, *Buffy*: Angel #2. Dark Horse)
(July *Buffy*: Angel #3. Dark Horse)
(*Buffy* Season 3)
29 September, S3E1 Anne. The WB**
6 October, S3E2 Dead Man's Party. The WB
13 October, S3E3 Faith, Hope and Trick. The WB
20 October, S3E4 Beauty and the Beasts. The WB
3 November, S3E5 Homecoming. The WB
10 November, S3E6 Band Candy. The WB
17 November, S3E7 Revelations. The WB
1 December, S3E8 Lover's Walk. The WB
8 December, S3E9 The Wish. The WB
15 December, S3E10 Amends. The WB**
(December, *Buffy*; Haunted #1. Dark Horse)

(1999)

12 January, S3E11 Gingerbread. The WB
19 January, S3E12 Helpless. The WB
26 January, S3E13 The Zeppo. The WB
(January, *Buffy*; Haunted #2. Dark Horse)
9 February, S3E14 Bad Girls. The WB
16 February, S3E15 Consequences. The WB
23 February, S3E16 Doppelgangland. The WB**
(February, *Buffy*; Haunted #3. Dark Horse)
16 March, S3E17 Enemies. The WB
(March, *Buffy*; Haunted #4. Dark Horse)

(April, *Buffy*: Willow and Tara #1. Dark Horse)
(April, *Buffy*: Spike and Dru #1. Dark Horse)
4 May, S3E19 Choices. The WB
11 May, S3E20 The Prom. The WB
18 March, S3E21 Graduation Day I. The WB**
13 July, S3E22 Graduation Day II. The WB**
(July, *Buffy*: Willow and Tara–Wilderness #1. Dark Horse)
21 September, S3E18 Earshot. The WB
(September, *Buffy*: Willow and Tara–Wilderness #2. Dark Horse)
(*Buffy* Season 4; *Angel* Season 1)
5 October, S4E1 The Freshman. The WB**
5 October, S1E1 City Of. The WB**
12 October, S4E2 Living Conditions. The WB
12 October, S1E2 Lonely Hearts. The WB
19 October, S4E3 The Harsh Light of Day. The WB
19 October, S1E3 In The Dark. The WB
26 October, S4E4 Fear Itself. The WB
26 October, S1E4 I Fall To Pieces. The WB*
(October, *Buffy*: Spike and Dru #2. Dark Horse)
2 November, S4E5 Beer Bad. The WB
2 November, S1E5 Rm w/a Vu. The WB
9 November, S4E6 Wild at Heart. The WB
9 November, S1E6 Sense and Sensitivity. The WB
16 November, S4E7 The Initiative. The WB
16 November, S1E7 Bachelor Party. The WB
23 November, S4E8 Pangs, The WB
23 November, S1E8 I Will Remember You. The WB
30 November, S4E9 Something Blue. The WB
30 November, S1E9 Hero. The WB
14 December, S4E10 Hush. The WB**
14 December, S1E10 Parting Gifts. The WB
(December, *Buffy*: Spike and Dru #3. Dark Horse)
(2000)
18 January, S4E11 Doomed. The WB
18 January, S1E11 Somnambulist. The WB
25 January, S4E12 A New Man. The WB
25 January, S1E12 Expecting. The WB
8 February, S4E13 The I in Team. The WB
8 February, S1E13 She. The WB
15 February, S4E14 Goodbye Iowa. The WB
15 February, S1E14 I've Got You Under My Skin. The WB
22 February, S4E15 This Year's Girl. The WB
22 February, S1E15 The Prodigal. The WB
29 February, S4E16 Who Are You? The WB**
29 February, S1E16 The Ring. The WB
4 April, S4E17 Superstar. The WB
4 April, S1E17 Eternity. The WB
25 April, S4E18 Where the Wild Things Are. The WB
25 April, S1E18 Five by Five. The WB

2 May, S4E19 A New Moon Rising. The WB
2 May, S1E19 Sanctuary. The WB*
9 May, S4E20 The Yoko Factor. The WB
9 May, S1E20 War Zone. The WB
16 May, S4E21 Primeval. The WB
16 May, S1E21 Blind Date. The WB
23 May, S4E22 Restless. The WB**
23 May, S1E22 To Shanshu in LA. The WB
[*Titan A.E.* premiere: 26 June]*
(*Buffy* Season 5; *Angel* Season 2)
26 September, S5E1 Buffy vs. Dracula. The WB
26 September, S2E1 Judgment. The WB*
3 October, S5E2 Real Me. The WB
3 October, S2E2 Are You Now Or Have You Ever Been. The WB
10 October, S5E3 The Replacement. The WB
10 October, S2E3 First Impressions. The WB
17 October, S5E4 Out of My Mind. The WB
17 October, S2E4 Untouched. The WB^
24 October, S5E5 No Place Like Home. The WB
24 October, S2E5 Dear Boy. The WB
7 November, S5E6 Family. The WB**
7 November, S2E6 Guise Will Be Guise. The WB
14 November, S5E7 Fool For Love. The WB
14 November, S2E7 Darla. The WB
21 November, S5E8 Shadow. The WB
21 November, S2E8 The Shroud Of Rahmon. The WB
28 November, S5E9 Listening to Fear. The WB
28 November, S2E9 The Trial. The WB
19 December, S5E10 Into the Woods. The WB
19 December, S2E10 Reunion. The WB
(2001)
9 January, S5E11 Triangle. The WB
16 January, S2E11 Redefinition. The WB
23 January, S5E12 Checkpoint. The WB
23 January, S2E12 Blood Money
(January, *Fray* #1. Dark Horse)*
6 February, S5E13 Blood Ties. The WB
6 February, S2E13 Happy Anniversary. The WB*
13 February, S5E14 Crush. The WB
13 February, S2E14 The Thin Dead Line. The WB
20 February, S5E15 I was Made to Love You. The WB
20 February, S2E15 Reprise. The WB
27 February, S5E16 The Body. The WB**
27 February, S2E16 Epiphany. The WB
17 April, S5E17 Forever. The WB
17 April, S2E17 Disharmony. The WB
24 April, S5E18 Intervention. The WB
24 April, S2E18 Dead End. The WB
1 May, S5E19 Tough Love. The WB
1 May, S2E19 Belonging. The WB
8 May, S5E20 Spiral. The WB
8 May, S2E20 Over The Rainbow. The WB
15 May, S5E21 The Weight of the World. The WB
15 May, S2E21 Through The Looking Glass. The WB
22 May, S5E22 The Gift. The WB**

22 May, S2E22 There's No Place Like Plrtz Glrb. The WB
[*Atlantis The Lost Empire* premiere: 3]*
(July, *Buffy*: Oz #1. Dark Horse)
(July, *Fray* #2. Dark Horse)*
(August, *Buffy*: Oz #. Dark Horse)
(August, *Fray* #3. Dark Horse)*
Angel Season Three
24 September, S3E1 Heartthrob. The WB
(September, *Angel*#1. Dark Horse)*
(*Buffy*: Oz #3. Dark Horse)
1 October, S3E2 That Vision Thing. The WB
Buffy Season 6
2 October, S6E1 Bargaining I. UPN
2 October, S6E2 Bargaining II. UPN
8 October, S3E3 That Old Gang Of Mine. The WB
9 October, S6E3 After Life. UPN
13 October, S3E4 Carpe Noctem. The WB
16 October, S6E4 Flooded. UPN
22 October, S3E5 Fredless. The WB
23 October, S6E5 Life Serial. UPN
29 October, S3E6 Billy. The WB
30 October, S6E6 All the Way. UPN
(October, *Fray* #4. Dark Horse)*
(October, *Angel* #2. Dark Horse)*
5 November, S3E7 Offspring. The WB
6 October, S6E7 Once More With Feeling. UPN**
12 November, S3E8 Quickening. The WB
13 November, S6E8 Tabula Rasa. UPN
19 November, S3E9 Lullaby. The WB
20 November, S6E9 Smashed. UPN
27 November, S6E10 Wrecked. UPN
(November, *Angel* #3. Dark Horse)*
(November, *Fray* #5. Dark Horse)*
10 December, S3E10 Dad. The WB
(2002)
8 January, S6E11 Gone. UPN
14 January, S3E11 Birthday. The WB
21 January, S3E12 Provider. The WB
29 January, S6E12 Doublemeat Palace. UPN
4 February, S3E13 Waiting In The Wings. The WB**
5 February, S6E13 Dead Things. UPN
12 February, S6E14 Older and Far Away. UPN
18 February, S3E14 Couplet. The WB
25 February, S3E15 Loyalty. The WB
26 February, S6E15 As You Were. UPN
(February, *Buffy the Vampire Slayer: Tales of the Slayers*. Dark Horse)*
March, S3E16 Sleep Tight. The WB
5 March, S6E16 Hell's Bells. UPN
12 March, S6E17 Normal Again. UPN
(March, *Fray* #6. Dark Horse)*
15 April, S3E17 Forgiving. The WB
22 April, S3E18 Double Or Nothing. The WB
29 April, S3E19 The Price. The WB
30 April, S6E18 Entropy. UPN
(*Fray* #3. Dark Horse)*
6 May, S3E20 A New World. The WB
7 May, S6E19 Seeing Red. UPN
13 May, S3E21 Benediction. The WB

14 May, S6E20 Villains. UPN
20 May, S3E22 Tomorrow. The WB
21 May, S6E21 Two To Go. UPN
21 May, S6E22 Grave. UPN
(May, *Angel* #4. Dark Horse)*
(August, *Fray* #8. Dark Horse)*
(*Buffy* Season 7; *Angel* Season 4; *Firefly*)
*20 September, S1E2 The Train Job. Fox***
24 September, S7E1 Lessons. UPN*
27 September, S1E3 Bushwhacked. Fox
1 October, S7E2 Beneath You. UPN
4 October, *S1E6 Our Mrs Reynolds. Writer. Fox*
6 October, S4E1 Deep Down. The WB
8 October, S7E3 Same Time, Same Place. UPN
13 October, S4E2 Ground State. The WB
13 October, S7E4 Help. UPN
18 October, S1E7 Jaynestown. Fox
20 October, S4E3 The House Always Wins. The WB
22 October, S7E5 Selfless. UPN
23 October, S1E8 Out Of Gas. Fox
27 October, S4E4 Slouching Toward Bethlehem. The WB
1 November, S1E4 Shindig. Fox
3 November, S4E5 Supersymmetry. The WB
5 November, S7E6 Him. UPN
8 November, S1E5 Safe. Fox
10 November, S4E6 Spin The Bottle. The WB**
12 November, S7E7 Conversations with Dead People. UPN
15 November, S1E9 Ariel. Fox
17 November, S4E7 Apocalypse, Nowish. The WB
19 November, S7E8 Sleeper. UPN
26 November, S7E9 Never Leave Me. UPN
6 December, S1E10 War Stories. Fox
*13 December, S1E14 Objects In Space. Fox***
17 December, S7E10 Bring on the Night. UPN
*20 December, S1E1 Serenity S1E Fox***
*20 December, S1E2 Serenity S2E Fox***
(2003)
7 January, S7E11 Showtime. UPN
15 January, S4E8 Habeas Corpses. The WB
21 January, S7E12 Potential. UPN
22 January, S4E9 Long Day's Journey. The WB
29 January, S4E10 Awakening. The WB
4 February, S7E13 The Killer in Me. UPN
5 February, S4E11 Soulless. The WB
11 February, S7E14, First date. UPN
12 February, S4E12 Calvary. The WB
18 February, S7E15 Get It Done. UPN
25 February, S7E16 Storyteller. UPN
5 March, S4E13 Salvage. The WB
12 March, S4E14 Release. The WB
19 March, S4E15 Orpheus. The WB
25 March, S7E17 Lies My Parents Told Me. UPN
26 March, S4E16 Players. The WB
2 April, S4E17 Inside Out. The WB
9 April, S4E18 Shiny Happy People. The WB
16 April, S4E19 The Magic Bullet. The WB
22 April, S7E18, Dirty Girls. UPN
23 April, S4E20 Sacrifice. The WB
20 April, S7E19 Empty Places. UPN

30 April, S4E21 Peace Out. The WB
6 May, S7E20 Touched. UPN
7 May, S4E22 Home. The WB
13 May, S7E21 End of Days. UPN
20 May, S7E22 Chosen. UPN**
(*Angel* Season 5)
1 October, S5E1 Conviction. The WB**
8 October, S5E2 Just Rewards. The WB
15 October, S5E3 Unleashed. The WB
22 October, S5E4 Hell Bound. The WB
29 October, S5E5 Life Of The Party. The WB
5 November, S5E6 The Cautionary Tale Of Numero Cinco. The WB
12 November, S5E7 Lineage. The WB
19 November, S5E8 Destiny. The WB
(December, *Tales of the Vampires* #1. Dark Horse.)*
(2004)
14 January, S5E9 Harm's Way. The WB
21 January, S5E10 Soul Purpose. The WB
28 January, S5E11 Damage. The WB
(January, *Tales of the Vampires* #2. Dark Horse.)
4 February, S5E12 You're Welcome. The WB
11 February, S5E13 Why We Fight. The WB
18 February, S5E14 Smile Time. The WB*
25 February, S5E15 A Hole In The World. Writer, Director. The WB
(February, *Tales of the Vampires* #3. Dark Horse.)
3, S5E16 Shells. The WB
(March, *Tales of the Vampires* #4. Dark Horse.)
14 April, S5E17 Underneath. The WB
21 April, S5E18 Origin. The WB
28 April, S5E19 Time Bomb. The WB
(April, *Tales of the Vampires* #5. Dark Horse)
5 May, S5E20 The Girl In Question. The WB
12 May, S5E21 Power Play. The WB
19 May, S5E22 Not Fade Away. The WB*
(July, *Astonishing X-Men* #1. Marvel)*
(August, *Astonishing X-Men* #2. Marvel.)*
(August, *Astonishing X-Men: Director's Cut* #1. Marvel)*
(September, *Astonishing X-Men* #3. Marvel)*
(October, *Astonishing X-Men* #4. Marvel)*
(November, *Astonishing X-Men* #5. Marvel)*
(December, *Astonishing X-Men* #6. Marvel)*
(December, *Astonishing X-Men: Gifted* #1. Marvel)*
(2005)
(January, *Astonishing X-Men* #7. Marvel)*
(February, *Astonishing X-Men* #8. Marvel)*
(March, *Astonishing X-Men* #9. Marvel)*
(May, *Astonishing X-Men* #10. Marvel)*
(July, *Astonishing X-Men* #11. Marvel)*
(July, *Serenity: Those Left Behind* #1. Dark Horse)*
(August, *Astonishing X-Men* #12. Marvel)*
(August, *Astonishing X-Men: Dangerous* #2. Marvel)*
(August, *Serenity: Those Left Behind* #2. Dark Horse)*

[*Serenity* premiere: 30th September]**
(September, *Serenity: Those Left Behind* #3. Dark Horse)*
(2006)
(April, *Astonishing X-Men* #13. Marvel)*
(June, *Astonishing X-Men* #14. Marvel)*
(August, *Astonishing X-Men* #15. Marvel)*
(September, *Stan Lee Meets Spiderman*. Marvel)*
(October, *Astonishing X-Men* #16. Marvel)*
(November, *Astonishing X-Men* #17. Marvel)*
(December, *Astonishing X-Men* #18. Marvel)*
(2007)
(January, *Astonishing X-Men: Torn* #3. Marvel)*
(February, *Astonishing X-Men* #19 and #20. Marvel)*
(March, *Buffy the Vampire Slayer* Season Eight #1. Dark Horse)*
(April, *Buffy the Vampire Slayer* Season Eight #2. Dark Horse)*
(May, *Buffy the Vampire* Slayer Season Eight r #3. Dark Horse)*
(May, *Astonishing X-Men* #21. Marvel)*
(June, *Buffy the Vampire Slayer* Season Eight #4. Dark Horse)*
(July, *Sugarshock!* #1. Dark Horse / MySpace)*
(August, *Buffy the Vampire Slayer* Season Eight #5. Dark Horse)*
(September, *Buffy the Vampire Slayer* Season Eight #6. Dark Horse)
(September, *Sugarshock!* #2. Dark Horse/ MySpace)*
(October, *Buffy the Vampire Slayer* Season Eight #7. Dark Horse)
(October, *Astonishing X-Men* #22. Marvel)*
(October, *Sugarshock!* #3. Dark Horse / MySpace)*
(November, *Buffy the Vampire Slayer* Season Eight #8. Dark Horse)
(November, *30 Days of Night: Beyond Barrow* #2. IDW)*
(November, *Angel: After the Fall* #1. IDW)*
(December, *Angel: After the Fall* #2. IDW)*
(December, *Buffy the Vampire Slayer* Season Eight #9. Dark Horse)
(2008)
(January, *Angel: After the Fall* #3. IDW)*
(January, *Buffy the Vampire Slayer* Season Eight #10. Dark Horse)*
(January, *Astonishing X-Men* #23. Marvel)*
(February, *Angel: After the Fall* #4. IDW)*
(February, *Buffy the Vampire Slayer* Season Eight #11. Dark Horse)*
(March, *Angel: After the Fall* #5. IDW)*
(March, *Astonishing X-Men* #24. Marvel)*
(March, *Buffy the Vampire Slayer* Season Eight #12. Dark Horse)
(March, *Serentiy: better days* #1. Dark Horse)*
(April, *Angel: After the Fall* #6. IDW)*
(April, *Buffy the Vampire Slayer* Season Eight #13. Dark Horse)
(April, *Serenity: Better Days* #2. Dark Horse)*
(May, *Angel: After the Fall* #7. IDW)*
(May, *Buffy the Vampire Slayer* Season Eight #14. Dark Horse)

(May, *Serenity: Better Days* #3. Dark Horse)*
(June, *Angel: After the Fall* #8. IDW)*
(June, *Astonishing X-Men: Unstoppable* #4. Marvel)*
(June, *Buffy the Vampire Slayer* Season Eight #15. Dark Horse)
Doctor Horrible's Sing-along blog
15 July, *Dr. Horrible* Act S1E Internet.**++
17 July, *Dr. Horrible* Act S2E Internet. **++
19 July, *Dr Horible* Act S3E Internet. **++
(July, *Angel: After the Fall* #10. IDW)*
(July, *Buffy the Vampire Slayer* Season Eight #16. Dark Horse)
(August, *Angel: After the Fall* #11. IDW)*
(August, *Buffy the Vampire Slayer* Season Eight #17. Dark Horse)
(August, *Serenity: The Other Half.* Dark Horse / MySPace)
(September, *Angel: After the Fall* #12. IDW)*
(September, *Buffy the Vampire Slayer* Season Eight #18. Dark Horse)
(October, *Angel: After the Fall* #13. IDW)
(November, *Angel: After the Fall* #14. IDW)*
(November, *Buffy the Vampire Slayer* Season Eight #19. Dark Horse)
(December, *Angel: After the Fall* #15 IDW)*
(December, *Buffy the Vampire Slayer* Season Eight #20. Dark Horse)
(2009)
(January, *Angel: After the Fall* #16. IDW)*
(January, *Buffy the Vampire Slayer* Season Eight #21. Dark Horse)
(*Dolhouse* Season 1)
13 February, S1E1 Ghost. Fox**
20 February, S1E2 The Target. Fox
27 February, S1E3 Stage Fright. Fox++
(February, *Angel: After the Fall* #17. IDW)*
(February, *Angel: After the Fall* #18. IDW)
(February, *Buffy the Vampire Slayer* Season Eight #22. Dark Horse)
6 March, S1E4 Grey Hour. Fox
13 March, S1E5 True Believer. Fox
20 March, S1E6 Man On The Street. Fox*
27 March, S1E7 Echoes. Fox
(March, *Buffy the Vampire Slayer* Season Eight #23. Dark Horse)
(March, *Angel: After the Fall* #19. IDW)
3 April, S1E8 Needs. Fox
10 April, S1E9 A Spy In The House Of Love. Fox
24 April, S1E10 Haunted. Fox++
(April, *Buffy the Vampire Slayer* Season Eight #24. Dark Horse)
(April, *Angel: After the Fall* #20. IDW)
1 May, S1E11 Briar Rose. Fox
8 May, S1E12 Omega. Fox
(May, *Angel: After the Fall* #21. IDW)*
(May, *Buffy the Vampire Slayer* Season Eight #25. Dark Horse)
(June, *Angel: After the Fall* #22. IDW)*
(June, *Runaways* vol. 8: Dead End Kids. Marvel)*
(July, *Angel: After the Fall* #23. IDW)*
(July, *Buffy the Vampire Slayer* Season Eight #26. Dark Horse)

(August, *Buffy the Vampire Slayer* Season Eight #27. Dark Horse)
(August, *Angel: After the Fall* #24. IDW)
(*Dollhouse* Season 2)
25 September, S2E1 Vows. Fox**
(September, *Buffy the Vampire Slayer* Season Eight #28. Dark Horse)
(September, *Angel: After the Fall* #25. IDW)
2 October, S2E2 Instinct. Fox
9 October, S2E3 Belle Chose. Fox
23 October, S2E4 Belonging. Fox++
(October, *Buffy the Vampire Slayer* Season Eight #29. Dark Horse)
(October, *Angel: After the Fall* #26. IDW)
(November, *Buffy the Vampire Slayer* Season Eight #30. Dark Horse)
(November, *Angel: After the Fall* #27. IDW)
4 December, S2E5 The Public Eye. Fox
4 December, S2E6 The Left Hand. Fox
11 December, S2E7 Meet Jane Doe. Fox++
11 December, S2E8 A Love Supreme. Fox
18 December, S2E9 Stop-Loss. Fox
18 December, S2E10 The Attic. Fox++
(December, *Angel: After the Fall* #28. IDW)

(2010)

8 January, S2E11 Getting Closer. Fox
15 January, S2E12 The Hollow Men. Fox
29 January, S2E13 Epitaph Two: Return. Fox++
(January, *Buffy the Vampire Slayer* Season Eight #31. Dark Horse)*
(January, *Angel: After the Fall* #29. IDW)
(February, *Buffy the Vampire Slayer* Season Eight #32. Dark Horse)
(February, *Angel: After the Fall* #30. IDW)
(March, *Buffy the Vampire Slayer* Season Eight #33. Dark Horse)
(March, *Angel: After the Fall* #31. IDW)
(April, *Buffy the Vampire Slayer* Season Eight #34. Dark Horse)
(April, *Angel: After the Fall* #32. IDW)
(May, *Buffy the Vampire Slayer* Season Eight #35. Dark Horse)
(May, *Angel: After the Fall* #33. IDW)
(June, *Angel: After the Fall* #34. IDW)
(June, *Serenity: Float Out*. Dark Horse)*
(July, *Angel: After the Fall* #35. IDW)
(August, *Angel: After the Fall* #36. IDW)
(September, *Buffy the Vampire Slayer* Season Eight #36. Dark Horse)
(September, *Angel: After the Fall* #37. IDW)
(October, *Buffy the Vampire Slayer* Season Eight #37. Dark Horse)
(October, *Angel: After the Fall* #38. IDW)
(November, *Buffy the Vampire Slayer* Season Eight #38. Dark Horse)
(November, *Angel: After the Fall* #39. IDW)
(November, *Serenity: The Shepherd's tale*. Dark Horse)*
(November, *Serenity: Downtime*. Dark Horse / USA Today)

(December, *Buffy the Vampire Slayer* Season Eight #39. Dark Horse)*
(December, *Angel: After the Fall* #40. IDW)
(2011)
(January, *Buffy the Vampire Slayer* Season Eight #40. Dark Horse)*
(May, *Astonishing X-Men: MGC* #1. Marvel)*
(August, *Angel and Faith* #1. Dark Horse)
(September, *Buffy the Vampire Slayer: Season 9* #1. Dark Horse)*
(September, *Angel and Faith* #2. Dark Horse)
(October, *Buffy the Vampire Slayer: Season 9* #2. Dark Horse)*
(October, *Angel and Faith* #2. Dark Horse)
(November, *Buffy the Vampire Slayer: Season 9* #3. Dark Horse)*
(November, *Angel and Faith* #3. Dark Horse)
(December, *Buffy the Vampire Slayer: Season 9* #4. Dark Horse)*
(December, *Angel and Faith* #4. Dark Horse)
(2012)
(January, *Buffy the Vampire Slayer: Season 9* #5. Dark Horse)
(January, *Angel and Faith* #5. Dark Horse)
(February, *Buffy the Vampire Slayer: Season 9* #6. Dark Horse)
(February, *Angel and Faith* #6. Dark Horse)
(March, *Buffy the Vampire Slayer: Season 9* #7. Dark Horse)
(March, *Angel and Faith* #7. Dark Horse)
[*The Cabin in the Woods* premiere: 9 March]*<>
(April, *Buffy the Vampire Slayer: Season 9* #8. Dark Horse)
(April, *Angel and Faith* #8. Dark Horse)
[*The Avengers* premiere: 11 April]**
(May, *Buffy the Vampire Slayer: Season 9* #9. Dark Horse)
(May, *Serenity: Firefly Class 03-K64–It's Never Easy.* Dark Horse)
(May, *Angel and Faith* #9. Dark Horse)
(June, *Buffy the Vampire Slayer: Season 9* #10. Dark Horse)
(June, *Angel and Faith* #10. Dark Horse)
[*Much Ado About Nothing* premier: 21 June]**<>
(July, *Buffy the Vampire Slayer: Season 9* #11. Dark Horse)
(July, *Angel and Faith* #11. Dark Horse)
(August, *Buffy the Vampire Slayer: Season 9* #12. Dark Horse)
(August, *Angel and Faith* #12. Dark Horse)
(September, *Buffy the Vampire Slayer: Season 9* #13. Dark Horse)
(September, *Angel and Faith* #13. Dark Horse)
9 October, *Dr. Horrible's Sing-along blog*. The CW**++
(October, *Buffy the Vampire Slayer: Season 9* #14. Dark Horse)
(October, *Angel and Faith* #14. Dark Horse)
[28 October, Mitt Romney 'endorsement' https://www.youtube.com/watch?v=6TiXUF9xbTo]
(November, *Buffy the Vampire Slayer: Season 9* #15. Dark Horse)
(November, *Angel and Faith* #15. Dark Horse)

(December, *Buffy the Vampire Slayer: Season 9* #16. Dark Horse)
(December, *Angel and Faith* #16. Dark Horse)

(2013)

(January, *Buffy the Vampire Slayer: Season 9* #17). Dark Horse)
(January, *Angel and Faith* #17. Dark Horse)
(February, *Buffy the Vampire Slayer: Season 9* #18. Dark Horse)
(February, *Angel and Faith* #18. Dark Horse)
(March, *Buffy the Vampire Slayer: Season 9* #19. Dark Horse)
(March, *Angel and Faith* #19. Dark Horse)
(April, *Buffy the Vampire Slayer: Season 9* #20. Dark Horse)
(April, *Angel and Faith* #20. Dark Horse)
(May, *Buffy the Vampire Slayer: Season 9* #21. Dark Horse)
(May, *Angel and Faith* #21. Dark Horse)
(June, *Buffy the Vampire Slayer: Season 9* #22. Dark Horse)
(June, *Angel and Faith* #22. Dark Horse)
(July, *Buffy the Vampire Slayer: Season 9* #23. Dark Horse)
(July, *Angel and Faith* #23. Dark Horse)
(August, *Buffy the Vampire Slayer: Season 9* #24. Dark Horse)
(August, *Angel and Faith* #24. Dark Horse)
(September, *Buffy the Vampire Slayer: Season 9* #25. Dark Horse)
(September, *Angel and Faith* #25. Dark Horse)
(*Agents of S.H.I.E.L.D.* season one)
24 September, S1E1 Pilot. ABC**++
1 October, S1E2 0–8–S4E ABC++
8 October, S1E3 The Asset. ABC++
15 October, S1E4 Eye Spy. ABC
22 October, S1E5 Girl in the Flower Dress. ABC
5 November, S1E6 FZZT. ABC
12 November, S1E7 The Hub. ABC
19 November, S1E8 The Well. ABC
26 November, S1E9 Repairs. ABC++
10 December, S1E10 The Bridge. ABC

(2014)

7 January, S1E11 The Magical Place. ABC
14 January, S1E12 Seeds. ABC++
(January, *Serenity: Leaves on the Wind* #1. Dark Horse)
4 February, S1E13 T.R.A.C.K.S. ABC
(February, *Serenity: Leaves on the Wind* #2. Dark Horse)
4, S1E14 T.A.H.I.T.I. ABC
11 March, S1E15 Yes Men. ABC
(March, *Buffy the Vampire Slayer* Season 10 #1. Dark Horse)
(March, *Serenity: Leaves on the Wind* #3. Dark Horse)
1 April, S1E16 End of the Beginning. ABC
8 April, S1E17 Turn, Turn, Turn. ABC++
[*In Your Eyes* premiere: 11 April]*<>
15 April, S1E18 Providence. ABC
22 April, S1E19 The Only Light in the Darkness. ABC
29 April, S1E20 Nothing Personal. ABC
(April, *Buffy the Vampire Slayer* Season 10 #2. Dark Horse)
(April, *Serenity: Leaves on the Wind* #4. Dark Horse)
6 May, S1E21 Rag Tag. ABC
13 May, S1E22 Beginning of the End. ABC++

(May, *Buffy the Vampire Slayer* Season 10 #3. Dark Horse)
(May, *Serenity: Leaves on the Wind* #5. Dark Horse)
(June, *Buffy the Vampire Slayer* Season 10 #4. Dark Horse)
(June, *Serenity: Leaves on the Wind* #6. Dark Horse)
(July, *Buffy the Vampire Slayer* Season 10 #5. Dark Horse)
(August, *Buffy the Vampire Slayer* Season 10 #1. Dark Horse)
(*Agents of S.H.I.E.L.D.* Season Two)
23 September, S2E1 Shadows. ABC++
30 September, S2E2 Heavy is the Head. ABC
(September, *Buffy the Vampire Slayer* Season 10 #7. Dark Horse)
7 October, S2E3 Making Friends and Influencing People. ABC
14 October, S2E4 Face My Enemy. ABC
21 October, S2E5 A Hen in the Wolf House. ABC
28 October, S2E6 A Fractured House. ABC
(October, *Buffy the Vampire Slayer* Season 10 #8. Dark Horse)
11 November, S2E7 The Writing on the Wall. ABC
18 November, S2E8 The Things we Bury
(November, *Buffy the Vampire Slayer* Season 10 #9. Dark Horse)
2 December, S2E9 Ye Who Enter Here. ABC
9 December, S2E10 What They Become. ABC
(December, *Buffy the Vampire Slayer* Season 10 #10. Dark Horse)

(2015)

(January, *Buffy the Vampire Slayer* Season 10 #11. Dark Horse)
(February, *Buffy the Vampire Slayer* Season 10 #12. Dark Horse)
3 March, S2E11Aftershocks. ABC++
10 March, S2E12 Who You Really Are. ABC
17 March, S2E13 One of Us. ABC
24 March, S2E14 Love in the Time of Hydra
31 March, S2E15 One Door Closes. ABC
(March, *Buffy the Vampire Slayer* Season 10 #13. Dark Horse)
7 April, S2E16 Afterlife. ABC
[*Avengers: Age of Ultron* premiere: 13 April]**
14 April, S2E17 Melinda. ABC
21 April, S2E18 The Frenemy of my Enemy. ABC
28 April, S2E19 The Dirty Half Dozen. ABC
(April, *Buffy the Vampire Slayer* Season 10 #14. Dark Horse)
5 May, S2E20 Scars. ABC
12 May, S2E21, S.O.S S1E ABC
12 May, S2E22 S.O.S S2E ABC++
(May, *Buffy the Vampire Slayer* Season 10 #15. Dark Horse)
(June, *Buffy the Vampire Slayer* Season 10 #16. Dark Horse)
(July, *Buffy the Vampire Slayer* Season 10 #17. Dark Horse)
(August *Buffy the Vampire Slayer* Season 10 #18. Dark Horse)
(Agents of S.H.I.E.L.D. Season Three)
29 September. S3E1 Laws of Nature. ABC++
(September, *Buffy the Vampire Slayer* Season 10 #19. Dark Horse)
6 October, S3E2 Purpose in the Machine. ABC
13 October, S3E3 A Wanted (Inhu) man. ABC
20 October, S3E4 Devils you Know. ABC

27 October, S3E5 4,722 Hours. ABC

(October, *Buffy the Vampire Slayer* Season 10 #20. Dark Horse)

3 November, S3E6 Among us Hide ... ABC

10 November, S3E7Chaos Theory. ABC

17 November, S3E8 Many Heads, One Tail. ABC++

(November, *Buffy the Vampire Slayer* Season 10 #21. Dark Horse)

1 December, S3E9 Closure. ABC

8 December, S3E10 Maveth. ABC

(December, *Buffy the Vampire Slayer* Season 10 #22. Dark Horse)

(2016)

(January, *Buffy the Vampire Slayer* Season 10 #23. Dark Horse)

(February, *Buffy the Vampire Slayer* Season 10 #24. Dark Horse)

8, S3E11 Bouncing Back. ABC

15 March, S3E1S2E The Inside Man. ABC

22 March, S3E1S3E Parting Shot. ABC

29 March, S3E14 Watchdogs. ABC

(March, *Buffy the Vampire Slayer* Season 10 #25. Dark Horse)

5 April, S3E15 Spacetime. ABC++

12 April, S3E16 Paradise Lost. ABC

19 April, S3E17 The Team. ABC

26 April, S3E18 The Singularity. ABC

(April, *Buffy the Vampire Slayer* Season 10 #26. Dark Horse)

3 May, S3E19 Failed Experiments. ABC

10 May, S3E20Emancipation. ABC

17 May, S3E21 Absolution. ABC

17 May, S3E22 Ascension. ABC++

(May, *Buffy the Vampire Slayer* Season 10 #27. Dark Horse)

(May, *Serenity: The Warrior and the Wind*. Dark Horse)

(June, *Buffy the Vampire Slayer* Season 10 #28. Dark Horse)

(July, *Buffy the Vampire Slayer* Season 10 #29. Dark Horse)

(August, *Buffy the Vampire Slayer* Season 10 #30. Dark Horse)

(*Agents of S.H.I.E.L.D.* Season Four)

20 September, S4E1 The Ghost. ABC++

27 September, S4E2 Meet the New Boss. ABC

[21 September, 'Important: Save the Day' https://www.youtube.com/watch?v=nRp1CK_X_Yw]

11 October, S4E3 Uprising. ABC

18 October, S4E4 Let Me Stand Next to Your Fire. ABC

25 October, S4ES5E Lockup. ABC

1 November, S4E6 The Good Samaritan. ABC

29 November, S4E7 Deals with our Devils. ABC

(*Buffy the Vampire Slayer* Season 11 #1 Dark Horse)

[Novemember 1, 'If congress was your co-worker' https://www.youtube.com/watch?v=YibDgSdo2Xk]

6 December, S4E8. The Laws of Inferno Dynamics. ABC

(December, *Buffy the Vampire Slayer* Series 11 #2 Dark Horse)

(2017)

10 January, S4E9 Broken Promises. ABC

17 January, S4E10 The Patriot. ABC

24 January, S4E11 Wake Up. ABC

31 January, S4E12 Hot Potato Soup. ABC

(January, *Buffy the Vampire Slayer* Season 11 #3 Dark Horse)

(January, *Angel* Season 11 #1 Dark Horse)
7 February, S4E13 BOOM. ABC.
14 February, S4E14 The Man Behind the Shield. ABC
21 February, S4E15 Self Control.++
(*Buffy the Vampire Slayer* Season 11 #4 Dark Horse)
(*Angel* Season 11 #2 Dark Horse)
(*Buffy the Vampire Slayer* Season 11 #5 Dark Horse)
4 April, S4E16 What if ... ABC
11 April, S4E17 Identity and Change. ABC
18 April, S4E18 No Regrets. ABC
25 April, S4E19 All the Madame's Men. ABC
(*Buffy the Vampire Slayer* Season 11 #6 Dark Horse)
2 May, S4E20 Farewell, Cruel World! ABC
9 May, S4E21 The Return. ABC
16 May, S4E22 World's End. ABC
(*Buffy the Vampire Slayer* Season 11 #7 Dark Horse)
(*Angel* Season 11 #3 Dark Horse)
[17 May, Unlocked: Planned Parenthood video https://www.youtube.com/watch?v=3vTG4lUl1PU]
Unaired *Firefly*
S1E13 Heart Of Gold
S1E11 Trash
S1E12 The Message*
Unaired *Dollhouse*
Echo, unaired pilot.**
Epitaph One (unaired but canon: episode S1E13)*++

References

Abbot, S. (ed.) (2005) *Reading Angel: The TV Spin-Off with a Soul*, London, I. B. Tauris.

Abbott, S. (2008) '"Can't stop the signal": the resurrection/regeneration of *Serenity*', in R. V. Wilcox and T. R. Cochrane (eds), *Investigating Firefly and Serenity: Science Fiction on the Frontier*, London, I. B. Tauris, 227–38.

Abbott, S. (2009) *Angel*, Detroit, IL, Wayne State University Press.

Abbott, S. (2012) 'Angel', in M. A Money (ed.), *Joss Whedon: The Complete Companion*, London, Titan Books, 161–7.

Abbott, S. and Brown, S. (2007) 'Introduction', in S. Abbott and S. Brown (eds), *Investigating Alias: Secrets and Spies*, London, I. B. Tauris, 1–8.

Adalian, J. (2001) *Variety*, 23 April 2001, http://www.variety.com/article/VR1117797571.html?categoryid=14&cs=1, accessed 23 November 2008.

Barnes, E. (2007) 'The new hero: women humanism and violence in *Alias* and *Buffy the Vampire Slayer*', in S. Abbott and S. Brown (eds), *Investigating Alias: Secrets and Spies*, London, I. B. Tauris, 57–72.

Bauder, D. (2001) '*Buffy* up for grabs after this season', *Napa Valley Register*, 9 January, http://napavalleyregister.com/lifestyles/buffy-up-for-grabs-after-this-season/article_b210526a-e0fb-5498–9ab8–8325be30172b.html, accessed 23 June 2009.

Beckett, S. (1953/2009) *Watt*, London, Faber and Faber.

Bell, J. (2005) 'Commentary' to 'Not Fade Away', *Angel* season 5 DVD, disc 6.

Bennet, J. and Brown, T. (2008) 'Introduction: past the boundaries of "new" and "old" media: film and television after DVD', in J. Bennet and T. Brown (eds), *Film and Television After DVD*, New York, Routledge, 1–18.

Bennett, T. (2011) 'Interview with Joss Whedon' in R. Edwards (ed.), *Worlds of Whedon: SFX Interviews*. Ebook.

Bercovici, J. (2012) 'Avengers director Joss Whedon on trying to be more like Buffy', forbes.com, 3 May, https://www.forbes.com/sites/jeffbercovici/2012/05/03/avengers-director-joss-whedon-on-trying-to-be-more-like-buffy/6/#4ec982726dd4, accessed 12 June 2016.

Berner, A. (2004) 'The path of Wesley Wyndham-Price', in G. Yeffeth (ed.), *Five Seasons of Angel: Science Fiction and Fantasy Writers Discuss Their Favorite Vampire*, Dallas, TX, BenBella Books, 145–52.

boxofficemojo.com (2017) boxofficemojo.com/people/chart/?view=Writer&id=josswhedon.htm, accessed 30 January 2017.

Brand, M. (2009) 'New formats test TV writers', *Day Today*, http://www.npr.org/templates/story/story.php?storyId=101716627, accessed 16 June 2016.

Breznican, A. (2011) 'The Avengers: your first look at the dream team', *Entertainment* Weekly, 30 September, http://ew.com/article/2011/09/30/avengers-your-first-look-dream-team, accessed 17 July 2013.

Brincker, F. (2017) 'Transmedia storytelling in the "Marvel cinematic universe" and the logics of convergence-era popular seriality', in M. Yockey (ed.), *Make ours Marvel: Media Convergence and a Comics Universe*, Austin, TX, University of Texas Press, 207–30.

Broadcasting Standards Commission (2001) *Bulletin* 39, 31 January. (This document is no longer publicly available via the web. It can be obtained through a Freedom of Information request addressed to OfCom https://www.ofcom.org.uk/about-ofcom/contact-us).

Broadcasting Standards Commission (2003a) *Bulletin* 67, 31 July. (This document is no longer publicly available via the web. It can be obtained through a Freedom of Information request addressed to OfCom https://www.ofcom.org.uk/about-ofcom/contact-us).

Broadcasting Standards Commission (2003b) *Bulletin* 68, 30 September. (This document is no longer publicly available via the web. It can be obtained through a Freedom of Information request addressed to OfCom https://www.ofcom.org.uk/about-ofcom/contact-us).

Brojakowski, B. (2015) 'Spoiler alert: understanding television enjoyment in the social media era', in A. F. Slade, A. M. Narro and D. Givens-Carroll (eds), *Television, Social Media, Fan Culture*, New York, Lexington Books.

Brown, E. (2014) 'Joss Whedon's $5 in your eyes Vimeo distribution is a vanity project, not a revolution', *International Business Times*, 21 April, http://www.ibtimes.com/joss-whedons-5-your-eyes-vimeo-distribution-vanity-project-not-revolution-1574484, accessed 19 July 2015.

Buckman, A. (2010) 'Go ahead! Run away! Say it was Horrible! *Dr Horrible's Sing-along blog* as resistant text', *Slayage: The Journal of the Whedon Studies Association*, 8(1), n.p.

Burnell, A. C. (2011) 'Rebels, rogues and sworn brothers: *Supernatural* and the shift in "White Trash" from monster to hero', in S. Abbott and D. Lavery (eds), *TV Goes to Hell: The Unofficial Roadmap of Supernatural*, Toronto, ECW, 47–59.

Bussolini, J. (2013) 'Television intertextuality after *Buffy*: intertextuality of casting and constitutive intertextuality', *Slayage: The Journal of the Whedon Studies Association*, 10(1), n.p.

Carman, J. (1998) 'TV season ends with a bang – of implosion', *San Francisco Chronicle*, 22 May, C.1.

Chalaby, J. K. (2016) *The Format Age: Television's Entertainment Revolution*, Cambridge, Polity Press.

Cochrane, T. R. (2008) 'The Browncoats are coming! *Firefly, Serenity*, and fan activism', in R. V. Wilcox and T. R. Cochrane (eds), *Investigating Firefly and Serenity: Science Fiction on the Frontier*, London, I. B. Tauris, 239–50.

Colvin, P. (2005) '*Angel*: Redemption and Justification through Faith' in S. Abbott (ed.) *Reading Angel: The Spin-off with a soul*, New York and London, I. B. Tauris, 17–30.

Consoli, J. (2008a) 'Fox to debut remote free tv format with Fringe', *Adweek.com*, http://www.adweek.com/tv-video/fox-debut-remote-free-tv-format-fringe-108404/, accessed 12 June 2016.

Consoli, J. (2008b) 'Fox: tests show remote free TV yields more ad-viewing content', Adweek.com, http://www.adweek.com/tv-video/fox-tests-show-remote-free-tv-yields-more-ad-viewing-intent-109619/, accessed 12 June 2016.

Cox, A. and Fülöp, R. (2010) '"What rhymes with lungs?" When music speaks louder than words', in P. Attinello, J. K. Halfyard and V. Knights (eds), *Music, Sound and Silence in Buffy the Vampire Slayer*, Farnham, Ashgate, 61–78.

Creeber, G. (2004) *Serial Television: Big Drama on the Small Screen*, London, British Film Industry.

Creeber, G. and Hills, M. (2007) 'Editorial – TVIII', *New Review of Film and Television Studies*, 5(1), 1–4.

Cruise, J. (2004) 'The assassination of Cordelia Chase', in G. Yeffeth (ed.), *Five Seasons of Angel*, Dallas, TX, BenBella Books, 187–98.

Da Silveira, L. H. Y. (2010) 'How cancellation told the story of the Dollhouse', in J. Espenson (ed.), *Inside Joss's Dollhouse*, Dallas, TX, BenBella Books, 147–60.

DeCandido, K. R. A. (2004) '"The Train Job" didn't do the job', in J. Espenson (ed.), *Finding Serenity Anti-heroes, Lost Shepherds and Space Hookers in Joss Whedon's Firefly*, Dallas, TX, BenBella Books, 55–62.

Dollimore, J. (2003) 'Art in a time of war: towards a contemporary aesthetic', in J. J. Joughin and S. Malpas (eds), *The New Aestheticism*, Manchester, Manchester University Press, 36–50.

Eaglestone, R. (2003) 'Critical knowledge, scientific knowledge and the truth of literature', in in J. J. Joughin and S. Malpas (eds), *The New Aestheticism*, Manchester, Manchester University Press, 151–66.

Edwards, L. Y., Rambo, E. L. and South, J. B. (2009) 'Preface: At sixes and sevens in Sunnydale' in L. Y. Edwards, E. L. Rambo and J. B. South (eds), *Buffy Goes Dark: Essays on the Final Two Seasons of Buffy the Vampire Slayer*, Jefferson, NC, McFarland and Co., 5–12.

Finke, N. (2007) 'Anyone care what Barry Diller thinks?', *Deadline Hollywood*, 12 November, http://deadline.com/2007/11/does-anyone-care-what-barry-diller-thinks-3840/, accessed 20 August 2010.

Forbes.com (2017) http://www.forbes.com/profile/isaac-perlmutter/, accessed 11 May 2017.

Francis, R. (2000) 'Blood lust', *DreamWatch*, August/September, issue 71–72, 28–35.

Frankel, V. E. (2015) 'Preface', in V. Frankel (ed.), *The Comics of Joss Whedon: Critical Essays*, Jefferson, NC, McFarland and Co., 1.

Frohard-Dourlent, H. (2012) 'Someone's Asian in *Dr. Horrible*: humor and racial representations in the Whedonverse', unpublished conference paper.

Furman, P. (1998) 'It adds up for WB network 'Buffy'-fueled programming pushes it past rival UPN', *New York Daily News*, 22 June: 52.

Fuss, D. (1995) *Identification Papers*, London, Routledge.

George, R. (2006) '*Astonishing X-Men* HC Vol.1 Review', *IGN*, http://uk.ign.com/articles/2006/05/17/astonishing-x-men-hc-vol-1-review, accessed 7 October 2014.

Gilman, L. A. (2004) 'True Shanshu: redemption through compassion, and the journey of Cordelia Chase', in G. Yeffeth (ed.), *Five Seasons of Angel*, Dallas, TX, BenBella Books, 179–86.

Gliatto, T. (1997) 'Picks and pans review: Buffy the Vampire Slayer', *People*, http://people.com/archive/picks-and-pans-review-buffy-the-vampire-slayer-vol-47-no-12/, accessed 29 April 2010.

Golden, C., Bissette, S. R. and Sniegoski, T. E. (2000) *Buffy the Vampire Slayer: The Monster Book*, New York, Pocket Books.

Golder, D. (2011) 'Interview with Anthony Stewart Head' in R. Edwards (ed.), *Worlds of Whedon: SFX Interviews*. Ebook.

Goltz, J. (2004) 'Listening to *Firefly*', in J. Espenson (ed.), *Finding Serenity: Anti-heroes, Lost Shepherds and Space Hookers in Joss Whedon's Firefly*, Dallas, TX, BenBella Books, 209–16.

Grant, P. S and Wood, C. (2004) *Blockbusters and Trade Wars: Popular Culture in a Globalized World*, Vancouver, Douglas and MacIntyre.

Greenwalt, D. (2001) 'Featurette: introducing *Angel*', on *Angel* season 1 DVD, disc 6.

Harrison, J. R. (2005) 'Gender politics in *Angel*: traditional vs. non-traditional corporate climates', in S. Abbott (ed.), *Reading Angel: The Spin-off with a Soul*, London, I. B. Tauris, 117–31.

Havens, C. (2003) *Joss Whedon: The Genius Behind Buffy*, Dallas, TX, BenBella Books.

Hawk, J. (2010) 'More than the sum of our imprints', in J. Espenson (ed.), *Inside Joss's Dollhouse*, Dallas, TX, BenBella Books, 247–57.

Hibberd J. (2013) 'Joss Whedon clarifies his SHIELD duties', *Entertainment Weekly*, 4 August, http://ew.com/article/2013/08/04/joss-whedon-shield/, accessed 13 February 2015.

Hill, A. and Calcutt, I. (2007) 'Vampire hunters: the scheduling and reception of *Buffy the Vampire Slayer* and *Angel* in the United Kingdom', in E. Levine and L. Parks (eds), *Undead TV: Essays on Buffy the Vampire Slayer*, Durham, NC, Duke University Press, 56–73.

Hills, M. (2007) 'From the box in the corner to the box set on the shelf', *New Review of Film and Television Studies*, 5(1), 41–60.

Hine, T. (1997) 'TV's teen-agers: an insecure, world-weary lot', *New York Times*, 26 October, sec. 2, 1.

Holder, N., Mariotte, J. and Hart, M. (2000) *Watcher's Guide*, Vol. 2, New York, Pocket Books.

Holt, J. (2003) 'Vertical vision: deregulation, industrial economy and prime-time design', in M. Jancovich and J. Lyons (eds), *Popular Quality Television*, London, British Film Institute, 11–31.

Hontz, J. and Petrikin, C. (1998) 'Whedon and Fox vamping', *Daily Variety*, 5 June, 1.

Jancovich, M. and Lyons, J. (2003) 'Introduction', in M. Jancovich and J. Lyons (eds.) *Quality Popular Television*, London, British Film Institute, 1–10.

Jensen, J. (2004) 'Why the *Buffy* and *Angel* creator is ditching TV, *Entertainment Weekly*, 21 May, http://ew.com/article/2004/05/21/why-buffy-angel-creator-ditching-tv/, accessed 12 July 2015.

Jensen, J. (2005) 'Serenity how', *Entertainment Weekly*, vol. 840, 16 September.

Johnson, C. (2005) *Telefantasy*, London, British Film Industry.

Johnson, C. (2007) 'Tele-branding in TVIII: the network as brand and the programme as brand', *New Review of Film and Television Studies*, 5(1), 5–24.

Johnson, D. (2007) 'Inviting Audiences In: The spatial reorganization of production and consumption in 'TVIII'' in G. Creeber and M. Hills (eds.) *New Review of Film and Television Studies*, 5:1, 61–80.

Jones, A. Z. (2010) 'The redemption of Topher Brink', in J. Espenson (ed.), *Inside Joss's Dollhouse*, Dallas, TX, BenBella Books, 79–94.

Joughin, J. J. and Malpas, S. (2003) 'The new aestheticism: an introduction', in J. J. Joughin and S. Malpas (eds), *The New Aestheticism*, Manchester, Manchester University Press, 1–23.

Jowett, L. (2005) *Sex and the Slayer: A Gender Studies Primer for the Buffy Fan*, Middletown, CT, Wesleyan University Press.

Jowett, L. (2008) 'Back to the future: retrofuturism, cyberpunk and humanity in *Firefly* and *Serenity*', in R.V Wilcox and T. Cochrane (eds), *Investigating Firefly and Serenity: Science Fiction on the Frontier*, London, I. B. Tauris, 101–13.

Jowett, L. (2014a) 'Stuffing a rabbit in it: character, narrative and time in the Whedonverses', in R. V. Wilcox, T. R. Cochrane, C. Masson and D. Lavery (eds), *Reading Joss Whedon*, Syracuse, NY, Syracuse University Press, 297–311.

Jowett, L. (2014b) '"I love him ... is that real?": interrogating romance through Victor and Sierra', in S. Ginn, A. R. Buckman and H. M. Porter (eds), *Joss Whedon's Dollhouse: Confounding Purpose, Confusing Identity*. Lanham, MD: Rowman & Littlefield, 127–40.

Jowett, L. and Abbott, S. (2013) *TV Horror: Investigating the Dark Side of the Small Screen*, London, I. B. Tauris.

Kackman, M., Binfield, M., Payne, M. T., Perlman, A. and Sebok, B. (eds) (2011) *Flow: TV: Television in the Age of Media Convergence*. New York, Routledge.

Kaveney, R. (2005) 'The sense of an ending: Schrodinger's *Angel*', in S. Abbott (ed.), *Reading Angel: The Spin-off with a Soul*, London, I. B. Tauris, 57–76.

Kimmel, D. M. (2004) *The Fourth Network: How Fox Broke the Rules and Reinvented Television*, Chicago, IL, Ivan R. Dee Publishing.

Knighton, A. (2014) 'Disruptive distribution: Joss Whedon and the release of *In Your Eyes*', curnblog.com, 4 May, http://curnblog.com/2014/05/04/disruptive-distribution-joss-whedon-release-eyes, accessed 19 June 2016.

Kociemba, D. (2009) 'Understanding the Espensode', in L. Y. Edwards, E. L. Rambo and J. B. South (eds), *Buffy Goes Dark: Essays on the Final Two Seasons of Buffy the Vampire Slayer*, Jefferson, NC, McFarland and Co., 23–40.

Koontz, D. K. (2008) *Faith and Choice in the Works of Joss Whedon*, Jefferson, NC, McFarland and Co.

Lacoue-Labarthe, P. (1990) *Heidegger, Art and Politics: The Fiction of the Political*, Oxford, Blackwell.

Landau, J. (2001) 'Designing *Buffy*', *Buffy the Vampire Slayer*, season 2 DVD, disc 6.

Landau, N. (2016) *TV Outside the Box: Trailblazing in the Digital Television Revolution*, Waltham, MA, Focal Press.

Lavery, D. (2002a) 'Emotional resonance and rocket launchers: Joss Whedon's commentaries on the *Buffy the Vampire Slayer* DVDs', *Slayage: The Journal of the Whedon Studies Association*, 2(2), n.p.

Lavery, D. (2002b) '"A religion in narrative": Joss Whedon and television creativity', *Slayage: The Journal of the Whedon Studies Association*, 2(3), n.p..

Lavery, D. (2014a) *Joss Whedon: A Creative Portrait*, London, I. B. Tauris.

Lavery, D. (2014b) '*Dollhouse*: an introduction', in R. V. Wilcox, T. R. Cochrane, C. Masson and D. Lavery (eds), *Reading Joss Whedon*, Syracuse, NY, Syracuse University Press, 201–4.

Lavery D. and Burkhead C. (eds) (2011) *Joss Whedon: Conversations*, Jackson, MS, University Press of Mississippi.

Littleton, C. (2001) *The Hollywood Reporter*, 23 April, 26.

Lury, K. (2005) *Interpreting Television*, London, Hodder Arnold.

Marder, K. (1999) 'WB joining the big boys', *Daily News*, 10 January, https://www.thefreelibrary.com/WB+JOINING+THE+BIG+BOYS.-a083599879, accessed 11 May 2013.

McCabe, J. and Akass, K. (2007) *Quality TV: Contemporary American Television and Beyond*, London, I. B. Tauris.

McCormick, C. (2012) 'Making sense of the future: narrative destabilization in Joss Whedon's *Dollhouse*', in M. Ames (ed.), *Time in Television Narrative: Exploring Temporality in Twenty-First-Century Programming*, Jackson, MS, University Press of Mississippi, 206–17.

McCormick, C. (2017) 'TV finales: on-demand endings', *Flow*, 23(5), https://www.flowjournal.org/2017/03/on-demand-endings/, accessed 30 March 2017.

McKee, A. (2007) 'Why is "City of Death" the best *Dr Who* story?', in D. Butler (ed.), *Time and Relative Dissertations in Space: Critical Perspectives on Doctor Who*, Manchester, Manchester University Press, 233–43.

Meyer, C. (2001) 'Designing *Buffy*', *Buffy the Vampire Slayer*, season 2 DVD, disc 6.

Middleton, B. (2012) *Undead TV–The Ultimate Guide to Vampires on TV*, Winchendon, MA, Light Unseen Media.

Mietkiewicz, H. (1997) '*Buffy* comes up short in vampire killing', *Toronto Sun*, 7 March, D14.

Miles, L., Pearson, L. and Dickson, C. (2003) *Dusted*, Des Moines, IA, Mad Norwegian Press.

Miller, J. P. (2003) '"The I in team": Buffy and feminist ethics', in J. B. South (ed.), *Buffy the Vampire Slayer and Philosophy*, Chicago, IL, Open Court, 35–48.

Milson, J. (2012) 'The power of fandom in the Whedonverse', in M. A Money (ed.), *Joss Whedon: The Complete Companion*, London, Titan Books, 270–84.

Minear, T. (2009) 'Making *Dollhouse*', *Dollhouse*, season 1 DVD, disc 4 featurette.

Minimum Basic Agreement (2004) Los Angeles and New York, Writers Guild of America, and Sherman Oaks, CA, Alliance of Motion Picture and Television Producers.

Mittell, J. (2015) *Complex TV: The Poetics of Contemporary Television Storytelling*, New York, New York University Press.

Murray, S. (2004) '"Celebrating the story the way it is": cultural studies, corporate media, and the contested utility of fandom', *Continuum: The Journal of Media and Cultural Studies*, 18(1), 7–25.

Nasdaq.com (2017) http://www.nasdaq.com/symbol/dis/financials?query=balance-sheet, accessed 23 February 2017.

Nelson, R. (2007) *State of Play: Contemporary High-End TV Drama*, Manchester, Manchester University Press.

Noxon, M. (2001) http://www.scifi.com/sfw/issue211/news.html (no longer available), accessed 3 June 2009.

Nussbaum, E. (2009) 'Split personality: Joss Whedon attempts to play it safe *and* weird in *Dollhouse*', *New Yok Magazine*, 8 February, http://nymag.com/arts/tv/features/54047/, accessed 19 October 2014.

O'Connell, M. (2017) 'Buffy at 20: Joss Whedon talks TV today, reboot fatigue and the trouble with bingeing', *Hollywood Reporter*, 10 March, http://www.hollywoodreporter.com/live-feed/buffy-at-20-joss-whedon-talks-tv-today-reboot-fatigue-trouble-binging-984885, accessed 20 April 2017.

O'Connor, J. J. (1997) 'Just the girl next door, but neighborhood vampires beware', *New York Times*, 31 March, http://www.nytimes.com/1997/03/31/arts/just-the-girl-next-door-but-neighborhood-vampires-beware.html, accessed 17 June 2002.

Oppenheimer, J. (1999) 'Young blood', *American Cinematographer*, 10(6), 90–101.

Palmer, L. (2011) 'The road to Lordsburg: rural masculinity in *Supernatural*', in S. Abbott and D. Lavery (eds), *TV Goes to Hell: An Unofficial Road Map of Supernatural*, Toronto, ECW, 77–89.

Parks, L. (2003) 'Brave new *Buffy*: rethinking "TV violence"', in M. Jancovich and J. Lyons (eds), *Popular Quality Television*, London, British Film Institute Publishing, 118–36.

Pascale, A. (2014) *Joss Whedon: The Biography*, Chicago, IL. Chicago Review Press.

Pateman, M. (2006) *The Aesthetics of Culture in Buffy the Vampire Slayer*, Jefferson, NC, McFarland and Co.

Pateman, M. (2012) 'Foreword', in B. Glynn, J. Aston and C. Johnson (eds), *Television, Sex and Society: Analyzing Contemporary Representations*, New York, Continuum Books, vii–viii.

Pateman, M. (2014) 'Firefly: of formats, franchises and Fox', in R. V. Wilcox, T. R. Cochrane, C. Masson and D. Lavery (eds), *Reading Joss Whedon*, Syracuse, NY, Syracuse University Press, 153–68.

Peristere, L. (2007) 'Mutant Enemy U', in J. Espenson (ed.), *Serenity Found*, Dallas, TX, BenBella Books, 117–30.

Petrie, D. (2000) 'Shooting Script for Fool For Love', hosted at Buffyworld.com, http://www.buffyworld.com/buffy/scripts/085_scri.html, accessed 23 May 2015.

Pope, K. (1997) 'Limping "Buffy" gets a lift from WB', *Wall Street Journal*, 14 May: B.1.

Radish, C. (2013) 'Show runners Maurissa Tancharoen and Jed Whedon talk Marvel's Agents of SHIELD, their two-year plan, Easter eggs and more', Collider.com, 20 November, http://collider.com/maurissa-tancharoen-jed-whedon-agents-of-shield-interview, accessed 27 January 2017.

Rice, L. (2001) 'Slayer it ain't so', *Entertainment Weekly*, 23 March, http://ew.com/article/2001/03/23/slayer-it-aint-so/, accessed 14 November 2003.

Ricoeur, P. (1985) *Time and Narrative*, Vol. 2, trans. K. McCloughlin and D Pellauer, Chicago, IL, University of Chicago Press.

Rixon, P. (2003) 'The changing face of American television programmes on British screens', in M. Jancovich and J. Lyons (eds), *Popular Quality Television*, London, British Film Institute Publishing, 48–64.

Rolinson, D. (2005) *Alan Clarke*, Manchester, Manchester University Press.

Rose, J. (2009) 'New formats test TV writers', *Day Today*, http://www.npr.org/templates/story/story.php?storyId=101716627, accessed 16 June 2016.

Ruditis, P. (2002) 'Interviews' in *'Once More with Feeling': The Script Book*, New York, Pocket Books.

Rutenberg, J. (2001) '*Buffy* moving to UPN, tries to be WB slayer' *New York Times*, 21 April, http://www.nytimes.com/2001/04/21/business/buffy-moving-to-upn-tries-to-be-wb-slayer.html, accessed 10 August 2009.

Ryan, M (2008) 'Joss Whedon talks Dollhouse and Dr. Horrible', *Chicago Tribune*, 23 July, http://featuresblogs.chicagotribune.com/entertainment_tv/2008/07/joss-whedon-on.html, accessed 15 May 2014.

Ryan, M. (2009) 'Sex, secrets and Dollhouse: Joss Whedon talks about the end of his Fox show', *Chicago Tribune*, 3 December, http://featuresblogs.chicagotribune.com/entertainment_tv/2009/12/dollhouse-fox-joss-whedon.html, accessed 15 May 2014.

Sandison, N. (2009) 'Fox abandons experiment to air fewer ads', *BrandRepublic*, hosted at Campaign.co.uk, http://www.campaignlive.co.uk/article/fox-abandons-experiment-air-fewer-ads/905770?src_site=brandrepublic, accessed 15 June 2016.

Sepinwall, A. (2009) '*Dollhouse*: Joss Whedon Q&A', http://sepinwall.blogspot.co.uk/2009/02/dollhouse-joss-whedon-q.html, accessed 15 June 2016.

Shull, I. and Shull, A. (2009) 'The Candide of Sunnydale: Andrew Wells as satire of pop culture and merchandising trends', in L. Y. Edwards, E. L. Rambo and J. B. South (eds), *Buffy Goes Dark: Essays on the Final Two Seasons of Buffy the Vampire Slayer*, Jefferson, NC, McFarland and Co., 75–82.

Smith, A. W. (2007) '"These children that you spit on": horror and generic hybridity', in R. J. Hand and J. McRoy (eds), *Monstrous Adaptations*, Manchester, Manchester University Press, 82–94.

Smith, M. (1995) *Engaging Characters: Fiction, Emotion and the Cinema*, Oxford, Oxford University Press.

Stafford, N. (2004) *Once Bitten: An Unofficial Guide to the World of Angel*, Toronto, ECW Press.

Stafford, N. (2007) *Bite Me! The Unofficial Guide to Buffy the Vampire Slayer*, Toronto, ECW Press.

Stafford, N. (2011) 'The great *Buffy* re-watch', *Nik at Nite*, http://nikkistafford.blogspot.co.uk/search/label/Buffy%20Rewatch, accessed 28 June 2016.

Steinberg, B (2008) 'So, does remote-free TV work?', *Advertising Age*, http://adage.com/article/media/remote-free-tv-work/130946/, accessed 14 June 2016.

Stevens, K. (2010) 'Battling the buzz: contesting sonic codes in *Buffy the Vampire Slayer*', in Attinello, P., Halfyard, J. K. and Knights, V. (eds), *Music, Sound and Silence in Buffy the Vampire Slayer*, Farnham, Ashgate, 79–90.

Sullivan, M. P. (2004) 'Interview with Joss Whedon', www.ogo.com/channels/filmtv/features/firefly/josswhedon, accessed 8 February 2004.

Sutherland, S. and Swann, S. (2005) 'The rule of prophecy: source of law in the city of angels', in S. Abbott (ed.), *Reading Angel: The Spin-off with a Soul*, London, I. B. Tauris, 132–48.

Terrance, V. (2016) *Internet Children's Television Series: 1997–2015*, Jefferson, NC, McFarland and Co.

Terranova, T. (2000) 'Producing culture for the digital economy', *Social Text*, 63(18), 33–58.

Topping, K. (2002) *Slayer: An Expanded and Updated Unofficial and Unauthorized Guide to Buffy the Vampire Slayer*, London, Virgin Books.

Topping, K. (2004) *Angel Hollywood Vampire: An Expanded and Updates Unauthorized and Unofficial Guide*, London, Virgin Books.
Tracy, K. (1998) *The Girl's Got Bite: The Unofficial Guide to Buffy's World*, Los Angeles, CA, Renaissance.
Turnbull, S. (2004) 'Not just another *Buffy* paper: towards an aesthetics of television', *Slayage: The Journal of the Whedon Studies Association*, 4(1–2), n.p.
Utichi, J. (2012) 'A Buffy-style kicking for torture porn', *Sunday Times*, 15 April, 15. https://www.thetimes.co.uk/article/a-buffy-style-kicking-for-torture-porn-xmdt6h33jfx, accessed 23 March 2015.
Westerfield, S. (2003) 'A Slayer comes to town', in G. Yeffeth (ed.), *Seven Seasons of Buffy*, Dallas, TX, BenBella Books, 30–40.
Wheatley, H. (2006) *Gothic Television*, Manchester, Manchester University Press.
Whedon, J. (2001a) 'Commentary' to 'Innocence', *Buffy the Vampire Slayer*, season 2 DVD, disc 4.
Whedon, J. (2001b) 'Bronze posting', 23 May, 08:24:44, http://www.cise.ufl.edu/cgi-bin/cgiwrap/hsiao/buffy/get-archive?date=20010523, accessed 4 June 2009.
Whedon, J. (2001c) 'Bronze posting', 23 May, 00:33:51, http://www.cise.ufl.edu/cgi-bin/cgiwrap/hsiao/buffy/get-archive?date=20010523, accessed 4 June 2009.
Whedon, J. (2002a) *Once More with Feeling: The Script Book*, New York, Pocket Books.
Whedon, J. (2002b) 'Commentary' to 'Hush', *Buffy the Vampire Slayer*, season 4 DVD, disc 3.
Whedon, J (2002c) 'Commentary' to 'The Body', *Buffy the Vampire Slayer*, season 5 DVD, disc 5.
Whedon, J. (2002d) 'Shooting Script' for 'Hush', *Buffy the Vampire Slayer*, season 4 DVD, disc 3.
Whedon, J. (2003) 'Q&A' with *The Hollywood Reporter*, 16 May, 27.
Whedon, J. (2004) 'Joss says', BronzeBeta.com, http://www.bronzebeta.com/Archive/Joss/Joss20040214.htm, accessed 29 September 2012.
Whedon, J. (2005) *Serenity: The Official Visual Companion*, London, Titan Books.
Whedon, J. (2006) *Firefly: The Official Companion, Volume One*, London, Titan Books.
Whedon, J. (2007a) 'Satin tights no longer', http://whedonesque.com/comments/12385#more, accessed 14 November 2013.
Whedon, J. (2007b) *Firefly: The Official Companion, Volume Two*, London, Titan Books.
Whedon, J. (2009) 'Commentary' to 'Epitaph 1', *Dollhouse*, season 1 DVD, disc 4.
Whedon, J. (2010) 'Heart broken', *This American Life*, https://www.youtube.com/watch?v=vM3Hme36gos, accessed 4 June 2011.
Whedon, J. (2012) 'Whedon on Romney', youtube.com/watch?v=6TiXUF9xbTo, accessed 3 November 2012.

Whedon, J. (2013) *Much Ado About Nothing: A Film by Joss Whedon*, London, Titan Books.

Whedon, J. (2017) tweet 27 April, hosted at http://www.mrctv.org/blog/joss-whedon-apologizes-after-right-people-weren-t-offended-tweet-mocking-cancer-survivors, accessed 5 May 2017.

Whedon, J., Whedon, Z., Whedon, J. and Tancaroen, M. (2011) *Dr. Horrible's Sing-Along Blog: The Book*, London, Titan Books.

Whedonesque.com (2011) http://whedonesque.com/comments/27504, accessed 28 August 2012.

Wilcox, R. V. (2001) '"There will never be a 'very special' *Buffy*": *Buffy* and the monsters of teen life', *Slayage: The Journal of the Whedon Studies Association*, 1(2), n.p..

Wilcox R. V. (2005) *Why Buffy Matters: The Art of Buffy The Vampire Slayer*, London, I. B. Tauris.

Wilcox, R. V. (2011) '"Let it simmer": Tone in "Pangs"', *Slayage: The Journal of the Whedon Studies Association*, 9(1), n.p.

Ziarek, E. P. (2003) 'Mimesis in black and white: feminist aesthetics, negativity and semblance', in J. J Joughin and S. Malpas (eds), *The New Aestheticism*, Manchester, Manchester University Press, 51–67.

Index